When Tom Went West

A Good Life, A Gang Slaying

Nedra J. Downing

Website: www.whentomwentwest.com

Facebook: www.facebook.com/nedradowning2

Cover Design and Book Layout: Eric Christensen

ISBN 978-1-943462-09-4
Library of Congress Control Number: 2016903775

First Printing July 2016
Second Printing November 2016

Printed in the United States of America
by CreateSpace, An Amazon.com Company

I dedicate this book to those who shared his life:
Laura, Margaret, and Christina.

Tom Hollar

The call in the night—the one every mother fears most—came in the early hours of July 23, 1993. It was my daughter, Laura, who said, "Mom, Tom's been shot! They wouldn't tell me anything. You need to call Gary at Denver General Hospital," and she gave me the 303-exchange phone number.

PROLOGUE

NOTHING IN MY LIFE had prepared me for enduring Tom's violent death and Christina's brutal beating. Having gone through medical school plus a hospital internship had exposed me to death, and having pronounced more than one person dead in the wee hours of the morning conditioned me somewhat. Maybe this was called "inner strength." Although our family has never been prone to public displays of emotion, I was devastated, completely drained, could not handle ordinary duties my day called for. I could only cry and wonder why this horrible thing had happened to Tom.

"Sorrow comes to all...
Perfect relief is not possible,
except with time. You can't
now realize that you will ever
feel better...and yet
You are sure to be happy again."

~Abraham Lincoln

Now, after more than twenty years, I know that people can survive a terrible tragedy and go on to have a good life; that simple family structure with traditions, expectations, and family dinners where all the family are present, including father, are good preparation for life and for moving on after a tragic event.

I wrote this narrative of my son's life and violent death to remember him and as a part of a healing journey for me. I was merely a chronicler of events. In writing this account, I could not keep from telling some of my own story.

When Christina entered Tom's life six years before his death, I could not write about Tom without including Christina, since she was his constant companion—his decisions were their decisions.

I suppose writing this book is a way to keep a bit of life with Tom. Seldom does a day go by without my thinking of him and his place in my heart. Things remind me of him, and tears well up inside. As I write now, more than twenty years after the event, the pain is largely gone, but the sense of loss is greater—all those years unfolded without Tom. A part of me died when he did.

Some unimportant details may not be completely accurate since I was not present in Denver with Tom during the last eight years of his life. I had difficulty eking out bits of information from those who were there; those with living memory are busy.

Big events are true-to-life and in the order they happened to the best of my knowledge, however there may be unimportant shifts in the timeline.

I used letters, old photos, old address books, my Franklin Planner notes from the time, phone conversations, e-mails, and my memory as well as that of Margaret, Laura, and Howard, with Christina chiming in every-so-often. This is my story about Tom; others have different stories about those days of 13th Avenue, Denver, in the 1980s—skateboards, punk, and raves.

CHAPTER 1: WHEN TOM WENT WEST

POPE JOHN PAUL II and President Bill Clinton were planning to travel to Denver for a conference on youth violence, a part of World Youth Day, at the same time my husband Howard and I were packing our bags to leave on July 29, 1993. From our windows at The Oxford Hotel, we could see street crews already distributing saw horses, which later would be placed to block Wazee Street for the Pope's motorcade through lower downtown, past the site for the future Coors Field, past Union Station and back up 17th Street.

Just hours earlier at Fairmount Cemetery, Alameda at Quebec, in southeastern Denver, I'd buried my son, Tom Hollar.

A few days before, Christina, his 27-year-old widow—accompanied by her brothers Michael and Gregory Schneider from Los Angeles—had chosen the cemetery plot at Fairmount, which has a good view of the Front Range off to the northwest. For me, with its view of the distant mountains, the place symbolizes eternity. The lovely plot is beneath a Western Maple frequented by flashy, noisy, black, white, and iridescent green magpies. Magpies are boisterously disrespectful of the solemn cemetery where they live—a bird Tom might have chosen.

FRONT RANGE

Massive sleeping shapes
purple and darker grey,
blue sky becomes
dark as the mountains.
My son slumbers on
in his final resting place—
Front Range snowy peaks
standing watch.
So go the days
year after year.
My son,
cold and still
as the mountains,
becoming part of
their dust.

Chapter 2: Tom's Story Begins

TOM WAS BORN on November 6, 1962 to my husband, Ed Hollar and me. A big, strong baby weighing nine pounds, seven ounces. He was round and ruddy with a bright red birthmark between his eyebrows, which faded over time. Alert and interested in everything and everyone, he seemed intense and older than his age. His sister Laura—a cute little girl with curly brown hair—had been an only child for two years, and her life changed dramatically when Tom was born.

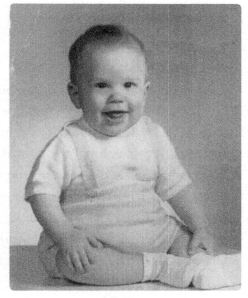

Baby Tom

For Thanksgiving that first year, I baked a turkey with our usual sage, celery and onion stuffing. Since Laura's birthday is November 25, we always celebrated her birthday at Thanksgiving time. She was happy to have some attention since she'd had to share with Tom and even had to help with his care, which was not so much fun for her. This new little brother seemed a bother: he'd wake up and cry at night, and at other times her mother would take care of him first, and she had to wait. So on this day, she had a chocolate birthday cake, which I'd made from a Duncan Hines mix, with chocolate frosting. She blew out the candles and liked opening her presents.

Wrapped in cotton blankets and lying comfortably in his reclining baby seat in the center of the table, Tom was happy sharing the festivities of her party.

The grandparents Hollar came for the day. Rachel was a kindergarten teacher, who loved little children—especially babies. When she came in the door, she said, "So we got a Tommy!"

She held Tom and smothered him with kisses. Then she fussed over Laura and exclaimed what a big girl she was at two. Tom laughed and grinned when we sang "Happy Birthday," and Laura blew out the candles.

Tom was fascinated by the little push toy she got. When she pushed it past him on the floor, it played musical notes and had lights in its wheels that sparkled.

Tom's First Christmas

Ed loved holidays and traditions, especially Christmas. He bought a large, lovely Douglas fir tree from Whispering Pines on Mt. Morris Road in Montrose near his dental office. He put on lights, and Laura and I hung the ornaments. We all enjoyed the lighted tree in the evenings when we played Christmas music, such as a 33 1/3 rpm recording of Tchaikovsky's *Nutcracker Suite,* which I have always enjoyed, and Bing Crosby's *Silent Night, White Christmas, Deck the Halls* and other Christmas songs. With a strong sense of family togetherness for his first Christmas, we held and rocked baby Tom, while we all enjoyed the lighted, decorated tree and festive music.

Mother's Day 1963

On Mother's Day 1963, we drove to Ohio to be with my parents, Bard and Julia Hall, with seven-month-old Tom in his carseat in the back of our sporty navy-blue Chrysler 300 E with tail fins and a powerful V-8 engine. My father, a Chrysler dealer, had given us a close-family discount on this car—otherwise we could not have afforded it. Laura rode in the back with Tom when all was well, but sometimes I sat in back so I could give him a bottle or change a diaper.

Tom was fussed over by his aunts Jan and Cara, his uncles John and Glenn, and his cousins Bard and Amy, and of course his grandparents. We set up in the back bedroom with Tom's bassinet. After a bottle and a good burping by Grandma Hall, Tom slept, while we had Mother's signature dinner of butter-fried chicken, mashed potatoes, peas, carrot-pineapple salad and apple pie. Tom's cousin Nick, one month younger than Tom, was there, too, but the two were too young to remember.

Neighborhood 1963

Ed and I lived in Ann Arbor when Laura was born. During that time he worked as an instructor at the University of Michigan Dental School, and I worked as a staff pharmacist at University of Michigan Hospital Pharmacy.. We moved from Stadium Boulevard in Ann Arbor to Flushing, Michigan in the fall before Tom was born in 1962.

We chose a split-level four-bedroom home with a good-sized backyard and a chain-link fence at the back. An old apple tree in the front yard had lovely, fragrant white blossoms each spring and produced a few gnarled apples, which we didn't eat. The family room on the lower level had a wall-to-wall sandstone fireplace with a foot-wide wooden mantle, which we decorated each year for Christmas with lights and evergreen boughs. The rest of the year, we displayed the children's artwork, photos, or paintings there.

We lived within walking distance of Springview Elementary School, and one block from Mutton Park with the blue water tower. The park had swings, monkey bars, and teeter-totters for the children to play on.

Each week, I would invite one or two neighborhood mothers and their children to come to our house for coffee, or I would be invited with Tom and Laura to go to their houses.

During one of these visits, Tom—in his high chair—decided to dump his bowl of oatmeal on the wall so it went sliding down and left a long, sticky mess. I think he was bored sitting in his chair while I was busy elsewhere; he liked to stay active.

Children in the Neighborhood

Many children lived in our subdivision and others flanking the school. Behind our back fence lived the Benedicts, with Michael, Christopher, Scott, Matthew, Patrick and Susan, the oldest.

Next door to the Benedicts lived the Lees, with B.J.—a few years older than Tom, Arthur Mitts ("Mitts," who was Tom's age) and Elizabeth a few years younger. David Van Brocklin lived two houses away on Clearview Drive.

Two doors down from the Lees lived Chris Bacon, who was about four years older than Tom and had a fenced-in swimming pool in his backyard.

Across our street and around the corner lived Stevie Dunn, a frequent visitor to our backyard while Tom was growing up. When they were old enough to ride two-wheeled bicycles, Doug Otero used to show up to spend an afternoon in our backyard. He lived a little further away, across Coutant Street.

Backyard Fun Begins

All the neighborhood boys liked to play in our large backyard because we had things to do: a large sandbox with buckets, shovels, trucks; a big swing hanging from a side branch of the old box elder tree; a large mowed lawn good for kicking balls or playing croquet or building on with wood.

The boys stayed busy for hours playing with little metal Matchbox© trucks, front loaders, and cars—as well as little green-plastic army men they sometimes nailed into the railroad ties that bordered the sandbox. The big draw for the boys was Tom, who cracked jokes and had spontaneous creative ideas for things they all could do.

CHAPTER 3: AS TOM GREW

LAURA HELPED ME FEED BABY TOM, mostly Gerber baby food, baby cereals, and formula from glass bottles, which I sterilized in a round electrical unit on the kitchen counter. Laura was not big enough to lift Tom, but if she sat down and held him, she could give him a bottle.

When he was about nine months old, Laura and I would sit at the round wooden table in the kitchen in front of the sliding glass doors to the backyard, while Tom sat in his high chair. We'd look out to the backyard, point, and make up things to get Tom to laugh, which he did with a hearty chuckle.

We'd say, "There goes Tommy, riding his horse!"

And Tom would laugh, rollicking in his high chair and slapping the tray. (When he cried or got excited, the birthmark on his face got redder.)

Or we'd say, "There goes Tommy climbing the tree!"

And Tom would guffaw, sometimes with drool spilling out of his grinning, toothless mouth.

We put little, round, colored cake-decoration candies on his high chair tray. It took him a long time to pick them up with wet fingers, so he didn't really get much, but it kept him busy. He would sit there laughing and slapping his tray, a happy silly time for all of us.

Tom always was drawn to sound, rhythm, and music. When he was old enough to grasp objects, he'd sit in his baby chair on the counter beside where I was working. Over and over, he'd drop a ringed set of metal measuring spoons onto the kitchen floor. He'd watch us as the spoons hit the floor, and then he'd grin. He liked the power of the noise he made.

Laura retrieved the spoons, made a fuss over them, and gave them back to him. Of course, he promptly dropped them again, watching our reaction to the sound he'd made, pleased with himself.

One of his favorite games was *kitchen musicians*. Once he could crawl, I'd let him empty the cupboards of pots and pans in the kitchen, and then I'd give him a wooden spoon, so he could bang on the lids and pans. He'd say, "Ban, ban" and laugh at the loud sounds.

He and Laura liked to play *Rhythm Bands* where he'd sit on the kitchen floor, and Laura would partially fill glasses with water, and the two of them would make music by tapping pans and glasses with spoons to make different musical sounds.

Sometimes, he'd clank two pan lids together like cymbals to add percussion to the tinkling musical sounds. We had a regular kitchen band going with Tom laughing and tapping and bouncing away with the rhythm of the sounds. Of course, they made a mess, but it was easy to clean up—just water on the floor and pots and pans to clean and put away—well worth the effort since it entertained them a while.

Little Brother Tom

By the time Tom was 18 months old, he could climb out of his crib. I'd put him to bed after the usual time spent getting him settled, and all too soon, he'd appear at the top of the short flight of stairs off the living room, grinning with pride at his achievement. By the time he was two, he could walk quite well on level surfaces and pretty much got into whatever he wanted. He called Laura, "Wawa."

We played 45 rpm records of songs like *Farmer in the Dell* and *Mary Had a Little Lamb*. He'd move his body and arms to the rhythm and really liked dancing around, trying to say the words.

Tom got into things in Laura's room and often left her toys all over the floor. He'd take what he wanted—marbles, Silly Putty, or Tootsie Rolls she'd hidden on the shelves. Laura called him, "a little brat."

Often at bedtime, I read to Laura and Tom or made up stories to tell them, which they liked the best. My mother, their beloved Grandma Hall, had told such stories to me and my two sisters, so I copied her example. They especially liked stories of Sampson the Giant, who was magic and saved people trapped in burning buildings or buried in blizzards.

Holidays

Holidays were always important for our young family. We decorated for Christmas, Easter, and Halloween. Ed loved to decorate Christmas trees, and sometimes he coated the tree with a white, soapy solution and let it dry. Ornaments looked very bright on this soap-snow-flocked tree.

As Tom grew, he liked to help put ornaments on the tree, but when he was two or three, he mostly liked to knock ornaments off. He liked to crawl under the tree to hide

Tom, Laura, Margaret with a flocked Christmas tree

in the wrapped presents, so we had to look carefully to see his smiling face among the colored wrapping paper. When he realized we had seen him, he'd laugh and hide again.

Halloween

For his first Halloween, when he was three or four, I made Tom a blue- and-white striped clown suit big enough for him to wear a warm jacket, pants, and boots under it. The suit had red balls for buttons and at the peak of its pointed hat. Laura had a similar one in red, yellow, and green stripes.

He was a little timid at first, but before the night was over, he'd discovered that it was fun to ring a doorbell, run a short distance away and then shout, "Trick or Treat!" Our neighborhood was quite safe. Those days, one didn't have to worry about razor blades hidden in apples, and there were hundreds of children roaming our neighborhood street accompanied by parents.

Christmas

When he was four, Tom started making his own Christmas ornaments. He and Laura colored, cut, and pasted paper ornaments for the Christmas tree. They made some from homemade dough, which they cut out or formed into shapes and painted.

Tom loved to make these ornaments and spent hours working on them. Then I baked them. I treasure these ornaments, which we still put on our tree each year.

Ed's parents, Earl and Rachel Hollar came for Christmas dinner. Earl had a round belly with a rosy complexion and full, round face.

Tom said, "Grandpa, you look just like Santa Claus. Say 'Yo-ho-ho,' Grandpa."

Rachel Hollar doubled over with laughter.

When Tom realized we were all giving gifts to each other, and he didn't have any to give, he scurried around the house to pick up things to give as Christmas presents: a banana, an apple, a hairbrush, a wooden bowl, an ashtray. He wrapped them as best he could, and then hand-delivered each gift, beaming proudly. This was a very happy holiday.

Chapter 4: Backyard
1967

TOM AND THE BOYS made mud in the sandbox, and they buried Tom—except for his head. He was delighted, allowing them to do this. They were all laughing, dumping bucket after bucket of wet, yellow sand on top of Tom, who wore blue jeans and a T-shirt. The other boys would be scolded if they got too dirty, so they were careful and had the vicarious fun of watching Tom being buried in soppy, yellow sand.

When he'd had enough, Tom pulled himself out of the thick, wet mud, assumed the posture of a bog monster and chased after some of the boys making threatening growls, then he appeared at the sliding-glass door off the kitchen. He was beaming, proud of himself for thinking up this slightly outrageous happening.

I made him strip to his underwear, hosed him down with the garden hose, then sent him to the shower.

I often made lunch for the gaggle of backyard boys. Standard fare back then was peanut butter and grape jelly sandwiches on white bread, with potato chips and Hi-C fruit drink. At some point, I started making better lunches— such things as chicken or turkey sandwiches, carrots and celery sticks, milk or real fruit juice, whole grain bread. This met with some resistance from Mitts.

When we invited Mitts to come for dinner, before accepting, he'd ask what we were having.

Mitts was Tom's best friend. One of the two boys climbed the fence every day so they could play together and get into trouble together. Mitts had a way of laughing with a silly little smile that encouraged Tom with whatever he was getting into. However, down through the years, Tom listened to and valued Mitts's suggestions.

Never a Dull Moment

Once when Tom and Mitts were about six, the next-door neighbors had a broken basement window with jagged glass. The two boys dared each other to put their heads into the opening.

Of course, they did.

Tom made it, but Mitts cut his head open at the temple, and blood streamed. Worried, I rushed him to the family doctor, Dr. Whites, for emergency sutures.

Tom was nervous and upset, trying to comfort Mitts as we rode to the doctor. Tom didn't, however, feel responsible for Mitts's injury, since Mitts didn't have to put his head into the opening. When Tom was nervous, he had a way of moving his head forward and tilting his chin, then tugging at the front of his shirt, as if trying to loosen a tight collar. He did it that day on the way to the doctor's office. Fortunately, Mitts healed without further problems, except the scolding he got from his parents.

An Unguarded Pool

Later that summer, Mrs. Lewis—a kindly white-haired woman, who looked and dressed like Miss Marple—was babysitting Tom and Mitts. I felt very lucky to have Mrs. Lewis as a babysitter.

In an especially devilish streak this particular day, the boys decided to give her some trouble. They left the house, cut across several backyards to the Bacon's backyard, where there was a fenced-in pool.

The boys scaled the fence and threw three or four plastic lawn chairs into the pool. Then they climbed partly into the pool on the metal ladders, getting their shoes wet. Neither boy could swim very well.

Mrs. Lewis followed them and ran around the outside of the fence shouting at them. They were laughing and having a wonderful time, not totally aware of the danger they were in. When it was no longer fun, the boys crawled back over the fence, not really taking in the stern reproach Mrs. Lewis was giving them about their stupid actions. I felt helpless to do anything about what they had done, other than talking to the Bacons, offering to fix anything broken, and scolding Tom.

Later that night, once in bed, Tom had time to think about the day's events and especially his father's version of dealing with his undesirable behavior. Tom most likely learned a lesson and wouldn't repeat his reckless behavior again.

Clear Lake

On weekends in June, July, and August in the early 1960s, we drove south to Clear Lake, Indiana, near Fremont, where my parents owned a six-bedroom cottage plus an inboard Chris Craft with a Chrysler engine and an outboard-motor fishing boat.

Lake weekends were usually crowded with relatives and other guests. Dad would take them for rides in his speedboat, and some people waterskied. Sometimes, Dad took us fishing, but Tom was too young to fish. Lake weekends were fun, but packing and watching the children did not allow much rest or recuperation for me.

Tom was a month older than his cousin, Nick Milnor, who lived in Kendallville, Indiana. Nick's Grandparents Milnor had a large cottage around the lake from ours. Nick was often at Clear Lake at the same time Tom was there.

So Tom and Nick played in the sand at Clear Lake and went swimming in little plastic pools we set up on the grass. They dug trenches in the dirt, filled them with water, splashed and got muddy. They pushed trucks around to move dirt and made ramps for the trucks to run down and crash in the mud.

The boys threw stones into the lake to watch them splash. They waded in shallow areas while holding someone's hand, since Clear Lake was mucky on the bottom on our side of the lake.

Fourth of July was always a big time at Clear Lake. Fireworks over the water plus loud firecrackers set off around the lake dominated the night until bedtime.

Tom covered his ears with his hands against the loud noises, but by the time he was five, he had learned about sparklers. We also let him light the little black discs that grew into long black snakes. He loved the rolls of caps he could hit with a hammer on the sidewalk. He had cap guns, wore leather holsters, and ran around our yard at home shooting off his cap pistol.

Across the State Line

When he was seven, he talked his Grandma Hall into taking him across the state line into Indiana to buy firecrackers. She bought him one-inch firecrackers he could light and toss. At home in the sandbox, Tom would pack his army men into a sand hill and then stick in a one-inch firecracker, light it, and run as the sand would blow up scattering the army men.

Minette 1966

We got Minette in the fall. She was a lovely, gentle, longhaired grey tabby cat with green eyes. Minette came from the home of Carol and Charles Rosmorduc, who early

Tom Hollar and Nick Milnor

Tom Hollar and Nick Milnor

on introduced their new kittens to being around humans so they would be good house pets. Charles would take a litter of kittens delivered by their mother cat, Bambi, into bed with him, and let the little kittens run around on top of the blankets where he could pet them and talk to them. Then they found homes for them.

The children loved Minette. Each tried to get her to jump onto his or her bed at night. They learned to feed her, to pull a string or toss a toy mouse to play with her, and we all spoke "cat talk" in a high-pitched voice to Minette. Tom felt very special when this cat chose his bed to settle on; this was a great comfort to him.

Margaret Was Born 1967

Tom was four-and-one-half when Margaret was born, and he thought she was a fine addition to the family. "Put her on the floor so I can play with her," he said.

He was interested, but not helpful. Once when I left Margaret on the living room floor on a large blanket before she could get around, Tom built a wall of wooden blocks around her. I think he hoped with all her wiggling she would knock it down. He sat there watching and waiting for the blocks to tumble. He kept moving the blocks closer until she did tumble a block wall, to Tom's delight. He retrieved the blocks, and set them up again.

Looney Tunes Cartoons

When Margaret was tiny, and Tom and Laura were small, they watched cartoons on Saturday mornings. They watched Scoobie Doo, Mr. Magoo,

Road Runner, Speed Racer, Fat Albert, Looney Tunes, and Bugs Bunny. I liked for them to watch *Sesame Street*. No big surprise, *Dennis the Menace* became Tom's favorite. From one of the episodes of Dennis played by Jay North, Tom learned the phrase, "Can't do it; gotta have a war dance first."

He used this often when asked to do something, and it was quite funny. Then he'd run around in a circle making war-whoop sounds and patting his mouth, a way to delay having to comply.

Tom the Builder

Tom had a large zippered plastic case of small Lego® pieces in white, blue, yellow and red, which we kept in his room. He built quirky shapes of buildings unlike any real ones. His had off-shoots or odd shapes with side appendages extending off in different directions, and he worked to keep them balanced. He made Lego® cars and sent them down ramps he'd made from his wooden blocks.

Tom set up a booby trap in his room. He put a bucket of marbles on his bookshelves attached to a string, which was tied to the doorknob. Whenever someone entered the room, the bucket of marbles would spill, making a loud sound and tricky footing.

He liked blocks, building tall towers with ramps and bridges—all for the joy of knocking them down. He raced his Matchbox® cars down the ramps and loved to have them "wreck up," as he called it. But Tom liked to stay active, so he never stayed with his blocks for more than an hour or so before he was off, usually going outside. By this time, he was old enough to be allowed to play outside in the backyard in the sandbox without a babysitter.

About this same time, Tom learned to belch at will. He was proud of his loud belch which he could do easily, sometimes as a way of changing the subject.

Tom and Laura liked their set of Lincoln Logs,® which they'd assemble into a log cabin with a green roof and a red chimney.

Tom and Laura were good at jigsaw puzzles, too. Very often, especially in the winter, we had a 1000-piece puzzle going on the 40-inch square white Formica® coffee table in the family room. Tom liked to take his breakfast down there so he could work on the puzzle while eating. And he liked to eat as he played games.

CHAPTER 5: SCHOOL YEARS
1968

IN SEPTEMBER 1968, TOM started school at Springview Elementary. He and Mitts, Stevie Dunn, Doug Otero, David VanBrocklin all attended at the same time. A group of students walked from our neighborhood. For young children, this was fairly far, about five blocks. I was very sad to see this little creative child of mine set off across the backyard with his notebook, entering a whole new chapter of his life.

Tom liked those teachers who liked him and inspired him to do his homework, praised him for his successes. Others were not so gifted. One day when Tom was ill with a sore throat when he was seven or eight, I was unable to get a babysitter on short notice.

So I settled Tom into his bed before I left for work. Minette sensed his distress. She jumped up on his bed and settled on his chest, purring. He really liked this.

Tom was not afraid. He could call me if need be, and Laura would be coming home for lunch. Gerry Benedict and Jan Lee were at home nearby. I called Jan to tell her Tom was home. She agreed to stop by to check on him.

When he got well and returned to school, one of his teachers said to him, "Tom, how does it feel to have your mother leave you when you are sick?"

Tom came home from school and told me this. This was not one of the teachers he liked and felt close to. He felt very bad, as if he had done something wrong, and I was angry. I would much rather have stayed home, but I could not abandon my pharmacy obligations and had no other pharmacist to run my pharmacy. I decided not to hire a pharmacist so I could take time off work to talk to this teacher.

Laura, Nedra, Tom, Uncle Dave, Ed holding Margaret, Rachel Hollar

Tom was a mix of fun-loving, rule-bending and integrity. Once he brought home a math-test paper, which had a grading error in his favor. When he found the mistake, he decided to take the paper to his teacher to tell her she'd given him a higher score than he had earned.

Savings

Tom opened a savings account in August of 1968 at Genesee Merchants Bank and Trust branch in Flushing. He played marbles for a penny a shot, and he traded or sold baseball cards he collected from packages of bubble gum. He sold things he'd picked up in the trash. He liked making money. His account accrued in value over the years from small deposits and interest. (His last transaction was a withdrawal in 1984 of $1100.00, leaving a small balance. He had a $75.00 US Savings bond from July, 1981.)

Backyard 1970

Tom started building tree houses in the box elder tree, which was hard to do since the tree was quite tall. The crew of boys built wooden steps, hammered into the tree trunk, so they could climb it. Tom also attached a strong, black-rubber bungee cord, which the boys used to bounce up and down on. This was great fun and good exercise. I don't recall anyone being hurt.

The little wooden tree houses morphed into forts built on the ground under the box elder tree. Made from scrap wood discarded at building sites in the many subdivisions around Springview School, forts were the best project ever.

A fort by the box elder tree with Margaret in the tree and Tom on a bungee cord to the right

The wooden forts the boys built, tore down, and rebuilt captured their total absorption. Then came the pleasure of hiding in them, a separate world of their own.

Rudimentary at first, the forts had roofs, which leaked when it rained. The boys loved to retreat into their fort then, and I sometimes made popcorn for them.

Soon the forts became more sophisticated with shingles on the roof, and later, electricity so they could have lights and listen to music. Our backyard was full of boys pounding nails into wood to change the fort. Boys from all over the small town gathered at our house, coming and going; new faces, old faces, neighborhood regulars: Mitts Lee, David Van Brocklin, Matt, Scott and Chris Benedict, Stevie Dunn, Doug Otero.

I'd come home from the pharmacy to find bicycles all over the driveway and front lawn. Around dinner time mothers phoned and asked me to send their sons home, which I did, of course.

I'll admit to getting "fed up" with Tom and his friends constantly pounding nails and running around our backyard. Every so often, I'd go out and send all the boys home just for a bit of peace and quiet.

Dreams of a Dawn Donut Boy

Every so often, I took Tom and Laura to McDonald's on Clio Road in northwestern Flint, a short drive from our home in Flushing. Across the road was a Dawn Donut Shop with a huge neon sign on a tall stand at the street corner.

The bright sign showed a smiling boy wearing blue bell-bottom trousers and a tall white chef's hat holding a large tray of doughnuts. Tom was fascinated with this sign.

When we asked him what he wanted to be when he grew up, he didn't say, "Fireman," or "Policeman," as many little boys did. Tom always said, "Dawn Donut Boy." He had a cute way of slurring it, saying it fast, with a rhythm to the sound, like a song.

CHAPTER 6: MAJOR FAMILY CHANGES
1970

IHAD GRADUATED from the University of Michigan College of Pharmacy in 1958 and pursued a career in pharmacy at the University of Michigan Hospital Pharmacy in Ann Arbor as a staff pharmacist at the time Laura was born in 1960. Since that time, I had stayed home to be a housewife and mother, except for working part time at Flint Medical and Surgical Supply on Saginaw Street in downtown Flint and later as a part-time pharmacist at Bejcek's Drug Store on Main Street in Flushing.

By 1970, I had become tired of being a housewife, realizing that life was not as I'd expected. I grew up in the fifties when outward appearances of a perfect marriage and implied happiness therein came from keeping a spotless home and being a good cook.

There were no real challenges for me now, and being wife of a professional man was not all it had been trumped up to be.

One day I sat in my kitchen after having washed and waxed the floors. I thought that life must hold more for me than this. Staying home with three children was harder than working outside the home. I filed for divorce. Of course, there were other compelling issues related to the divorce, but this is Tom's story.

Ed and I Were Divorced 1971

Laura was eleven, Tom was nine, and Margaret was four when Ed and I were divorced. After this disruption to our household, Ed moved into an apartment across town, and we began the routine of alternating care on weekends. The divorce affected Laura the most. Tom's backyard world changed little; but now he was pressured to mow the lawn.

Tom and his father had never been close. They didn't do things together. Ed loved gardening—especially growing roses and tomatoes. He kept our yard looking beautiful with blooming flowers, mowed lawn, and neat gardens. And he was an avid University of Michigan football fan, never missing a home game.

Tom was interested in building with wood, creating with mud and clay, working with wheels and motors, remaking bicycles and cars. Tom did attend some football games with Ed, but he was not a huge fan. Tom certainly realized that our beautiful lawn and gardens were the result of his father's care, but he took it for granted.

At the time of the divorce, I was forced to go back to work full-time. I had a degree in pharmacy, so the judge didn't award alimony. This was a turning point in my life.

I took a full-time job as a staff pharmacist at McLaren Hospital in Flint. (After that, I continued to work for the next 37 years, including doing the hard work of going back to school for advanced degrees.) At present, I needed a good babysitter so I could work full-time.

The Babysitter and the Backyard Buddies 1971

I met Colleen Heatwole, R.N., an IV nurse, who worked in the space next to the pharmacy at McLaren. She knew Nancy and Clair Smoker, newlywed Mennonites from Pennsylvania, who'd recently moved to Flint. Clair, a conscientious objector from the Vietnam war, was doing alternative service driving a Goodwill truck. Nancy was looking for a job. I hired her and have always felt that divine intervention played a role in providing her to help me.

Nancy was perfect: she kept the house cleaner than ever, watched the children, made dinner and fed them while I worked. Clair was good-natured and liked the children. He often brought his guitar to play songs so we could sing: *She'll be Comin' Round the Mountain When She Comes, Stewball*, or *Jesus Loves Me*.

Nancy was a match for Tom and his backyard buddies. Having grown up in a large family with brothers and sisters and cousins, Nancy was up to the challenge. She could keep them in line with no nonsense, and she had a good sense of humor. She had the energy to go outside where they were, stand there with hands on her hips, little white voile cap on her smoothed-back light-brown hair. She wore an apron over full skirts and short-sleeved white blouses most of the time.

Nancy said to Tom, "Get down there and pick up your room, and make your bed before you go outside to play."

But Tom had his own thoughts about Nancy. "You think you're big," he told her. "You think you can tell me what to do. My mom hired you to clean the house, and you tell me to clean my room! You're just trying to get out of work."

"Listen, Buddy, a big part of my job is teaching *you* to do your part, and making sure you mind when we ask you to do things. Now get down there before I have to *make* you go!"

Tom reluctantly ambled into the house and made his bed and picked up his room, but he wore a mad look on his face under his red railroader's cap with white polka dots.

Nancy Smoker was many things, but lazy was not one of them.

Tom learned that he could disappear into his room, close the door, and crawl out the window without being discovered for quite a while. Tom's room was on the lower level next to the family room with windows at ground level. When this no longer worked, he discovered the vanishing cleaning-lady trick: he'd take the small vacuum into his room, turn it on, and exit via the window. Tom's world—his creative space—was his backyard where his ideas took shape, and he was free in his element.

That's why peers were attracted to Tom: he had a sense of purpose, he always had some project they could help with, and he did things they dared not do. He fed on this admiration, open to any opportunity to do something a little outrageous, always in good fun, never harming nor making fun of anyone. But he saw humor in everything.

Tom welcomed all comers, treated them fairly, made them feel accepted; there were no fights. Boys took turns, and Tom doled out jobs for them. I could see boys waiting to saw two-by-fours. Two or three boys sat on the long end steadying the board, waiting for a turn to saw, while one boy sawed off the other end.

Nancy Smoker had a time with Tom when he insisted upon putting a fireplace into his fort. He built a fire from sticks in an empty Folger's coffee can and put another empty coffee can with two open ends in the roof to serve as a chimney. She was afraid he'd set fire to the fort, but he insisted there was no problem since he had put in a chimney. She made him keep a full bucket of water just outside the door to the fort—just in case. Tom reluctantly complied.

On nice summer nights, Matt, Chris or Scott Benedict, Mitts, Tom, and perhaps other boys slept in the fort in sleeping bags. Of course there was less sleeping going on than talking.

Once I had to send the boys home at 3:00 A.M. because there was too much noise; they were blasting music in the fort.

Woes of a Single Mother

When I was a single mother with three healthy children, I had trouble. I'd grown up in the 1950s when women were expected to be good housekeepers, while Tom grew up in the 70s and 80s when things were quite different--

casual, laid back, rebellious. While growing up, my two sisters and I, along with our mother, Tom's Grandma Hall, cleaned the house thoroughly and then took baths and washed our hair each Saturday before dinner.

I recall getting really mad at Tom when I wanted him to help or to pick up his room. We had a good understanding and were close, but he just stared at me, questioning me with his big dark-brown eyes, as if to ask why he needed to pick up his room. Why was it so important to keep a neat and clean house? Why did it matter?

He had a wisdom I didn't appreciate then, but later began to understand.

Kit, one of my 11-year-old patients, reminded me of Tom. This cute boy's creativity was slowly being smothered by the constant need for him to conform.

KIT FLYNN

Kit Flynn, just 11,
drew pastel pictures
with colored pencils:
neat, even marks
on the paper.
A pineapple, a tree,
a house.
Good in school,
young Kit
still had
a twinkle
in his brown eyes.

I once had a boy
like Kit,
but his eyes danced
with irreverent impish glee.
Eyes black like a crow's—
glints of purple, neon blue,
unfathomable pools
deep, deep into his soul—
knowing, pleading,
wanting to say it all as it was.

I once had a boy
who drew pictures—
strong, black lines,
with chaotic reds, oranges,
raw, passionate cobalt, magenta—
flowing, twisting, screaming life.
Angry, black pictures of me—
bloodshot eyes, missing teeth, moles.
        Massive shapeless forms
like amoeba
when he was hurt by me
or I didn't understand,
and we argued.

Bored in school,
        he tried so hard to tell me
he'd never stay in the lines—
no point, no time.
He drew outrageous, compelling,
knowing pictures at age 11,
as if he knew.

Chapter 7: Tom—More Woes of a Single Mother

WHEN TOM AND I were mad at each other, we drew pictures of each other that were funny so that after a while our anger disappeared, and we'd laugh. Each of us kept drawing more outrageous pictures, trying to outdo each other.

One time when I asked Tom to do some task around the house, he said to me, "I won't do it, and you can't make me."

He was right. At nine or ten, he was as tall as I was and stronger. He worked hard at what *he* wanted to do, but not at tasks *I* wanted him to do.

Tom was never an easy, compliant child, but kept doing imaginative things such as heating coins in a pan on the stove and then forgetting about them until smoke filled the kitchen. He'd planned to hammer the hot coins into a wooden table he was making, but instead, they burned round holes into the kitchen carpeting.

I was very upset since the carpeting was still fairly new, but after a time, we all laughed about how life with Tom was so unpredictable.

Popping Corn

One time, when Tom was about ten, he started to pop corn upstairs in the

Tom's Drawings

kitchen, then went down to play a game. He forgot about the popcorn until black smoke filled our kitchen. The bottom of the pan had started to melt, so we threw it into the grassy backyard and had to repaint the kitchen ceiling, and repair the carpeting.

Dish Duty Strategies

The children were expected to do the dishes. There was always a hubbub about who would do what. Margaret and Laura would usually start, but Tom learned that he could disappear into the lavatory off the kitchen by the door to the garage.

He'd not be missed for a while. Sometimes the girls pounded on the locked lavatory door and shouted, "Tom, you get your lazy self out here to help."

And he did eventually come out, but didn't hurry to the sink. He'd suddenly need a tissue to blow his nose, or he'd pick up something left on the table that absolutely had to be taken downstairs.

This was also the time of "toilet jokes." Tom and the Milnor boys had many a phone call where the only reply from the Milnors was the sound of a toilet flushing. They had a card that made this sound, so all they had to do was open the card and hold it near the phone. The phone would ring, then I'd hear loud laughter.

Each time it happened it was funny again.

Tom Was Like Grandpa Hall

Tom took after the Hall side of the family. He was much like his Grandpa Hall (Bard Kenneth Hall); both were happiest with grease up to their elbows and working on engines and motors.

Like Tom, my father spread his things around, but always knew where they were. My father was considered to be an honest car dealer. While he knew how to trade cars, he always worked on used cars to be sure they were in good shape before he sold them. Tom seemed to inherit this integrity, as well as an ability to make a sound deal.

My father loved being a Chrysler dealer. He was so proud of the flashy new cars when they came in, especially the Chrysler Town and Country with its red-plaid wool upholstery and real wood on the outside. He liked to take us for a ride in these cars.

He provided us with a convertible to drive in the summertime. Grandpa Hall died when Tom was two, so they never really knew each other. But as a boy, Bard Hall played every prank a country boy could dream up—including leading a cow up the church bell tower in Evansport, Ohio and tying the bell rope to the cow's tail; and releasing a snake from handlebars of his bicycle outside the ice cream parlor just as girls were walking out the door. It was so obvious that Tom shared this same spirit of fun.

Of course, Tom was a favorite of his Grandma Hall who said, "Just leave him alone! He'll find himself one day. He needs to work with his hands." She was right.

Born to parents who were products of the 1950s, both professional, there was always pressure on Tom to conform, fit in, pursue a professional career. Tom was not meant for this, but this was hard for a parent to see. His Grandpa Hall was a garage mechanic, who became a car dealer. They were born six days apart (Scorpios), and they died on dates six days apart, different years, of course.

Tom's caring about people without judging them came mostly from Grandma Hall. There are many stories of people she befriended, never expecting to be paid back. Arthur Garbers was a good example. He wandered into her yard one day, homeless. She, widowed at the time, had a large lawn with trees, so she gave him a job keeping up the lawn.

As it turned out, Arthur was a runaway from family in West Virginia, who were trying to have him committed as being unable to manage his affairs. He stayed in Ohio with Mother as his caregiver until he died in a nursing home. She found a place for him to live, took food to him, and later visited him in the nursing home.

There are others on the list of recipients of Mother's good will. Tom picked up this attitude of kindness and generosity from his Grandma Hall.

And Grandma Hall indulged him. He loved to stay with her in Wauseon, Ohio where I grew up. She turned her garage over to Tom, took him to junk yards and to visit friends of his Grandpa Hall.

They got a kick out of Tom's interest in cars, parts, wheels, motors, bicycles, electricity, just like his grandpa. Grandma Hall would buy him what he wanted—wheels, pieces of cars, tools, and batteries.

Then he worked for hours and days in her garage building things like wagons, three or four-wheeled go-carts often without a seat or steering wheel, and one special one he called "Monster." One had towers made of junk with an electric light at the top. He made an interesting one from metal bicycle-wheel rims with spokes, rusty chains, and handlebars, all mounted on a weathered six-by-six piece of wood. (When he grew up this sculpture was displayed in his Corona Street apartment in Denver.)

Howard Downing Came to Dinner

When Tom was about nine, I decided to learn how to ski and took lessons at Mt. Holly near our home. When I moved from Ohio, I decided that to like living in Michigan, I must appropriately dress for the colder weather and learn to like all the snow.

I liked to go skiing in northern Michigan at Boyne Mountain. Often a group of skiers from Flint and surrounding towns was there. On one of these ski trips, I met a Flint man, Howard Downing, Jr., in the Snowflake Lounge at Boyne Mountain. Howard asked me to ski with him the next day. Thus began a long-lasting friendship.

Margaret and Tom ready to greet Howard before dinner

Back at home, I invited Howard to come for dinner. The children didn't know what to make of this new situation, but they were excited and curious. For one thing, Howard smoked cigarettes at that time and regularly drank Coca Cola and ate Lay's potato chips before dinner. At times he carried a giant bottle of Coke with him when he came to dinner. I usually cooked staples like fried chicken, meatloaf, hamburgers or sloppy joes, sometimes fish or roast beef.

When Howard rang the doorbell, Laura would rush to the piano and start playing to show off a little. She was in John Thompson Book No. Two and liked to play etudes, which she'd learned while practicing for her piano lessons.

Tom and Margaret also liked to hide in the coat closet that opened to the living room not far from the front door. Once Howard was inside, they'd jump out.

Tom greeted Howard with such endearing comments as, "What are you doing here?" or "Why do you keep coming back here?" He'd stand with his hands on his hips, actually pleased that Howard was there. Before long, he and Howard would be tussling on the carpet, rolling around, having a good time.

Sometimes Margaret and Tom dressed up in outlandish outfits for Howard's visits. One time they wore black bowler hats and neckties and put clown makeup on their faces.

Soon the children started to tell Howard he should quit smoking since it was bad for him. They sat on the steps going upstairs just off the living room and watched him with disapproval. They made remarks like, "You know, smoking makes you stink," or "We don't like the smell of your smoke; it makes us cough." Then they'd start making hacking cough noises. Or "Why don't you quit smoking?"

Routinely, the three children lined up, arms folded, to greet Howard with heckling remarks about his smoking.

Likewise they commented on his consumption of Coca Cola. By this time, I had not been buying soda of any kind for the family to drink for a year or so, and I never had bought very much. I taught my children that soda is not good for us, especially young girls.

The net result of the children's efforts was that Howard stopped smoking, and he gave up drinking Coca Cola.

When Tom got used to the idea that Howard was coming back, he still tackled him at the front door and had a good session of rolling on the floor before dinner.

While Howard had no experience with children, his background of having been a Lieutenant in the U.S. Army's 1st Armored Division, including a stint as company commander, gave him enough background that he was undaunted. I think Howard liked the idea of being part of this unlikely group, where there was always something going on.

On December 16, 1972, Howard and I were married at his parents' home on Circle Drive near Flint Golf Club. My family from Ohio and Indiana came. Howard's sister, Gail, and her husband, Michael Smith and their daughters, Maureen and Sydney, were present.

Someone commented that Howard and I were married between appointments since I was quite busy setting up my new pharmacy, which opened for business in Genesee County Community Mental Health Building in February, 1973, just two months after the wedding.

When Howard moved into our house with the children and me, things changed. He believed in routine, discipline, duty, schedules, manners, responsibility, and fairness. Tom was then a lanky ten-year-old with a notable dislike for work around the house.

Family Schedules

Soon after Howard moved into our home in Flushing, we set up charts of duties for the children with reimbursement, so they could earn an allowance. Charts on the refrigerator listed duties, with a rotating schedule.

We put X-X-X in the appropriate squares when tasks were finished. Such things as scraping and stacking dishes, washing and rinsing dishes, drying and putting away dishes, emptying wastebaskets into the garage bin for trash collection, mowing front lawn, mowing back lawn, shoveling front sidewalk in winter, vacuuming family room, picking up one's bedroom, picking up the family room, and washing the table in the family room, doing laundry.

This plan worked better for Tom, but he still needed to be prodded to get started. He had picked up a few jobs mowing lawns, so he felt a bit independent with his own income stream.

The schedule sheet kept disappearing from the front of the refrigerator. No one knew where it had gone or how it happened to disappear.

After a few times, we abandoned the schedule, since it took quite a bit of time to set it up each time; we did not have computers to help back then. We went back to the familiar pattern of expecting the children to do the dishes, pick up their rooms, make their beds each day, and help with other tasks as assigned.

One time when it was Tom's turn to wash dishes, I came upon him in the kitchen standing about two feet from the sink where dirty dishes were stacked. He held a large squirt gun and was squirting water at the dishes—his attempt to make the job tolerable.

Next, Tom bargained with Laura and Margaret to do his share of the dishes for money. This worked a few times. Laura usually did her share without hesitation, and when she was waiting for Tom to do his part, she'd come to me to say, "Tom's not working."

No amount of talking could get Tom to move faster, but once he got started, he and Laura and Margaret actually seemed to have fun joking and laughing while they washed, rinsed, sprayed each other, and dried the dishes.

About Tom

Tom was a vortex spinning off good-will energy that caught others in it and took them along. He had a kind of humble good sense like his Grandpa Hall. His life was about accepting others, about creativity, about his projects. Always he had something creative going on, a purpose—usually building something, with a place for others to fit in and participate. No questions asked.

Everyone was welcome to just pitch in, get dirty, work together, cooperate, get engrossed in the project at hand, crack jokes, go into the house for water and to use the lavatory, go home when your mother called.

His life was about his humor; he could laugh about almost any situation without hurting others, and he made people feel included in his jokes. Tom's way:

Accepting others was his creed,
having fun was his goal,
being a little outrageous along the way.
He saw the fun and good in everyone.

"Have fun." Tom lived his watchwords with everyone around him.

Junk-Bikes and Other Treasures

Tom loved junk and bargains. On garbage pickup day, he'd junk pick and come home with a discarded television or appliance he'd take apart to work on. (Much later, in Denver, Tom became a dumpster diver, reveling in his "finds," which he brought back to his apartment to rework or repaint.)

In our garage in Flushing, he'd build one bicycle after another from parts he'd pick up from curbs on junk-pickup day. He didn't follow the rules; his bikes were different, creative—maybe three wheels of different sizes or two wheels with a very high seat that could have been in a circus. We called his bikes, "gronky."

He and Margaret would take off down our quiet street peddling one of his bikes, struggling to keep balance. Soon they'd return laughing, and I was always glad when they'd come back unharmed.

Mitts and other boys were there most days working with the bicycle parts lying on the garage floor to be put together to make a new bike.

One day Tom finished a gronky bike with a lawnmower wheel in front. This was especially challenging for him to ride. A Flushing high school physics teacher, who was visiting in the neighborhood, came outside to the porch to watch, laughing at the spectacle of Tom struggling down Clearview Drive on this odd-looking bike with mismatched wheels. Tom loved this kind of attention.

School For the Deaf 1973

Because Tom didn't respond when Nancy or I told him to do things or even during ordinary conversation at times, I became concerned that maybe he had a hearing problem. My father was hard of hearing, and so am I. So I made an appointment for Tom to be tested at the School for the Deaf in Flint in the old brick building on Miller Road. After several hours of testing, therapists declared that Tom's hearing was perfectly normal. So it seems that Tom conveniently had selective hearing.

Chapter 8: Outings and Ski Trips

W HILE GROWING UP, Howard had spent some summers with friends who had a home along the Boardman River near Traverse City, Michigan. He had fond memories of good times there. He suggested a family outing on the Boardman.

Canoe Trip Boardman River, Ranch Rudolph 1973

On a Friday after work in June, Laura, Tom, Margaret, Howard and I drove to Traverse City and out Brown Bridge Road to Ranch Rudolph, where we stayed in the motel, all in one room with a bunk bed, a folding bed, and a double bed.

We ate dinner in the dining room where the children had burgers and fries, with Tom preferring a cheeseburger.

Tom and Laura played ping pong in the game room off the dining room, but soon Tom found the pin-

Howard, Margaret, and Tom in canoe
on Boardman River

ball machines, which he loved, but being Tom, he often got the loud honk for tilting the table.

I played several games with him, which was fun even though he trounced me. The children were excited to be staying in a motel, a new experience for them.

Saturday morning we ate pancakes and sausages in the restaurant before setting out on a four-hour canoe trip down the Boardman River. We rented two canoes with Howard, Tom, and Margaret in one, and Laura and me in the other. Staff took us to Forks Campground, where we fitted each child with a life preserver and launched the canoes from a gentle slope on the river bank.

The strong currents of the Boardman carried us back down the river toward Ranch Rudolph. Little paddling needed to be done, but steering was critical since fallen trees and branches cluttered the river. They were not cleared away because they provided good habitat for fish.

Groups of fishermen were set up all along the banks of the river as we approached Ranch Rudolph. Some people had picnics spread out on blankets, and others had camper trailers parked along the road.

As we floated and paddled to steer down the Boardman, we pushed away from fallen trees using a paddle or with our hands on the branches. It was great fun.

Laura kept hitting her thumb on trees so it became sore; all of us endured deer fly bites, which cannot be described adequately. These bites are more like a gouge of flesh bitten out with formic acid insect venom injected, really nasty. We all got more sun than expected, even though we were mostly in the shade of large trees along the banks of the river. Our faces were ruddy and tanned, close to sunburn.

The children had small seats attached to the canoe seats, while Howard and I sat on a regular canoe seat in the rear to help steer with a large paddle or on the floor of the canoe in the middle. We stopped for a picnic (which the dining room had packed for us) at a wooden bridge across the Boardman. We pulled our canoes onto the banks of the river and scrambled up to sit on the bridge to eat.

Since there were no outhouses, we all had to find cover in the bushes to relieve ourselves. Laura complained that Tom was peeking at her through the bushes. Later, at home, he drew a picture of what he said he saw and taunted her with it. We all had fun on this outing, a memorable time together.

Drummond Island

Later that summer, we rented a two-bedroom cabin at Lyke Marina on Drummond Island. Laura, Tom, and Margaret liked the adventure of traveling from the Upper Peninsula of Michigan to the island on a ferry which also carried the car.

On dirt roads, we hiked around the island and picked raspberries as we went. We purchased licenses and rented boats to fish in Lake Huron near the marina.

The children dropped lines from the long dock and caught a few rockfish and blue gills. Tom liked to fish as long as they were biting, but when the lines were quiet Tom said, "I'm sick of doing this; let's do something else."

I caught the largest fish I'd ever caught, a fourteen-inch northern pike. We cleaned the fish, I rolled it in flour, cooked it, and we ate it along with potatoes and salad for dinner. While the fish was delicious, there were so many bones that it

Tom and Howard on Drummond Island

was hard to eat.

We rented bicycles and rode around the island on roads near Lake Huron. We came upon a dolomite quarry near the road where this chalky white mineral was being dug up and shipped for commercial usage. Chalky pits with vertical sides in tiers lined the quarry where dolomite had been chopped out of the hillside. Piles of dolomite rocks of several sizes were along roads going down into the quarry.

Front loaders and yellow dump trucks were parked near the main road leading down to the big pit. We rode our bikes part way down this road to the quarry, but turned back since it was so dry and dusty. Tom was eager to go all the way down so he could see the trucks and equipment up close, but it turned out to be more than we wanted to do.

Ski Trip to Sugar Loaf Winter 1973

We rented a chalet at Sugar Loaf, where I enrolled the children in ski school. Tom decided he didn't want to go to ski school, so he hid. We searched for him and finally found him under the bed in the room where the children slept on bunk beds. We hauled him out, and he attended ski school. The ski instructors made it fun.

Pretty soon he appreciated his improved ability to turn and to ski on steeper hills. When we were all on the same hills at the same time, we had fun skiing past each other. Tom liked to cut it close, and would shout, "On your left," or "On your right," and go skiing by fast. I was never a very good skier, and sometimes this was enough to make me lose balance and fall, especially if I was in a turn.

Ski Trip to Shanty Creek Winter 1973

At Shanty Creek Ski Resort we rented a nice chalet with a balcony facing the slopes, where Howard and I enjoyed a glass of wine before dinner.

Margaret was just starting to ski on red wooden skis that didn't slide very well, but this made them safer. However, she developed chicken pox with red spots on her face, arms, and trunk. We had to keep her from the other children in the dining room, but she was not very sick and wanted to ski.

Tom skiing at Shanty Creek

So Howard and I took her on the bunny hills, one of which was called, "Chicken Run." We had a good laugh about this and took pictures. I loved these days of easy skiing with the children—good exercise followed by a good dinner.

Tom had become an agile skier and on our many ski trips, he would take off to go up the chair lift and down the hills as fast as he could. Sometimes Tom skied with Howard and me, and sometimes with Margaret. He was kind and patient with Margaret, helping her get on and off the chair lift, or up after a fall, but she was able to manage quite well without help.

Camping Trip to Pictured Rocks, Mosquito River June 1974

Margaret and Tom, Howard and I spent five days hiking and camping near Mosquito River in Pictured Rocks National Lakeshore on Lake Superior. Pictured Rocks, a popular tourist attraction, is near Munising.

Howard liked maps and had

Tom and Margaret at Mosquito River in Pictured Rocks National Lakeshore in Michigan

49

learned orienteering in the army, so we started out by trying to hike through the woods to our destination following directions on the map, but we had to turn back and drive in the long way since we were not sure where we were, and the hiking was difficult through the underbrush.

Tom feeding black ducks

The next day, we followed trails along the sand to the mouth of Mosquito River and set up our big tent at the top of a sand hill above the river. Margaret and Tom had fun building a bridge of fallen logs across the river, which was only a few feet wide at this point near its outlet to Lake Superior.

They then walked across their bridge several times, lost balance and fell down into the cold water, only to get up and do it again. We had freeze-dried food to eat and water filters to prepare river water for drinking and to use in preparing the freeze-dried dinners. We ate dinner around a small campfire in a pit we made in the sand.

Tom and Margaret followed trails from the river that led to Lake Superior. They came back and asked if it was OK for them to moon the tour boats traveling along the shore, where passengers could view the colorful pictured rocks.

We said, "No!"

They told us that other campers along the crest of the rocks were mooning the tour boats. We never knew for sure whether they actually did moon the tour boats or not.

In the morning when we awakened in our tent, we all had fine, red, itchy rashes on our arms, legs, faces and trunks. We could not figure out why until the following morning when we awakened to find the inside of our tent covered with tiny sand fleas which had thoroughly bitten us during the night. They were small enough to enter through screens on the tent walls. Although these bites were minor, it was enough to cause us to break camp and decide to set up another place for the next night.

Camping Trip to Wilderness State Park, Mirror Lake August 1975

I was able to trade my pale-green Buick Skylark for a nice, big, pale-yellow Oldsmobile station wagon in 1975. We decided to use this car to make the journey to Porcupine Mountains State Park at the west end of the Upper Peninsula and to include some of the neighborhood boys.

Howard had been a Boy Scout, had camped during his teens, and liked the idea of taking extra children. Earlier, Howard, Margaret, Tom, and I had spent a weekend at Wilderness State Park, at Waugoshance Point in the Lower Peninsula, where we enjoyed the facilities, including a water pump, and the proximity to Lake Michigan.

Tom and Margaret ready for camping trip to Mirror Lake

So we invited three Benedict boys: Patrick, who was Margaret's age, Scott, and Matthew. The wilderness cabin had capacity to sleep eight people.

In no way, under any possible set of circumstances was Laura interested in traveling ten hours in the same car with her little brother and three Benedict boys. She had quite enough of them at home. She spent time with her father while the rest of us were away, and she had become an avid reader.

I packed food for each day, carefully measuring portions of rolled oats, Cream of Wheat, powdered milk, and brown sugar to cover the number of days and the number of people.

Since we carried everything in to the cabin in our backpacks, we didn't take canned goods or bulky items. We did take a little bread and peanut butter. We planned on catching a few fish to augment our food supply. What I didn't plan for was the hearty appetites of young boys, so the morning oatmeal was not enough to fill them up.

On the third day, Tom, Matt, and Patrick decided to go down the river to fish. From Mirror Lake, we had caught only one small fish, which was infested with parasite cysts and inedible. It was not enough to help feed us anyhow. I packed their lunches in brown paper bags, and they set out. Much later, they came back all excited and very hungry. They told us squirrels and chipmunks had gotten their lunches, which they had left behind to go fishing, so they didn't have any. We were running out of food, but I gave them more.

This plus because the fact that there was no water pump, we had to boil all our water, we decided to head for home in the morning. We packed our backpacks and started our trek to the car after a meager breakfast of granola, coffee, water, and dried apples. We all were tired and hungry. After reaching the car, we piled in and headed home. We stopped at the first restaurant we came to, ordered lunch or breakfast and devoured every bit of it.

Boyne Highlands, Bartley House Ski Trip 1974

We took all three of our children for a long weekend ski trip to Boyne Highlands, where we stayed in Bartley House and ate in their dining room. The lodge presented a good buffet dinner, and they were used to children. The children took ski lessons, and we all enjoyed the hills at Boyne Highlands.

At dinner, as we were serving ourselves at the buffet, Tom pointed to a bowl of green beans, and said, "What's that?" prepared to reject them.

The host, who was good with kids, said, "Buzzard puke."

This was the right thing to say, and Tom immediately said this was his favorite and piled green beans on his plate. To this day, we still make Bartley

House green beans and call them "buzzard puke." The recipe is actually green beans in a butter-garlic sauce.

Ball Chalet at Sugarloaf

One year we rented the Ball Chalet at Sugarloaf for the family to stay in while skiing. A very modern, fun place to stay with an open floor plan. We all sat in the glass-ceilinged great room with stars above our heads to talk about our day on the hills.

Laura had brought a friend, Kathy Maxwell, to go skiing with us. Mitts came with Tom. The chalet had a large carved wooden totem pole in the landing of the stairway to the second floor. The totem pole reached to the ceiling. Tom climbed this totem pole, and was able to look down into Laura and Kathy's bathroom on the first floor to taunt them. Laura yelled, "Tom, you get down right now!"

Tom, enjoying the power of his vantage point said, "Make me!" He was hanging on with his legs and one arm around the pole.

Laura and Kathy could use other bathrooms to avoid using theirs until Tom shinnied back down the totem pole, but each time they wanted to use their bathroom, they first checked to see whether Tom or Mitts had climbed the totem pole.

We had dinner sitting at a round table off the kitchen. Tom spilled cocoa on the floor on his way from the kitchen to the table.

Before I had a chance to tell him to clean it up, he had taken a dishrag, placed it under his foot, and was, in his way, cleaning it up, smearing the cocoa on the floor.

I said, "Tom, get water and soap suds and clean it up."

He made a big deal of it, but he found a bucket, added Mr. Clean and water, and wiped up the floor so it would not be sticky.

CHAPTER 9: ADVENTURES AT HOME

AT HOME, the children liked to make snowmen in the yard. Tom's snowmen had mustaches and beards. Sometimes, he drew black cuts on them and added stage blood, or he put bandages around a stick arm or added a crutch. He liked to draw hicks and hayseed-type yokels that he called "Elmer" with a prominent Adam's apple and baseball cap, sitting in a truck cab.

Backyard 1974-1976

As the boys grew older, their interests changed from sandbox, dirt bikes, and forts to cars, racing, pinball, skateboards.

These days, sometimes they would ride away on their bikes to the pits at the end of Clearview Drive where there were hills, and they could "pop wheelies." When he was about fourteen, Tom had a red dirt bike with strong deeply

Tom popping a wheelie on Clearview Drive

treaded tires. He became good at jumping short distances with his bike off a small hill and landing without falling. He and Matt rode at the pits regularly; Matt could ride about the same as Tom. These were gravel pits, and there was always a certain amount of danger related to the possibility of their falling into the deeper pits, which held water.

When Nancy Smoker was quite pregnant with her first child, Carl, she quit working for us. She jokingly said that she had made all her mistakes with my children, so she could get it right for her own. After that, I was fortunate to find good babysitters for after school among neighbors and other acquaintances. Mrs. Tierney, Mrs. Archambault, Mrs. Lowe, and some high school girls, including Eleanor Fras, were regulars.

One day, I came home from my pharmacy mid-afternoon unexpectedly to find three older boys, whom I didn't know, in the fort smoking pot. I made Tom and his friends tear down the fort, and it was never to be rebuilt again. Tom understood.

Monster 1975

Each summer, the children spent a week or two with Grandma Hall in Ohio. Often we met at Howard Johnson's Restaurant in Ann Arbor, which was about half way for both of us. Tom always had fried clams at Howard Johnson's, sometimes a double order. Grandma Hall was always glad to have the children come, and she was glad when they went home again.

Tom and Margaret with Grandma Hall in Ohio

One summer Tom built an open three-wheeled car with steering wheel, lights, and a motor. He spent weeks in Grandma Hall's garage building it. His Ohio friend, Mike Metzger and his cousin, Nick Milnor often came to help.

Grandma Hall was a good seamstress. She started a small non-profit business patching jeans for Tom's cousin, Bard Dielman and his friend Steve Tedrow. She would take scraps of fabric or leather, and stitch a good-sized patch over worn spots or holes in the jeans without changing the way they fit. This caught on, and boys from around Wauseon started bringing jeans for her to patch. Most of the time, she didn't charge, but sometimes, the boys insisted upon paying. She signed her work with a logo: GHJ (Grandma Hall's Jeans.) Tom and Laura had their jeans patched, and were very proud of the resulting stylish jeans.

Years later, Nancy Smoker and a group from her church in Pennsylvania used some of these GHJ patches to make quilts for us. I treasure these quilts, which are still in use.

Skateboard Ramp 1976

Back in Michigan, one day in June the steady pounding of nails resumed. A new project required wood, hammers, and nails. Six-to-eight boys dumped their bikes in our driveway after school and began hammering, putting sheets of wood together—standing back, pointing, talking, redoing. I did not know what was up, but knew it was important since the boys were so focused and were working so hard.

Tom and his helpers continued steadily every day for about three weeks. Finally, there emerged an eight-foot wide, twenty-foot high U-shaped plywood ramp, supported by a two-by-four understructure. The ramp filled half of our backyard from the box elder tree to the cement patio. We didn't question where they got materials since all of them had allowances or some sort of job.

Then boys with skateboards from all over town showed up. It made the local newspaper, the *Flushing Observer*. Asked how I felt about having a large skateboard ramp in my backyard with all the local boys clamoring to try it, I said, "At least I know where my son is; it is a creative project where they get good exercise and work together."

Except when it rained, the ramp was always full of boys riding their skateboards. Matt Benedict became quite adept and could actually turn around in the air at the top of his ride up the ramp. Tom was good at building the skateboards and learned to repair them. He'd buy a deck, attach trucks to the deck to hold the wheels and allow turns with weight shift. He kept an Allen wrench, a half-inch socket wrench, and a Phillips screwdriver in his little red metal tool box, along with spare kingpins, large bolts, and rubber bushings—just in case.

One evening, an irate builder appeared at our door telling us that his plywood was now in the skateboard ramp in our backyard. A new subdivision was being built seven or eight blocks away, and the boys apparently scavenged wood from houses being built there.

When we confronted Tom about where the plywood came from, his face turned red, and he started making the nervous gesture of loosening his shirt collar. To him, it was there lying on the ground for the taking, just like junk on trash pickup day. "I didn't think of it as stealing," he said. "I thought it was thrown away."

We paid for the plywood, and put Tom under restrictions. He couldn't use the skateboard ramp for one week, plus extra turns doing dishes and doing dishes all alone and lectures about stealing. We withheld his allowance for helping around the house and doing dishes to contribute to the cost of the wood. He complained bitterly about how unfair it was, but he understood.

Ymot

When he was about fourteen, Tom started signing his name as "Ymot," almost Tommy spelled backwards. He thought this was funny. Perhaps it was a sign that he didn't want to walk into the future, since he had no plans. He didn't know what his direction might be, and he would rather cling to his past years of fun, being in command and having the freedom of his backyard space.

Halloween

Tom and the neighborhood boys went Trick-or-Treating together most years. They put together costumes themselves, and dressed as hobos, pirates, or zombies.

Tom liked to use stage makeup to paint his face black and white like a skeleton. He also liked to use bright-red stage blood that came in a little squeeze tube. He'd paint a cut on his face in black and then put blood on it, or he'd put a little in the corner of his mouth and let a red drip run down to his chin.

He sometimes did this with stage blood in the summertime, delighting in the surprised reactions of his backyard chums. Other times he'd wrap part of his head with gauze as if he were injured and then add stage blood.

Dinner 1977

Even though I worked fairly late most nights, we still had dinner together sitting at the round wooden table in the kitchen. Surprisingly, Tom liked to cook. His favorite was Kraft Macaroni and Cheese from a box. Laura and Tom learned to make tuna noodle casserole. Tacos were a favorite for dinner, and Laura and Tom could prepare the chopped lettuce, hamburger with taco seasoning, chopped tomatoes and onions, and get out a bag of shredded cheese and the bottles of taco sauce for dinner.

Often, I'd put in a roast on time-bake with potatoes, or a whole chicken with sweet potatoes, or we had grilled hamburgers and salad. One of Tom's specialties was breakfast eggs. He'd melt butter in a skillet, pull a round hole in a slice of bread, toast the bread in the skillet and then flip it over and drop a raw egg into the hole. He'd cook the egg, turning the bread once more, and serve.

Tom delighted in eating really unhealthy food—such as from vending machines—partly because he thought it was cool and partly because he knew I didn't approve.

Many afternoons, he'd ride his bicycle a few blocks to Gina's Pizzeria on the point of Main Street and Chamberlain in Flushing. There, he played pin ball and ate a slice of pizza. When it was time for dinner, one of the girls would ride her bicycle to go get him, complaining about the fact that we always had to do this. Tom didn't come home on his own very often. He'd say he wasn't hungry, but we still made him sit with us during dinner. I was always a bit discouraged that Tom didn't seem to fit into the mold I had for him in my mind. I didn't register that my idea of what Tom should be was not what he was best suited for.

That summer, Laura had the bright idea of installing a large brass bell on the back of the house near the back door. The bell was easily reached from the top step outside the sliding glass door of the kitchen. It made a pleasant, resonant and unmistakable "Bong, bong, bong," which carried quite far like a church bell. When we rang the bell, after a little while, Tom magically appeared at the door for dinner. Laura and Margaret both liked to ring this bell. We did not have cell phones in those days. I felt good about having us all together for dinner, even though it was hectic at times. There is a resonance deep inside, which becomes part of the unseen, internal miasma when a child is wanted, needed, and expected to be with the family group.

Chapter 10: High School Years
1977

WITH LITTLE FANFARE, Tom, Mitts, and the rest of the backyard gang entered high school. This was further from home than Springview Elementary, a half-hour walk on sidewalks through several subdivisions ending with cutting through an empty lot just before reaching the road to the high school. The children always wanted me to pick them up after school, and sometimes I was able to indulge them, joining the queue of idling cars filled with parents waiting along the road to the school.

Most of the time, Tom walked home from school. He always wanted an after-school snack. I kept bananas, oranges and apples for them, but they usually wanted a bowl of cereal: Fruit Loops or Cocoa Puffs. In those days, I did not realize the sugar load from these cereals, and gave in to the children's wishes when shopping for cereal.

Tom's Art

Tom loved art classes in high school. He brought home many pictures he'd colored or painted. His was an impish, original style with bright colors, exaggerated features. Many of his works resembled African or primitive art.

Tom, Howard and I took a pottery class at Flint Institute of Arts. He did several primitive pottery masks with crooked noses and warts. I could always find features that looked like Tom's in these masks.

A print Tom made

He made coil cups and ashtrays, bowls, and trays—one with a little elephant walking across the top leaving footprints. He cut his initials: "TEH" (Thomas Edward Hollar,) in the bottom of his pottery, which was glazed and fired in the art center kiln. He did a few watercolors, but this was not his best medium.

Photography in High School

He learned photography from Richard Wolfgang at Flushing High School. Tom loved this class! He distorted photos and added his impish, creative touch to photos of his Grandma Hall, various cats, and a self-portrait with four versions of himself. He was always after something a little different, not necessarily flattering, but maybe funny or weird.

The Camaro 1978

After Tom got his driver's license at age 16, he bought an old Camaro. He and Mitts tuned it and raced it on country roads outside of Flushing. When he shifted gears the muffler made a nice, loud rumble that pleased Tom and was one more thing the neighbors endured. I always worried about this disturbance, but it didn't last long, and I could usually hear Tom's car at the end of the block when he was returning home, so I actually came to like the rumbling sounds of the Camaro.

One day when I came home from work, Tom and a bevy of his boisterous friends crowded the garage. They were very intent, spray painting the Camaro forest green. Cans of paint and murky fluids cluttered the floor.

I was upset, but the girls and I had come to expect such things from Tom. This reminded me of my father's garage, where similar cans of dark fluids sat around. The fluids were volatile organic solvents, which were unhealthy to breathe or to absorb through the skin, plus some of them were surely combustible.

I told Tom about the dangers, which he probably knew, and made him dispose of the fluids at the end of each day so they'd not be sitting around in the garage, which was attached to the house. He found a weedy area by the nearby gravel pits where the soil was exposed and dumped the fluids into the cracked clay where they were absorbed.

Laura and Margaret stayed far away from the Camaro project, coming home from school to retreat into their rooms to do homework, and sometimes going to the family room to watch television. Tom and his projects dominated the outdoors around our house, but we were used to Tom and his ways, and it seemed natural for him to be busy with such projects. I was always glad he was occupied with his creative projects and that I knew where he was and what he was doing.

Another time, when I arrived home, eight bicycles blocked the entrance to the garage, but the Camaro sat in the front yard under the old apple tree.

Tom had rented a hoist to lift the engine out of the car. He and his friends pushed the car frame out of the way, putting it on saw horses, and lowered the engine to the ground again to work on it.

I said, "Oh, no! What are you doing now?"

Tom and Mitts were intent,

Tom's green Camaro

leaning over the engine, seeming to know what they were doing, with other boys looking on, holding wrenches or screwdrivers. Tom said, "Tuning the engine."

There was quiet chatter going on with different boys offering opinions about what to do next. The boys were completely engrossed in this project and felt very important to be working on a real car. They may have been replacing spark plugs. This was serious business, for the Camaro needed to make a statement about who Tom was soon to become when he and Mitts drove it. It had to be cool, and it had to run; others needed to be envious.

Visiting boys put their tools away in the garage as they finished and headed home on their bikes, but Tom and Mitts worked until dark.

I prayed it would not rain to delay the finishing of this phase of work on the Camaro. Our home looked like a junkyard, and I had red tulips and lavender creeping phlox growing next to the sidewalk from the driveway to the front porch that I didn't want the boys to trample.

I just shook my head. "This, too, shall pass." I wrote in my journal, "At the end of the day, we have a crate of fresh corn-on-the-cob for dinner and a very green, freshly painted Camaro up on saw horses in the front yard under the apple tree. And the engine sits nearby on the grass."

Our tolerant neighbors kept their comments to themselves. I noticed Carl Wolf, who lived across the street, pausing when he arrived home after work to stare at our house. I can only imagine the dinner table conversation he and his wife Jean must have had that night!

Summers

In addition to working on the Camaro, Tom and Mitts became partners in a company called "Green Grow Complete Lawn Care." I have a photo of Tom and Mitts, each with a red power lawn mower, from this time. The boys distributed flyers to homes in the Springview School subdivisions, and had regular paying customers.

CHAPTER 11: AFTER HIGH SCHOOL
1981

TOM GRADUATED from Flushing High School in 1981. He had grades good enough to go to Western Michigan University in Kalamazoo, but he had no particular field he was interested in preparing for, so he signed up for General Studies.

Our family valued academics, so we expected that Tom would go to college to pursue some sort of professional career, but he chose otherwise. Tom's father and Uncle David were dentists, his aunt and grandparents were teachers, and I was a pharmacist at that time. Tom was not eager to go to college, but Mitts was going to Western, and spending the next year at home was not something Tom wanted to do.

Tom had a job working in Flint at Genesee Packaging on Dort Highway right after graduation. He had to be on the job at 7:00 A.M. with a brown bag

Tom in the box elder tree in his backyard

lunch. Howard helped him get this job.

Tom was punctual and came home with stories about all the unusual small parts that went into General Motors vehicles, which it was his job to label and shrink wrap, and then package in corrugated cardboard boxes for shipping.

We helped Tom buy a sturdy used black Honda Accord sedan, so he'd have wheels to drive back and forth from home. Laura was envious since we'd never helped her buy a car.

We all agreed it was time for him to move on to the next stage of his life. He did not want to make working at Genesee Packaging a career. He had no specific job training, so we thought a college setting would give him opportunity to look around to see what others were doing and perhaps find a line of study that interested him. So college was the next step. We hoped he'd turn his talents toward his future.

Music 1981

In 1981, Detroit was known as "Rock City." AM and FM radio played rock 'n' roll all night and all day. Tom was a big fan of Keith Richards, who played guitar for The Rolling Stones. Mick Jagger was vocalist. The Rolling Stones played their number-one album "Tattoo You" at the Silverdome in Pontiac in 1981. Tom, then nineteen years old, drove to this concert with Mitts in the passenger seat of his used black Honda Accord sedan. Tom owned the album "Physical Graffiti" by Led Zeppelin.

Green Camaro Is Sold

During this summer, Tom repainted the green Camaro with a fresh coat of green paint and sold it. He'd earlier replaced the engine with a newer, more powerful one, so the car performed well and looked good.

Western Michigan University 1981-82

When we packed Tom's clothes and things to go away to school in late August of 1981, I was sad. My free, creative son was leaving his familiar world where he was completely at home, to enter a larger, distant world with expectations and rigid standards, where he needed to fit in to succeed. I was hoping he'd like it and get excited about some new things he'd be exposed to.

We had signed Tom up rather late, so he was lucky to get a room in Eldridge Hall on campus. When we reached his assigned room on the third floor, his roommate was already there—a transfer student in his third year, who had little interest in palling around with a very green freshman. So Tom had to seek friends elsewhere.

Tom and Mitts with totaled Honda Accord

Mitts was in a different dorm. We unpacked Tom's jeans and shirts, his sneakers and tube socks, his supply of pens, pencils, and three-ring notebook paper.

He was subdued, but dealing with his new situation. He carried a weak little smile on his face, but didn't make his usual spirited quips. He did not have self-confidence in this new situation. We all ate dinner in the cafeteria of the dormitory, which would be Tom's dining room for the next year. The food was OK, and Tom liked the fact that he could get a cheeseburger and fries.

One day in early October, we had a call from Tom from Kalamazoo. He had totaled his Honda Accord with Mitts in the passenger seat at the time. They were very lucky since the car was damaged, having been sideswiped and moved off its normal position on the frame, with only the right front fender smashed, and no one was injured. The accident happened in town at low speeds when both cars veered the same way at the same time. Earlier, the boys had played chicken at higher speeds on roads outside of town, but luckily hadn't collided then.

After that, Tom bought a used black Dodge pickup truck to drive back and forth to college.

In late October, Tom was moved into a room with two sets of bunk beds, closets, a TV, and three roommates his own age. Any chance that Tom might have found classes he was interested in and want to study were dashed completely by the new setting. TV was on most of the time, and Tom could not resist watching. He missed his home with his space, and he missed his cat jumping onto his bed.

One weekend when he went home with Bill, a friend who lived on a farm near Kalamazoo, Tom brought back a barn cat to live in his dorm room. He let her sleep in the closet and brought cafeteria food for her to eat. Poor kitty was timid and terrified in the new home. The cat, named Kalamazoo, got used to her bed in the closet and did jump onto Tom's bed at night, where she purred and snuggled, to Tom's delight.

Thanksgiving Weekend 1982

While I was in medical school, I was driving an International Scout back and forth to East Lansing, and I paid to park in a church parking lot across Fee Road from Fee Hall where all my classes were held. (I started in the fall of 1982, and Tom was enrolled at WMU at the same time.)

As I left classes on Wednesday afternoon before a greatly-anticipated long Thanksgiving weekend, the Scout wouldn't start. Luckily, Lansing had an International® dealership and garage, which was willing to tow my Scout across town for repairs. I was lucky to have contacted them before the mechanics had left the garage for the long weekend. Howard made the long, boring drive from Flushing to pick me up at the dealership in Lansing.

On Sunday after the holiday, I rode with Tom in his black Dodge truck back to school. He dropped me off at the dealership in Lansing where my Scout was waiting. Tom drove, I sat in the middle, and some girl sat beside me. Tom was chewing tobacco and kept a coffee can on the floor where he could pick it up with his left hand to spit into it. A faded round mark on his back right jeans pocket came from carrying a can of Skoal. This was a new addition for Tom, which I was unhappy to see. I decided not to comment. I had several lectures ready, about chewing tobacco causing cancer and it being a disgusting habit, but Tom was finding his way toward entering a new world and growing up, and this was part of it. He was making his statement, choosing his image by chewing tobacco, not what I would have chosen for him.

He had his cat, Kalamazoo, in a grocery bag on the floor of his truck, with a towel in it for her to lie down on during the trip back to school. I felt sorry for the cat, and realized what an awful life she must be having living in a dormitory room.

After this trip, I rescued Kalamazoo and brought her to our home in Flushing. Tom agreed with this plan, since he knew it was stressful for Kalamazoo, and he had to

Kalamazoo, dorm cat

handle the kitty litter box in his closet, as well as the smell. This beautiful, longhaired, green-eyed grey cat had a good life in Flushing, becoming a playmate of Margaret's cat, Atilla. We called her "TV Kitty," because she'd jump on someone's lap and fall into a deep sleep while we watched TV, something she had learned to do while living with Tom in the dorm. When TV was on, it was safe to come out and jump on the bed. No one would chase her or pay much attention to her then.

Western Michigan University 1982-1983

At Western Michigan University, Tom had fun whenever possible. His weekends began on Thursday night and lasted until Tuesday morning. Western was known as a "party school," so he had plenty of company with this schedule.

During Tom's second year in college, he and Mitts rented a house on Buckout Street. A large, black trampoline filled the front yard. Inside the front door was a Pac-Man machine. Tom was a skilled Pac-Man player, knowing just how long it took for each part of the game. He found it easy to play Pac-Man, rather than study.

Nedra and Howard Vist Tom and Mitts

When we visited Tom and Mitts, piles of unwashed clothes lay on both bedroom floors. The kitchen had been "cleaned up," so there were no stacks of dirty dishes on the counters, but the dish drainer was filled with recently-washed dishes and the still-wet dishcloth was not especially clean-looking. Tom was not enthusiastic about any of his courses, although he was able to do art projects in one of them and was learning to use new media.

He was taking some courses in the School of Communication where he liked being a videographer. He and a classmate, Stephanie, videoed a spoof newscast of a weather report where Tom assumed a serious, tight British accent, and the news was zany: "It is 80 degrees in Longview, snow is closing freeways throughout the city."

Stephanie invited Tom to go to some house parties on campus, where age restrictions on drinking alcohol were loosely observed or completely ignored.

Even away from his backyard, in the confines of college life, where he had to show up for classes some of the time, Tom still found ways to have fun and play.

During final exams his last year at Western, Tom walked into a large room where a final was being given in a class he was not enrolled in. He signed in using a bogus name, Billy or Eddie Briss, took the final and left, proud of himself for thinking of doing this. In his way, showing irreverence for the system, he found a way not to have to go to college.

Tom's totaling the Honda Accord, as well as our realizing we were wasting our money, were the reasons we all, including Tom, decided that another year at WMU was not a good idea.

CHAPTER 12: WYOMING RANCH
1983

AFTER MUCH DISCUSSION and many phone calls, we all decided that an experience working on a ranch might bring new ideas for Tom's future. The plan was for him to work with Juan Reyes, the Cuban manager on a ranch owned by Tom's Aunt Cara and Uncle John Milnor of San Antonio.

The ranch at Tie Siding, Wyoming sat at an elevation of 8000 feet. John and Cara thought it was a good idea for Tom to come, and Juan agreed to take on a greenhorn helper. Tom liked the idea of working outdoors at the ranch where he'd had fun with his San Antonio cousins. We'd visited the ranch several times, and everyone involved figured it would be a win-win situation.

John had bought Italian cattle, Chianina, and Juan bred them with Black Angus. These hefty bulls from Italy were taller, with longer legs, and carried more weight per animal than Black Angus. The Milnors named some of these heavy cattle: *View Blocker* and *Pound Maker*.

Cara remembers her phone call to Juan about Tom. Both Cara and John thought having Tom live in the big ranch house during the winter and work

A Chianina bull and two black Angus cattle
on the 5M ranch where Tom worked

for Juan on the ranch would benefit them—having a caretaker for the house, and benefit Tom with a different kind of experience. Tom had his share of misgivings about how it would be to work for a Cuban ranch manager, since he would not be dealing with his mother or Nancy Smoker, but a tough ranch foreman.

Tie Siding, Wyoming is on U.S. Highway 287, which winds for sixty miles through hills and valleys, foothills of the Rocky Mountains. In southern Wyoming just north of Colorado, Route 287 is a rural highway connecting Laramie, Wyoming with Fort Collins, Colorado, two college towns. Colorado State University is at Fort Collins, and University of Wyoming is at

Laramie. Tie Siding is just seven miles north of Colorado, marked only by a small filling station with a used-book exchange. Route 287 is known as a pumpkin-vine road, made dangerous in winter due to ice, snow, and fog.

Juan Reyes had lived in foster homes after his parents got him out of Cuba, so he understood

Joni and Juan Reyes in their truck

that his role of working with a young man from Michigan, who was finding his way, was important. Juan had worked for the Union Pacific Railroads as an interpreter, a good job. He had a reputation for being a tough bar fighter and for having a hot temper. He also rode unbroken horses in rodeos before he accepted John Milnor's offer to become ranch manager at the Tie Siding Milnor Ranch.

After accepting this job, Juan settled down a little, married Joni, with whom he lived on the ranch in a trailer not far from the big ranch house and barn, where they kept horses. The barn had a small bedroom for ranch staff to use during calving in the spring when they had to keep an eye on newborn calves to protect them from freezing. Later Juan and Joni built a home where the trailer had been.

In August of 1983 Tom packed his clothes and dirt bike, and in his black Dodge pickup truck he headed for Wyoming. He also took his Grandpa Hall's red tool chest, which his grandpa had used during the days when he'd been a garage mechanic. Tom traveled just south of Lake Michigan, bypassed Chicago and pretty much followed the same path across Iowa and Nebraska as the Union Pacific Railroad.

Wyoming Milnor Ranch home where Tom stayed

Arriving in Cheyenne in southeastern Wyoming, he then drove through Laramie, down the Laramie-Tie Siding-Cherokee Park Road (Route 287), past the small gas station just before the long driveway to the big ranch house. Tom had visited his cousins, Nick, Sarah, and Dan Milnor at the ranch house, so he knew what it looked like.

After Tom drove to the ranch house with its wide porch, nearby pond where Cara liked to fish for trout, and barn, he parked and walked toward the trailer where Juan and Joni lived.

Juan came out to greet him, and Joni invited him in for a meal. They had a beer after eating, and Juan came over to unlock the big ranch house.

The spacious log ranch house faced east with a view of rolling foothills of the Laramie Mountains. A scene out the big picture-window in the living room was peaceful and beautiful, with distant mountains seeming closer than they actually were. Cara had chosen leather furniture grouped around a large fireplace, with wool hand-loomed brightly patterned Native American rugs on the wooden floors and a long wooden table filling the dining area, which was open to the living room.

The walls held Native American antiques: a gathering basket with hammered metal discs hanging from a leather fringe decoration, a long-stemmed peace pipe and paintings of western landscapes or cowboys riding horses or herding cattle.

Tom chose a bedroom upstairs toward the front of the house with twin beds and a TV mounted so he could watch from his bed. The air was very dry; Cara kept a bottle of water-based spray for her skin near the sink in the master bath.

Later, Tom unpacked and agreed to meet Juan in the morning at the barn to start work at 7:00 A.M.. The first day, Juan showed him how to dig a hole for a fence post and then hammer it in using a sledge hammer. He also showed him how to attach the wire to the fence post, and how to cinch it tight using a tool called a *come-along*.

Much of Tom's work was to be building and fixing fences. Another very important job was to help with calving in the spring—to find the new calves and bring them back to the barn so they wouldn't freeze to death; and also to help with fall branding of new cattle.

Chapter 13: Tom at the Tie Siding Ranch
1983

ONE YEAR, DAN MILNOR nursed a calf back to life after it was born out in the winter weather and had its ears and tail frozen off. At branding time in the fall when the calves were old enough, Tom helped with branding the cattle with the Milnor Ranch brand: **5M**. This was hard work. Tom learned to grab a calf, and help hold him while another man placed the hot branding iron on the calf's rump to burn in the brand.

Another time, Dan Milnor caught his pants on fire in the first ten minutes of helping with the branding. Nick Milnor worked quite a bit to help out at branding time. Tom didn't like this job, especially the smell, the smoky scent of burning fur and flesh, but he did it without comment.

The ranch was on rolling, sage-covered, sandy hills, where winds stirred sand that blew in the dry air. Rolling dead sage bushes collected at fences Juan had built. Tall, straight, lodge pole pines were abundant, and aspen trees turned golden in the fall creating an unforgettably beautiful vista from the ranch at Tie Siding.

A dry creek bed with scrubby, dwarfed trees and shrubs lay behind the ranch, as well as a hill Tom climbed to get a better view of the acreage. One time we built a cairn on this hill, and I wonder whether this cairn is still there. Medicine Bow Mountains loomed behind the ranch to the west.

The Milnors' Horses

The Milnors kept horses in their barn, and it was Joni's job and her choice to care for the horses. Sarah's horse, Rebel, had been shipped from Texas. Juan's horse was named Pissant, and Joni's horse was Wardlaw. Tom rode a big white horse named Liberty. He rode horseback some of the time when he was working on fences at a distance from the house. Other times, he drove a pale green flatbed truck, which belonged to the Milnors.

He'd never been interested in riding Laura's 4-H horse, a half-Arab named Synfara or Sam, but now he learned to put a girth, blanket and saddle, a bridle, bit and reins on a horse and to ride Western style.

Juan was tough, but fair. He and Tom became friends, and Juan respected Tom, who was trying his best and was funny. His humor helped relieve the boring everyday work of fixing fences. One day while he was ratcheting tight the fence wires, Tom broke the come-along tool.

Juan was madder than hell, and he cut loose with an angry tirade about how clumsy and stupid Tom was, but he slipped into Spanish, so Tom didn't understand the words, but there was no question about the intent. Tom's face got red so his old birthmark showed, and he made his nervous gesture of loosening his collar.

Loss of the come-along slowed fence work dramatically, but they continued to work on fences every day. Juan never mentioned the incident again, but there was a new tension in the working relationship for a while. Pretty soon they were back to normal chatter and joking.

Tom said to me more than once, "Mom, if you ever came out here, you would never go back and live in Michigan."

Tom earned Juan's respect by showing up, working hard, and being himself. Tom proudly showed me a freezer at the big ranch house where neatly wrapped packages of frozen elk meat were ready to be cooked and eaten.

Juan had shown Tom how to shoot and field-dress an elk. Juan and Tom had bagged an elk from the bountiful herds around the ranch. And the two working together put away a large supply of food for Tom during his stay in Wyoming. My thoughts were that Tom might not have chosen to cook much for himself—maybe the ground elk meat and the steaks, but probably not roasts or stews. Cara kept several large grills in the garage since the Milnors frequently had guests at the ranch, and Cara needed to grill steaks or hamburgers for a crowd.

This was the only time in his life that Tom was not surrounded by other people. He called home fairly often just to chat, but at no time did I detect any depression on his part from living alone. He was busy learning new things each day, and by the time he found something for his dinner, he was tired and ready to settle in for the night.

Tom at a rodeo

He stayed alone in the big ranch house with its antiques, spacious rooms, fireplaces, and gorgeous views of rolling mountains, beautiful sunrises. Bleak in the winter, snowdrifts could close the small dirt driveway from the ranch to the paved road. Tom spent a lot of time watching television, and every so often, he and Juan drove into Laramie to go to one of the local bars for a beer. They went to rodeos regularly.

Many evenings, when Tom went to the big ranch house after working, he got out his red dirt bike to ride over the rolling sand hills dotted with sage bushes around the Tie Siding ranch.

The Milnors spent spring and summer at the ranch in Wyoming, but spent winters in San Antonio. These busy summers with Nick, Dan, and Sarah,

John and Cara, were fun for Tom, but he still had to work. Nick and Dan occasionally worked with him, making things go faster. Food was notably better when Cara was there to cook her chicken salad, barbecued beef, potato salad, green beans, salads, and hamburgers. She cooked quite a few of the elk pot roasts from the freezer.

When I visited Tom the first time for Thanksgiving in 1983, the ranch house had been lived in: the lavatory sink and kitchen needed some cleaning. In his upstairs bedroom, all around the bed where Tom slept and watched TV, were large-sized empty bags of cheese curls, Fritos, potato chips, and popcorn. I suspect he ate this instead of an elk dinner, at least some of the time. During this time, I tried to bake a turkey in the oven as I did at home, but found that it simply did not cook. I forgot about the altitude affecting cooking, and ended up trying to cook the turkey on one of Cara's grills in the garage. There was a small amount of snow on the ground.

Injury at the Ranch October 1984

I received a phone call from Tom while I was working in the kitchen making dinner. Tom said he had cut his knee while honing a log to be used as a fence post. The saw had jumped and cut his left knee, which had been holding the log. It cut just above the kneecap, through his jeans and long underwear, through the skin and fat layer underneath showing white bands of tendons attached to his quadriceps muscles and patella, the knee bone, so that blood was gushing out. Tom said that he could feel blood filling his boot. He said

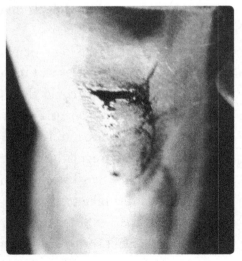

Tom's injured left knee, photo taken by Tom

that Juan had said to him, "We don't go to the emergency room for things like this."

I told Tom long-distance: "Go to the emergency room, now!"

I never heard details of what happened after that, but many years later when we had dinner with Juan and Joni in San Antonio, Juan apologized and felt very bad for how he handled that situation.

Ski Trip with Mitts and Jeff

That same year two and a half months after Tom's knee was cut, Mitts and his roommate, Jeff, flew to Laramie for Christmas break to ski with Tom. Juan gave Tom a two-week vacation. In his black Dodge pickup truck (with his skis, boots, poles, dirt bike and suitcase in the back) Tom picked up Mitts and Jeff at the Laramie airport. They drove to the Cowboy Bar in Laramie for a hamburger and a beer before heading south into Colorado.

The bar had a mounted brook trout, a hawk, and a set of elk antlers on the walls near the ceiling, as well as signs for beer companies: Budweiser, Coors, Corona, and Molson. O'Doull's was in green neon. Music was constantly in the background from a jukebox, sometimes a piano player. Tom liked *God Must Be a Cowboy* and *Nothin' Left to Do but Cry*, recorded by Dan Seals. While driving, Tom played tapes he'd made of these songs.

Tom saw Jennifer, a girl he knew, who was from Flushing, Michigan. She was attending University of Wyoming in Laramie. Mitts knew her, too. So Tom and Mitts walked over to the table where she was sitting with another girl and started chatting with her.

While Tom might not have drawn attention due to his weathered black cowboy hat, bleached hair with unkempt bangs straggling down his tanned face, Mitts, who was quite tall, pale, and handsome in his bright red ski jacket and ski hat, was too much for the locals. Several young men got up from their table, clattering across the wooden floor in their cowboy boots toward Tom and Mitts.

They said, "You got business with the lady?"

Tom and Mitts knew enough not to say anything, but turned tail, motioned to Jeff to join them, and quickly left the bar without getting their butts kicked. They headed south on the Laramie-Tie Sidings-Cherokee Park Road, planning to pick up 14 West to Steamboat Springs, Colorado to go skiing. This route took them past the ranch.

They drove up the long driveway for a quick look about. Tom pointed out where he had been working and the Roosevelt National Forest, which bordered the ranch to the south.

Mitts asleep on the trip to San Antonio

Proceeding south on the Tie Sidings-Cherokee Park Road, soon they came to snow and decided to turn around and head for Route 80, a major road, which connected with I-25 South and would be kept plowed.

Tom drove the truck south on I 25 until Denver, where they headed on West 70 to Vail. They had enough money to pay for lift tickets, but not enough for a room near the ski hill. After skiing they tried to find a cheap room outside of town, but they were all full. The three spent the night in the cab of the truck trying to sleep. Mitts told me that he awakened outside in a snowdrift, covered partly with fresh snow. It's a wonder that he didn't suffer injury or frostbite, and that none of the boys got sick.

After they had breakfast, they decided to head south on 25 heading for Tom's Grandma Hall's house in San Antonio. She'd moved from Ohio at age 75 to live on Silver Spruce in San Antonio in a nice home that the Milnors bought for her.

The boys reached New Mexico sometime in the early afternoon. Tom stopped the black truck in the desert and got out his red dirt bike. The three of them took turns racing around cacti on the flat sands of the desert. Then they headed southeast to Raton, through Sterling City, New Mexico on 87 to San Angelo, Texas, and then south to San Antonio.

During this ride from Denver to San Antonio, Jeff, who sat in the center of the truck's cab, fell asleep. Tom took the opportunity to put a small bit from his plug of tobacco into Jeff's gaping mouth as he snored. Jeff promptly woke up, sneezed and coughed, and they all had a good laugh.

Tom's Grandma Hall was extremely happy to see him and knew the young men were hungry. She fried bacon and made each of them three eggs, toast, and orange juice. They finished the eggs, and she made more for them. They were laughing, rowdy, and tired. She had known Mitts from earlier days, and this visit was a high point of her time in San Antonio. She was pleased to see Tom in this stage of his life looking fit and happy.

She had enough beds for all of them, and not too long after eating and taking a shower, the boys took a long nap until they all went out for a good San Antonio Mexican dinner at Jacala.

After this visit, they headed back to Michigan, where Tom took each of the boys to his home before coming home himself.

At the time, I knew nothing of the ski trip.

I was overjoyed to see Tom: He had a new steadiness born of being self-reliant in a lonely, tough world of ranchers and cowboys, men who lived off harsh land.

He'd driven the entire trip to Michigan with his left leg propped up and straight since he pulled open the cut whenever he bent his knee. (The cut hadn't kept him from skiing.)

When his two-week vacation was over, I didn't want him to return to the ranch because his leg was not healed, but he packed his small black metal suitcase with all the travel logos pasted on it, and said, "Juan needs me to help. I told him I'd come back."

I cried when my son left; I felt proud and sad at the same time. I watched as he crawled into his black Dodge truck, holding his left leg stiff as he walked.

Tom loading his black truck for return trip to Wyoming

CHAPTER 14: BACK TO MICHIGAN
1984

IN MARCH, after calving season, Tom returned to Michigan in his black truck with his quilted, red down winter jacket and black wool-knit headband holding back his bleached, fairly long hair. That spring, he went back to his former clients and began mowing lawns for the summer.

He mowed lawns for and played chess with Dr. Manwaring, who lived in a suburb of Flint, and met his daughter Martha. Dr. Manwaring liked to play chess with Tom because Tom didn't let him win.

Tom rode his dirt bike by the gravel pits at the end of Clearview Dr., hiked along the river in Flushing Park, stayed active. But he had pretty much outgrown his old backyard buddies except for Mitts, who had put in another two years of college and would eventually graduate with an associate degree in business management. Before very long, Tom was bored living at home with no job.

When Dr. Manwaring died in April that year, Martha was distraught since she'd been close to her father and lived with him in the family home. She needed a change and a fresh start on her life. She had previously lived in Denver and still had good friends and family there. So she moved back to Denver.

A few months later, Tom thought about moving to Denver to try his luck. He knew nothing about Denver other than that there were ski hills nearby, and it was West—a thriving, lively city out West, and that was enough. He was excited and motivated to pack up and go.

Mitts and Tom in Michigan

Chapter 15: Tom Moves To Denver
1985

AFTER TWO YEARS WORKING for Juan Reyes, Tom was strong, tanned, funny and full of tales of ranch and rodeo people he'd met, but he was no closer to finding a career path. Both Tom and his cousin, Nick Milnor, had decided that they didn't want to make ranching a career.

While Tom had gotten used to the routine at the ranch, he was lonely there and felt "stuck." He knew that his future didn't lie in being a ranch hand. Tom and Nick knew the hard labor involved, some of the risk and expense of raising cattle; things could go wrong. While Tom was at the ranch, some of the herd of Chianina cattle developed a lung disease called brisket and needed to be moved to a lower altitude to recover. Juan was planning to relocate the entire herd to a ranch about fifty miles away at a lower altitude.

Tom was sure of one thing: he loved the people he'd met in the West. They had proved to be friendly, genuine, tough, and reliable.

He packed his bags, and set out in his black Dodge truck on Interstate 70 across the plains to Denver. Tom set out with what he had.

His fun-loving, creative life didn't end when he moved to Denver. In fact, Denver became his new backyard, and the young people there were his new playmates. He carried in him the knowledge that if he just started out in his space and did not force anything, creative things would happen. He was still a leader, grounded, with something going on to interest others. He took his love of skateboards with him.

He drove straight through with stops only for gas, food, and restrooms, arriving in Denver in May, 1985.

Denver took him in as it had welcomed new residents for more than a century. He showed up in Denver, an authentic, more mature Tom, with no pretenses.

He had many strong qualities which drew others to him: spirit of optimism, self-esteem, terrific sense of humor, honesty, creativity, acceptance, vitality, fairness; he still carried uncertainty about his future. He saw the good in others—even those who had done bad.

Tom planned to stay with friends of Martha's until he could find lodging elsewhere. He slept on daybeds and enclosed front porches at first.

Stapleton Airport in Denver

Tom sought work at Stapleton Airport in northeast Denver. He was lucky to get a job right away driving a courtesy van for Dollar Rental Car. He was a good driver, friendly, quipping with passengers he picked up at arrival gates or delivered to departure gates. After his strenuous stint at the Wyoming ranch, he had no trouble lifting the luggage and

Tom wearing Arthurs' black coat with Howard at Stapleton airport

swinging it up to the chrome racks inside the van. He was able to load his van swiftly and get the passengers seated.

Tom, with his straggly bangs and relatively innocent face got better-than-average tips for his work, often more than a dollar a bag, and he carried small-bill change for a $10 or a $20 bill, making it easier for clients to tip him.

CHAPTER 16: SOME DENVER HISTORY

TOM'S JOURNEY TO DENVER was the kind that Horace Greeley made famous in the 1860s: "Go West, young man to seek your opportunity to succeed." Greeley was referring to opportunity under the Homestead Act of 1862.

The government provided a parcel of public land for settlers to build on, to use for farming or raising cattle, thus allowing them to become established landowners. Greeley was saying that for young men willing to work, the West held opportunity to succeed, and that is exactly what Tom did, with help from Christina, whom he met later.

Greeley was editor of *The New York Herald Tribune* and saw westward movement of workers as a way to reduce high unemployment rates in the East and something that could benefit Civil War veterans.

Greeley took the stagecoach west to cover the Gold Rush of 1859, where a small amount of gold had been found in the South Platte River near the confluence of Cherry Creek and the South Platte River. William Byer, an editor who published the first newspaper in the region, *Rocky Mountain News*, had painted a better-than-real picture of the Gold Rush of 1859, so large numbers of gold-seekers, called the 59ers, traveled to Denver. These prospectors were seeking gold on Indian Land.

Indian wars began, and in 1864, The US 3rd Cavalry headed into the plains east of Denver, where at Sand Creek, southeast of Denver, Colonel John Chivington killed off nearby camps of Cheyenne and Arapaho Indians, including women and children.

This was known as the Sand Creek Massacre. *Rocky Mountain News* praised these soldiers since confrontation between new settlers staking claims to the land and Native Americans, who had lived on the land for centuries, was inevitable.

Artifacts found in the area suggest that Native Americans had lived there for more than 10,000 years. These residents hunted in eastern Colorado and depended upon camping at the same water spots that the new European-American settlers had used. These battles are part of the history of Colorado and fodder for many novels by authors such as Zane Grey and Louis L'Amour and many John Wayne movies.

In the 1860s, a steady flow of homesteaders from the East settled on farms and ranches in the area. Denver became a cattlemen's town, since cattle were brought to the city, held in stockyards, processed as meat, or shipped by rail.

In 1861, General William Larimer had marked a square mile of land near the site where gold was found in the South Platte River (near where it meets Cherry Creek), during the Pike's Peak Gold Rush of 1859. This land is in the current Lower Downtown (LoDo) area, the oldest neighborhood in Denver.

Larimer had been a gold prospector in 1858, and he officially staked out towns to hold claims of prospectors in his group along Cherry Creek. He organized these prospectors into the Denver City Town Company and staked out this one square mile of land in LoDo, which he named for the governor of the Kansas Territory, John Denver. At that time, Denver was in Kansas Territory, but in 1861, Colorado became a territory, and a few months later the city of Denver was incorporated.

Larimer's group named the streets after themselves: Bassett, Wynkoop, Blake, McGaa, Larimer, Lawrence, Curtis, Welton—all of whom were part of the Denver City Town Company.

Other street names came from Indian names: Arapahoe, Champa, Cheyenne, Wapoola, and Wewatta.

Before WW II, Denver's economy was dependent primarily on processing and shipping minerals from mining and ranch products, mostly beef or lamb. Denver had always been a cattlemen's town.

Denver in the 1980s When Tom Arrived

Denver's residents in the 1980s included former military men, who had trained or recuperated in Denver, and later returned to live there after World War II. Large corporations, including Honeywell, Hewlitt-Packard, IBM, Ball Aerospace, and Lockheed Martin had brought jobs and money to Denver in the 1950s. The business center now at 16th and Larimer had shifted away from its beginnings in lower downtown at 15th and Blake.

At this time, important skyscrapers like The Republic Plaza Tower on California Street, Tabor Center, Daniels and Fisher Tower, Wells Fargo Center and the high-rise Equitable Building had been completed.

The Wells Fargo building is shaped like a cash register at the top making it a distinguishing landmark in the Denver skyline.

By 1985 when Tom arrived, Denver was a diverse city with many industries, including a major manufacturing center and many federal agencies with large numbers of federal employees. Denver's growth had consistently outpaced the national rate for cities. It was listed as the number-one metro area for population gain in the 25-to-34-year-old range.

Denver had a long history of being a destination for Easterners. It was an appealing place. Skies were blue and sunny most days; businesses were thriving; jobs for all skill levels were available; coffee shops were all around town serving a good cup of espresso or regular strong coffee with inviting outdoor tables where the coffee could be enjoyed. From any direction, gorgeous views of the Rocky Mountains beckoned.

CHAPTER 17: DENVER
1985

W HEN TOM ARRIVED IN DENVER, LoDo had seen a re-
birth and was a hopping place, with new residents living in trendy
lofts being built in old warehouses. Many new restaurants with
attractive menus had opened, making it a fun place to visit. Real estate agents
selling lofts at astronomically high prices were busy, and scaffolding around
buildings, where space for new lofts was being developed, could be seen all
over LoDo. When we walked to Cherry Creek, we noticed new lofts built
across 17th Street from The Oxford Hotel and along Wynkoop and Wazee

Across the street from The Oxford Hotel, Jax Fish Restaurant replaced an
old bar on the corner of 17th and Wazee. We frequented a European theme
restaurant and an Italian restaurant on Market Street, within walking distance from The Oxford Hotel. I remember the upstairs dining room of the
Italian restaurant and the pasta with shellfish I liked to order there. When
these restaurants moved or closed, we were sorry.

First Latino Mayor
Mayor Federico Pena, Denver's first Latino mayor, who had been elected
in 1983, was in office in 1985. By this time, older pioneer families, who had

settled in downtown in the 1800s around the then-fashionable 14ᵗʰ Street neighborhood, had moved further out, first to Brown's Hill as it was known, or Capitol Hill, and later, further out to such neighborhoods as Littleton and Arvada.

Denver in the 70s

Denver had changed from an urban center in LoDo, surrounded by ranches, to a busy downtown surrounded by suburbs. Denver had changed from a western cattleman's town, with gun-carrying, whiskey-drinking poker players roaming around LoDo at night, to a modern city, which kept its cattleman's fondness for a good steak.

Urban renewal projects in the 1950s had demolished blocks of old-frontier-era buildings, including the grand old Tabor Opera House built by Horace Tabor in 1881. In place of these historic buildings, new apartment and office buildings were built, but in the 1960s a movement to preserve Denver's history and old buildings began. Some old saloons and buildings in downtown Denver were renovated.

The 80s See Progress

By 1985, Denver downtown had lost population to the suburbs, and the city was falling into disrepair. Mayor Pena was able to convince Denverites to reinvest in their city and to approve a new $3 billion airport—Denver International Airport (DIA), a new convention center, and funding for improved infrastructure and schools. He was instrumental in causing to be passed an additional sales tax earmarked to help pay for a new baseball stadium in LoDo—Coors Field—for the Colorado Rockies.

In the mid-1980s, Stapleton Airport, the existing airport in Denver, was very busy, the seventh largest and the fourth busiest in the United States. It could no longer expand since the city had grown around it.

DIA, the new airport, is considered to be Mayor Pena's most important contribution to the city. The primary road leading to and from the new airport is aptly named, "Pena Boulevard."

When Tom first moved to Denver, we flew into Stapleton and learned the route down to Colfax, which like most of Denver, is on a north-south, east-west pattern, and into the LoDo grid, which is parallel to Cherry Creek and at an angle, where we traveled down 18th Street to Wynkoop, past Union Station, and back up 17th to The Oxford Hotel, where we always stayed.

Dynamic Denver in 1985 attracted a steady flow of young people from the East—skiers, runaways, those seeking jobs or a new life. But there was also a new influx of young people from the West. Specifically, gang members from Los Angeles were moving east to Denver to avoid sentences, probation, or being on wanted lists. Mothers of LA gang members moved with their sons and hoped for something better for them.

Tom's Places in Denver

In Denver, Tom found his way around quickly. He watched TV Channels 4, 7, and 9, stopped to eat at the Blue Bonnet Café or Tom's Tavern or My Brother's Bar for his favorite—a cheeseburger, or at Platte Coffeehouse for a break.

Right away Tom found dive bars, punk rock bars—his places in Denver where he felt at home and could have fun. Bumper stickers on cars in 1985 read, "Denver by a Mile."

When we visited, he took us to the Jerusalem Restaurant on Conifer Road in southeastern Denver and Las Delicias near Colfax and E. 19th Avenue. He liked to go to Sancho Broken Arrow on Colfax at Clarkson in Capitol Hill for a beer.

DENVER

Shiny ribbon-wrapped buildings,
tall masses against a blue sky,
Closer, sand-washed brick,
double-hung windows,
trendy LoDo, Coors Field.

Fast foreign sports cars,
convertibles, Jeeps,
four-wheel drive trucks
16th Avenue busses
busy streets.

Moving mix of people:
ponytails and earrings
business suits
cowboy boots
platforms, 4-inch spikes,
Doc Martens, mini-skirts,
green or purple hair,
wrinkled sun-bronzed skin,
ten-gallon hats, bolo ties,
trimmed moustaches,
big diamonds.

Braced by the mountains
off in the west
vast expanses of rock and trees,
his city nestled
in a flat, sweeping plain:
bustling, exciting,
moving—fresh.

He fed on the energy
of this place
he called home.

My son, a city boy,
a DENVERITE.

Chapter 18: Life in Denver
1985

Tom had a steady job and was making good money, so he decided to take an apartment. He looked around town, found the best deals in Park Hill and Capitol Hill, then chose a cheap apartment on Clarkson in Capitol Hill.

Not long after that he moved to a nicer two-bedroom first-floor apartment at the Shana Marie Apartment Building on Corona in Capitol Hill. It had a big kitchen, dining room, back and front porches. He liked this location across from a supermarket with a big parking lot adjacent to the apartment building. And he liked the front porch, which was close enough to the sidewalk that he could talk to passersby. In this way he came to know the people in the Capitol Hill neighborhood.

The Shana Marie Apartment Building on Corona

The apartment had plain grey walls and white woodwork with polished oak floors. Tom moved in with

very little, but soon checked out Goodwill and Salvation Army stores, garage and estate sales, Mile High Flea Market and used-furniture stores. He
bought a bed, a bureau for the bedroom, and a kitchen table and chairs. Always he was attracted to style—funky, interesting, formerly stylish furnishings. He took a real liking for Art Deco style and antiques that carried their own stories. He'd always loved art.

At an estate sale on 17th Avenue, he found an old Art Deco chandelier with dangling sockets that took colored bulbs of many differing styles, and he hung it in the dining room above a polished black wooden table and chairs beside a decorated-tile fire place, truly an attractive, stylish setting in his home.

Tom sitting on porch railing of his apartment on Corona

He liked "found items" with artistic value, so when he saw a discarded Cadillac grill in good shape with all its gleaming chrome, he recognized its potential and used it to make a bench for the entrance to his apartment.

He used a two-by-ten piece of wood, which he sanded and finished. The Cadillac had a Colorado license plate with a silhouette of mountains in green on a white field, which just suited his love of funky original things with a story. License plate on this Cadillac grill had **609** on it.

Business Ventures and Vehicles 1985

Tom and Martha Manwaring became business partners. Combining their names, they formed the Tomar Company using a Stapleton Airport PO Box mailing address. At about this same time, Martha moved into Tom's apartment. Both were trying to make their way in Denver, so they decided to share expenses as well as business endeavors. Martha had stayed with friends long enough and needed to move on.

Tabor Center Cart 1985

They rented a cart in Tabor Center, a thirty-floor-high skyscraper built in 1984 in downtown Denver. From the cart, the transplanted Michiganders sold pens, sunglasses, and refrigerator magnets. I recall visiting the cart with Tom on the second floor at Tabor Center and being impressed with the nice facility with its inviting food court.

The cart was about four-by-eight-feet with large panels where the refrigerator magnets were on display. Trays of pens were on view; two demo pens on tethers could be tried on paper mounted on the cart. On either side of the cart stood racks of sunglasses that could be tried on using a small mirror.

I came home with a batch of cute magnets: a fat, pink pig; a slice of watermelon with seeds; a plastic dollar bill; and a large clamp where I could attach notes. At the time, I was urging Tom to consider being a food vendor at Tabor, since I didn't see much future in selling pens, sunglasses, and refrigerator magnets, but Tom had his own sense of things.

Rent at Tabor Center was very high, so Tom decided to move the cart to a more favorable location, choosing an outdoor site on 16th Avenue just below Larimer. Business was just as good there as it had been at Tabor Center.

Tom wearing Wayfarers sunglasses

Sunglass Cart At Stapleton

An opportunity to rent a vendor-cart at a prime location at Stapleton Airport presented.

Tom felt sure he could do well, so he and Martha signed on. Tom, as well as two other vendors, had carts in this very busy location with almost constant traffic, near the junction of Concourses B and C, the United and Continental concourses.

The sunglass cart looked like a smaller version of a covered wagon with a peaked wooden roof. At the end of the day, he placed boards on the sides of the cart to cover the merchandise. These boards were stored under the cart during the day.

Tom had a paper receipt book and used hand-written receipts. In the beginning, he had a carbon-paper system for imprinting credit cards, but had to walk to a pay phone down the concourse where there was a special line to verify the cards for large sales. Business was good.

High-End Products

Tom made two large, white, four-by-six-foot Plexiglas® boards, one for each side of the cart. He cut round holes just right for holding a pair of sunglasses. Each Plexiglas® board held fifty pairs of sunglasses.

One end of the cart had locked glass cases, where the higher-ticket Ray-Ban® glasses, including Wayfarers, were on display. Tom liked Wayfarers and the nerdy 50-ish clothing that went with them. He often wore Wayfarers himself.

He sold a variety of styles. He had a section of very fussy turquoise, fuchsia, and yellow glasses with butterflies, flowers, and oversized frames that he called, "Ugly lady sunglasses." Mirrored-lens sunglasses were popular then, and these reflected the bright overhead and neon lights along the concourses, so his display attracted attention. He made a big sign that said: **"SUNGLASSES $7.00."**

He found wholesalers where he could buy low, sell high, and yet retain good quality, something he seemed to be skilled at doing. Business was brisk, and at times, shoppers trying on sunglasses surrounded the cart. Even when some were stolen, Tom had such a big markup that he still made money.

Tom and Martha also did Christmas Gift Shows at the Convention Center in Denver and had estate sales out in front of their apartment on Corona on weekends to try to bring in more money. For Christmas in 1986, Tom sent a pair of sunglasses to each family member.

Denver Sunglass Company

Tom liked being a retailer. He sold so many sunglasses that he formed another company, The Denver Sunglass Company. Tom took out a virtual office with a Colfax Avenue address and put ads in *Gentlemen's Quarterly* and *Westword* for mail-order sunglasses. He had a knack for choosing styles with attitude.

He also signed with a company that produced a merchandise catalog, with Tomar Company and his Colfax address on it.

He didn't have to stock anything or fulfill orders, but he got a cut of the sale. From this catalog, he chose a kitchen knife to give to me for Christmas. It was a Mac knife. He thought it was funny to give me "Mac the Knife" for Christmas. Whenever I use this knife, Tom and his humor are with me.

Sunglasses with attitude that Tom advertised
in Gentlemen's Quarterly

Chapter 19: Visit to Michigan
1986

T OM DROVE HIS Dodge truck home to Michigan in late spring. The first thing he did was to trade this truck for a new, white Dodge Ram, which was much roomier and more comfortable than his old black truck with so many miles on it.

Tom with white Dodge truck packed for trip to Denver

Coney Island Hot Dog Sandwiches

Tom had the idea of selling Coney Island hotdog sandwiches in downtown Denver. Coney Islands were born in Michigan in the early 1900s and very popular in Flint. Tom was fond of them, and saw a business opportunity. Koegel Meats had made the original hot dog traditionally used in the Flint Original Coney Island sandwich. This preferred hotdog is considered better quality and flavor than other brands.

TOM HOLLAR   MARTHA MANWARING

CONEY ISLAND

DENVER ORIGINAL

A TOMAR CO.   (303) 832-6702

Business card from Denver Original Coney Island sandwich from Tomar Company

On this trip home, Tom made an appointment to talk with Al Koegel about making Coney Island hotdog sandwiches in Denver.

Al was cordial and even gave Tom the recipe for the Coney Island Sauce, the key to making the sandwich. Tom and Martha made a batch of the sauce and set up a hotdog cart in downtown Denver on 16th Avenue just down from Larimer, where their pen, refrigerator magnet, and sunglasses cart had been in 1985. They'd sold this cart when they got the hotdog stand.

iMi JiMi Coined

In the alley behind Tom's Corona Street apartment lived a man, who'd been at Iwo Jimo at the end of WWII. He was down on his luck and had trouble describing his experiences on Iwo Jima. He slurred his words, calling the place, "Imi Jimi." He often walked from his Capitol Hill neighborhood to where Tom was selling Coney Island sandwiches. Tom gave him free sandwiches; they talked and became friends.

This same man had a cat named, "Ferry Boat," who had a litter of kittens. As a token of good will and partial payment for the hotdog sandwiches, he gave Tom an orange cat, which Tom promptly named, "Speed Boat." Tom was happy to have a cat friend again in his home.

The name, "Imi Jimi" caught Tom's fancy, so later in 1987, when he took out a business license and formally opened his store, he named it iMi JiMi.

Tom drew the name with wiggly letters, and made all the I's lower case since he liked the impish look of the dots on the I's, almost as if the letters were alive.

The Hearse

On his trip back to Flushing, Michigan in 1986, Tom spotted a vintage black 1940 Cadillac hearse parked behind the Rossell Funeral Home on Main Street with a "FOR SALE" sign on it. Tom pulled up his white Dodge truck near the hearse, inspected the old car, peered into its windows, checked under the hood, and kicked the tires.

He had to have this car! He made a deal with Ray Rossell and found a shipper to secure the car so it could ride on a flat rail car to Denver. Tom's friend and neighbor, musician Dan Dhonau went in with Tom to buy the car.

It was a proud day when Tom went to Union Station to await the arrival of his vintage hearse from Michigan. The car was drivable, so once it arrived and was unloaded from the railroad car, he and Dan drove it carefully up 17th Street, across Broadway, and then south on Washington, crossing Colfax, and on down to 9th and Corona, where

Rusty hearse when it first arrived in Denver, 1986

they parked it in the row of parking spaces next to their apartment.

From Day One, the car drew attention from passersby, sometimes with groups of three or four young men standing around talking and gesturing, pointing to the car. This just suited Tom.

The Cadillac hearse needed work on the engine and the wood-and-velvet interior. Tom set to work. He loved this job of restoration just as his Grandpa Hall would have. Tom sanded and treated the wood, and he oiled and re-placed engine parts, no easy task since the car was old and parts were difficult to find.

Summer in Denver 1986

After Howard and I bought our new home, Tom wrote a letter on his new *stationery*. To create it, he'd photocopied three one-dollar bills onto a single sheet of paper. He wrote, "So you finally bought a house! What's the new address? Did you know that the interest you pay with each payment is tax deductible and that at least 95% of each payment is interest? So make sure you deduct the proper amount on your income tax form." The humor here was that Howard is trained in accounting, has a business degree from University of Michigan, and that Tom was telling us what he very well knew we already knew, and he was talking to us as we might have spoken to him.

✦

Meanwhile, in Other Parts of Denver

In northeastern Denver, a young black man named Terry Smith decided to join a newly formed gang (Crips) because he thought this might help protect him, since he'd recently lost his Dad. Tom, in his own world, paid little attention to gang activity in Denver.

Visit To Tie Siding

One nice day in June, Tom decided to pay a visit to Juan and Joni at the ranch in Tie Siding. He'd felt responsible for the broken come-along and had kept Juan's upset over it in the back of his mind for two years now. He went to a hardware store, bought a new one, and set out north out of Denver on I-25, west to Laramie, and then on 287 to the ranch.

He pulled up, proud of his new white Dodge truck and knowing that ranchers pay attention to trucks. He knocked at the door of Juan and Joni's house. Joni was there; Juan was out working. She was very glad to see Tom, and he was delighted to see his old friend again.

So Tom set out among the familiar sage bushes on the rolling land of the ranch to where Juan was working, and when Tom saw him, he pulled out the new come-along, walked over, and presented it to Juan.

Juan was surprised and very pleased, never expecting this, and very glad to see Tom looking so good.

Joni made a pot of good, strong coffee, and came outside with a tray of brownies and coffee cups. She summoned Juan and Tom from the field to come for a break. The three sat at the picnic table for a happy reunion while sharing a cup of good coffee and a brownie. Tom knew Juan didn't want to spend time during a working day drinking coffee, for he never took breaks. After they'd had their chat, Tom said his goodbyes and headed back to Denver in time for dinner.

CHAPTER 20: iMi JiMi is Born
1987

WHILE DRIVING AROUND Capitol Hill, his new home, Tom noticed kids cruising on skateboards along 14th Avenue, Colfax, and on Washington Street. He couldn't resist. He bought a new skateboard deck, attached the wheels, while sitting on a bench on the corner of Washington and 13th Avenue, and then got on his board and took off north on Washington, then past several apartment buildings on 14th Avenue. Pretty soon, he had company. Three boys—about twelve or thirteen-years-old—came out of nearby buildings to skate with him.

Before long he was helping them fix their boards when a wheel started to wobble or the T-bar came loose. He carried a tool in his pocket with Allen wrench, Phillips head, and socket wrench all in one.

Word spread, and soon skateboarders from a wider area began to show up. Tom liked to skate

iMi JiMi business card with Denver Sunglass Company

with them, to show off what he knew, and to live a bit of his childhood again.

The next time he skated on 13th Avenue, six or eight boys appeared to skate with him. Some had come from further north on Washington Street and had heard about Tom from the others. Tom was fascinating to them since he was an older "kid," who was really cool and knew how to skate, someone new they could have fun with.

Tom and his new pals mostly street skated, finding their way into underground parking decks beneath apartment or office buildings, where they glided on the smooth grades and turns until some security guard threw them out.

One of these skateboarding boys was Antonio, who knew Ted—the owner of the liquor shop on the corner of 13th and Pearl.

609 East 13th Avenue

Tom struck up a conversation with Ted. One thing led to another, and after a few days, Ted opened the front door of a closed retail store at 609 East 13th Avenue for Tom. Ted was the landlord. A former row of businesses along the street had closed, and he was eager to rent the space, so he offered the store space to Tom free of charge until fall, when a meager $50 rent would come due each month, with increases expected later on.

Tom looked around the huge interior, dirty with dust and cobwebs, litter and dirt from mice, shredded paper, broken metal shelving, empty paint cans, and beer cans here and there on the floor. Round metal support posts ran from the floor to the high ceiling. There were two back rooms, a lavatory with sink and a lower level, which was really dusty, dirty, cobwebby, and filled with broken boxes, bent clothes racks, hangers and chipped mannequins.

At the front of the store two large glass display windows faced 13th Avenue. (Ten years prior, the location had been a sportswear store.)

In 1985, 13th Avenue was a cultural hub of Denver's underground alternative scene.

Tom agreed to Ted's conditions and from that day forward, he began repairing skateboards inside the store for his boarder friends. At first, they had only boxes and old five-gallon paint cans to sit on.

Tom had been thinking he'd like a home for his Denver Sunglass Company, so he moved it from its Colfax Avenue virtual office to his new "store" on 13th Avenue.

Tom with skateboard "Chopper" in early iMi JiMi

At first, Tom sold and repaired skateboards. He had all colors and kinds of boards, wheels, and kneepads on display on the store walls. He was very busy, happily selling the boards to eager Denver kids. He helped them assemble their boards and repair them when needed. He liked to take a break and glide down 13th on his board on nice days with the 13th Avenue neighborhood kids, reminding him of his backyard while he was growing up. There was little difference between these kids and his old friends in Flushing: just kids wanting to have fun. They had no money and so were not good customers, but were good kids.

Tom liked having traffic in the store even if some were not buying anything. He ordered stock from the wholesaler he'd used for the cart at the airport to begin selling T-shirts, baseball caps, and sunglasses from iMi JiMi. Martha screened T-shirts in the back room of iMi JiMi to sell in the front of the store.

Fashionation

Paul Italiano was setting up his store, Fashionation, a punk clothing and shoe store next door to iMi JiMi during summer of 1987. Fashionation opened

117

in April, while iMi JiMi opened in August as a skateboard, T-shirt, and sunglasses shop. Paul started a Facebook site called 13ᵗʰ Avenue Story, which includes Tom, and when remembering the 1980s there, he said, "Remember the good times."

Interesting Folks

Before Tom rented the space at 609 East 13ᵗʰ Avenue the landlord had allowed a man to live there, mostly in the back rooms where the lavatory was, in exchange for being a caretaker. This man cleaned the gutters, swept the sidewalk in front, and removed snow. He had Dissociative Identity Disorder—formerly known as Multiple Personality Disorder. His persona *Terry* knew Tom, his persona *Jim* knew Paul Italiano. But when he was *Jim*, he didn't know or speak to Tom; when he was *Terry*, he didn't know or speak to Paul. Tom was always friendly to Terry or Jim, greeting him with a smile and, "What's up?"

Finding His Niche

For a time Tom sold punk clothing and black studded leather items similar to Fashionation, but changed to selling streetwear, which better suited Tom's personality. As Tom's store changed from being a haven for skateboarders into a punk-clothing store, iMi JiMi was in direct competition with Fashionation. But as iMi JiMi moved on to streetwear, the stores went in different directions.

Tom fit in with what was happening in Denver without planning to. When he was nine or ten years old, he'd acquired vintage clothing that had belonged to Arthur Garbers, a drifter that his Grandma Hall had befriended. Tom's small, metal suitcase plastered with travel stickers and whacky package stickers had belonged to Arthur. This was the beginning of his interests in "vintage" items. Tom liked to wear Arthur's long black wool overcoat and scarf, which looked very punk. He'd been a fan of KISS rock band with their stage glamour, face paint, zombie skeletons, and colors of death: black, purple, maroon, and blue. He liked the Rolling Stones and had the album *Goat's Head Soup,* whose cover I didn't like to look at.

Tom's Persona

Tom was neat about his appearance and was clean-shaven except for a small "love patch" under his lower lip. He had no tattoos that I know of. He worked at being cool, although it also came naturally to him. He had a pierced left ear where he wore a small gold loop earring, but at times he'd place a safety pin there instead to gross out his square Michigan friends.

I suspect he chose Jaegermeisters as his signature drink because he thought it was cool, and for a period of time, about when he was at Western Michigan University, choosing a liqueur like Jaegermeisters was considered making a statement. Tom might have chosen Jaegermeisters also because it is an alcoholic blend flavored by herbs, roots, flowers, blossoms with a hint of orange peel, vanilla and cinnamon.

In a way, Tom was a runaway, too. He'd left behind him all the "shoulds" and rules he'd had imposed on him while he was growing up. Now he could express himself and be his fun-loving self without Nancy or me telling him to clean his room, but he carried within him what he had learned—honesty, decency, respect for others' dignity. He didn't take advantage or make fun of others.

The Store Grew

Tom's store became a regular skateboard repair shop with parents arriving in cars with their children's skateboards. Now he could charge more for his work. So he got to know a wider group of people and skateboarders. Some of the regulars were Antonio, Beast, Rocko, William, and Julian Martinez, who called himself a "Denver street kid."

Julian became especially good at skateboarding and became very close to Tom.

Skateboard Contest

One of the parents had the idea of holding an informal skateboard contest between nearby Denver neighborhoods. Tom worked on many of the skateboards of skaters from these different neighborhoods, so he knew the kids. He thought this was a great idea, and he decided to sponsor a skateboard team made up

Beast on skateboard in Denver

of kids, who skated around iMi JiMi, the 13ᵗʰ Avenue neighborhood.

Tom tuned all the skateboards to be sure they were in good shape, just like his Grandpa Hall repaired used cars before selling them, and the 13ᵗʰ Avenue team practiced on the jumps, turns, and ramps chosen for the contest. Tom's team included Beast and Julian, two skilled skateboarders.

Tom's team beat the more affluent teams and won the tournament, but the parents of the other skateboarders didn't want them to win, and didn't at first acknowledge the victory. Eventually the winning ribbon was awarded to the 13ᵗʰ Avenue team, however. Tom posted the ribbon just above the cash register at iMi JiMi for all to see. It was the brightest, happiest time of Julian Martinez's life, as he had never before achieved as much, had such self-esteem, or had so much fun.

Since Tom was busy with his store, he had no time for the hotdog cart, so he sold it. Making fresh batches of Coney Island sauce was time-consuming, even though he enjoyed making it and kept developing variations of the recipe. Profit from selling one pair of Wayfarers sunglasses was greater than selling six hotdog sandwiches.

Mural Off 13th Avenue

Just past two doors down from Tom's new store was an alley named "Anarchy Alley," which cut from 13th to 14th Avenue. A giant mural on the wall was an icon of the 13th Avenue alternative-arts scene. The mural had been painted by twins Roy and Royce, who formerly had a

Tom by mural off 13th Avenue

shop on 13th Avenue. But in 1987 when Tom opened iMi JiMi, they were in jail. I have no further information about the twins.

Two Locations 1987

Sunglasses were not selling from the store the way they had been at the airport, so Tom decided to keep the cart at Stapleton. Martha split her time between the airport and the 13th Avenue store, and that meant Tom needed more help.

Margaret Heads West

He focused on the skateboard customers and the increasing number of retail clothing customers on 13th Avenue. He asked his old pal, his sister Margaret, to come to Denver to help for the summer. With misgivings, I allowed Margaret to go since she wanted to, Tom knew the ropes, and he had an

Margaret and Tom at Coors Brewing Company in Golden, Colorado

extra bedroom in his apartment.

Margaret remembers that they bought an Art Deco dusty rose-colored sectional sofa for the living room of the apartment that summer. Tom found an oval, glass-topped table with a globe fitted into its base under the glass, which fit in perfectly with the sofa, and along with a corner television set in a cabinet, an Andy Warhol print and a spider plant, finished the living room.

Margaret spent time tending the cart at the airport and had fun selling sunglasses. Hawking goods to passersby didn't come as easily to her as it did to Tom, but sunglasses sold themselves with Tom's cart display and favorable price. The cart was usually busy.

Margaret remembers one day while she was tending the sunglass cart at Stapleton, when some big event was taking place in the mountains at one of the ski resorts, and hordes of well-heeled travelers surrounded the cart. She sold $700.00 worth of sunglasses during her eight-hour shift.

When she arrived home from Denver fall of 1987, she had orange hair.

CHAPTER 21: TOM'S LETTER
JUNE 17, 1987

"HI MOM, HOW (Howard), Things are progressing right on schedule. Marg's working the airport most days and doing just fine. The store looks better all the time. Skateboards are coming in on Thursday, so now we can advertise exactly what we sell. The dog on this card looks like Chopper, our new boxer. Our friends Dean and Clair gave us their old Tabor Center inventory-cards, cat and dog toys."

Note: Tom evidently needed a break here and finished the letter two days later.

"The burglar alarm was installed today, and boy is it loud! Almost time to go to the airport to give Marg a break. I think I'll call G Hall and talk for a few! Bye for now, Love, Tom."

I could sense his pride and feelings of well-being from the tone of this letter, and his expansive handwriting.

This letter (card) was mailed August 24, 1987, and included a folded promissory note for a loan we'd made to him in July. The note was written on a pad of paper with the heading: "Call Your Mother, She Worries." Tom's note read:

"I OWE YOU $1000.00; I=THOMAS EDWARD
HOLLAR;YOU = NEDRA J. DOWNING;
$1000.00 = One Thousand Dollars.
This is a note stating that I borrowed $1000.00 at the
annual interest rate of .08 or 8%. Payable upon request
or at the rate of $25.00 every quarter starting October
15 and every 3 months thereafter!
Signed, Thomas E. Hollar."

I loved Tom's version of a promissory note, and his terms for repayment
which would not be too hard on him.

Chapter 22: Store Makeover

TOM DECIDED IT WAS TIME to clean up his store. He bought brooms, buckets, cleaning solution, and rags. He, Martha, and Margaret swept, mopped, and scrubbed. When the floor had been thoroughly swept and washed, Tom bought five-gallon drums of floor paint in a dark battleship grey and painted the entire floor using paint rollers. Once the paint dried, the workers left white dusty footprints when they walked across the shiny dark-grey floor.

Awesome Findings

After the floor was painted, Tom disappeared in his white truck and reappeared hours later with items he'd found in dumpsters and junkyards, or bought at used furniture stores or estate sales. He found glass showcases and an old cash register. When a sale was rung up, the cash register made a loud, "Ding," the drawer opened, and black-and-white numbers displayed the amount of the sale in a window at the top. Martha sprayed Windex on the glass showcases to clean the corners from the inside.

On one of his junk-seeking missions, Tom found a six-foot-long plastic banana, which he picked up, took to his new store, cleaned and affixed with wires to the high ceiling. On another escapade, he found a discarded antique red-metal dental chair complete with appendages: a tray, a spittoon, and a footrest. He couldn't resist. Most people do not like to go to the dentist, often experiencing discomfort or pain when they do, so in a way, suggestion of this by the presence of the red dental chair added Tom's twist to the new punk attitude at iMi JiMi. He brought back the dental chair and placed it just inside his store, where it could be seen from the front display windows.

In early 1988, the left display window of iMi JiMi housed a woman in a coffin, and the right window showcased TV screens that turned on at night.

Neon

Tom also began picking up pieces of discarded neon signs—bent glass tubes that held inert gases, which created color when electricity was introduced. Tom loved working with neon. He made a pale-blue neon light to fit around the right display window at iMi JiMi and also around the ceiling of his apartment porch on Corona, and he even planned to put neon on his cars. As soon as Tom opened iMi JiMi, he made a neon sign for the front of his store with its wiggly letters and dotted i's. Later, he made more neon signs with the same wiggly letters. He was seriously considering taking training to become a creator of neon signs as his next career.

iMi JiMi at night with Tom's neon sign

Neon on Tom's apartment porch

Punk Clothing Arrives

As the skateboard craze faded, Tom used his talents to make studded black-leather collars, wristbands, and belts. But about 1989, as the store grew, iMi JiMi moved toward selling streetwear, replacing its punk clothing and studded leather.

Punk clothing, hair, makeup, music, and shoes arose as a movement which started in Europe—Germany, Netherlands, and Great Britain. At first, Punk clothing was popular in New York City. But Denver punkers, who hung out in the 13th Avenue neighborhood, soon found a home at iMi JiMi, where Tom made them feel welcome.

Punk music was an attempt by kids to be noticed for their talents and to compete with what they considered to be the phoniness of big-band sounds and commercial music of the day with their often spontaneous, very original, quite different sounds. These punk musicians had no money.

Small start-up punk bands played an audacious mix of rhythms and often discordant sounds, shouts or screams.

Instruments wandered where the lead didn't necessarily take them. They made no attempt at being lyrical or having a hummable melody. Confusing, clashing, edgy, upsetting, this completely original music spontaneously played by punk bands appealed to Tom and the mix of unsettled customers in his store. Tom could recognize its creativity.

Punk bands appeared in Denver venues like Mercury Café on California just off 22nd, where Marilyn Megenity provided a stage and a dance floor, and Kennedy's in the 17th Avenue neighborhood in Capitol Hill, where Nancy K welcomed the young musicians and gave them a place to play their slightly outrageous music.

Punk At Imi Jimi

Tom greeted the punk crowd by their first names. iMi JiMi was about attitude, and Tom made it fun. He was caught up by the outrageousness of punk, and could even see a bit of slanted humor in it. But for all the blunt black-and-white statement of the style, punk clothes carried an aesthetic of violence or cruelty and SM Punkers, often shy and introverted, maybe angry or depressed, sometimes inflicted self-injury.

Goth Punkers

Goth punkers were called the Undead, Muerto punk, black heart, predator, skull, Gothika, Crypts, Demon, Charade, or Dank. These dark themes in Goth punk were supposedly inspired by dark and spooky shadows cast by European Gothic architecture, usually churches.

Tom liked hard, hard punk-rock music, including The Ramons, The Dead Kennedys, Steel Pole Bathtub, GBH, and he was a big fan of Sex Pistols Band. He listened to their album, "Here's the Sex Pistols," and copied "God Save the Queen," and "Holidays in the Sun," to listen to on his car tape player. (By 1990, Tom liked to listen to Billy Bragg and the Poughs and others.)

He frequented Rock Island on 15th near Wazee, a haven for punk musicians. This is where Dan Dhonau, who had a five-member punk band named Peace Core, sometimes played. Dan sang and played guitar. Dan and Tom were friends, and Dan worked for a short time at iMi JiMi. He lived in the same apartment building as Tom on Corona, and was part owner of the 1940 black Cadillac hearse.

I remember a visit I made to iMi JiMi one afternoon when the store was busy. I looked like the embodiment of what the punkers were rebelling against—khakis, sneakers, mainstream middle-class dress.

When a tall, punk man about 18-years old strode in with a shaven head, scars, and pinches of skin sticking up on his head with pins through them, I could only stare. He wore face paint: white around the head like a skull with deep grey around the eyes. He wore torn, cutoff black jeans and boots.

Tom said, "Hi, David. What's up?"

Tom probably got a good laugh from my reaction to seeing this poor man, who had inflicted self-injury of the sort I'd never seen before. I've often wondered how Ed and I, about as provincial and conservative as parents can be, spawned a creative son like Tom, who came to embrace people with such far-out style.

New Honda, 1988

Tom came to Michigan to buy a new Honda because he thought he could get a better price than in Denver. He asked me to co-sign. He knew what he wanted, a sporty-but-substantial black Honda with dual tailpipes. He went to Mark Allen Honda on Saginaw Street in Grand Blanc. I met Tom at the dealership

Tom with his new Honda

after I finished work at my pharmacy. He chose a new black Honda Accord sedan. I was quite pleased with Tom wanting a new car since I knew that a man's self-image is closely tied to the car he drives. I felt that Tom wanted to present himself well. He never mentioned that he and Martha were not getting along or had just split up, and that he had an interesting new friend.

Tom traveled from Denver back to Michigan again in November of 1988 to attend the wedding of his sister, Laura, to Richard Kovalcik, held on Saturday, November 11. He had a

Tom with Margaret and Anne Hollar at Laura and Richard Kovalcik's wedding reception, November, 1988

good time with his family and friends while home and headed back to Denver in his new black Honda on Sunday after the wedding. Tom was a good driver, and he was very proud of his new black Honda.

CHAPTER 23: TOM MET CHRISTINA, 1988

STEVE SIMMONS, a friend of Tom's set him up with a beautiful girl named Christina. Steve was quite the matchmaker—he told Christina about Tom, and he gave Tom Christina's phone number.

Tom called the number, and when Christina picked up, he said, "Hi, this is Tom Hollar."

Christina replied, "Oh, I wondered if you'd call!"

"What's up?" said Tom.

"I'm staying home because I hit my shoulder in a car accident. It wasn't my fault. Someone ran into me at a stop light."

"Oh! Does it hurt?" asked Tom.

"Only when I move my right arm and when I try to sleep," said Christina. "I have had trouble studying because I am tired from not sleeping well, and I can't concentrate, but I am trying to study for my classes."

"Too bad," said Tom, "Anything I can do?"

"Not really," replied Christina.

At this time, Christina was staying home a short time because of the accident and was off work. She worked part time while taking classes at Metropolitan State College of Denver. Tom started calling every day, and each time, they talked for hours. He had flowers and soup delivered to her. She said that Tom was "such a kind person."

By the time Tom and Christina met face-to-face, they knew each other, and so it seemed easy and natural for them to be together. Once together, they shared their lives on a day-to-day, hour-to-hour basis.

+

When talking about Tom and his life in Denver, we are really talking about Christina's life, as well. She was with him, day and night, for the last six years of his life. They lived together, worked together, and very much enjoyed being together—so creativity spawned at iMi JiMi was their creativity, with Christina's flare for style showing through in selection of clothing and shoes for the store, advertisements, and window designs.

Penny Miller, who owned Pegasus Bar and Restaurant across 13th Avenue from iMi JiMi said that she would see Tom and Christina working together on window displays at the store at all hours of the night. Working together on such projects, time flew by as they kept thinking of new ideas, adding to or changing what they'd already done. They floated on the creative energy they shared, going for hours not needing food, but sipping on bottled water or maybe an energy drink from Alfalfa's.

When I visited Denver one time, Tom proudly took me to Alfalfa's where he ordered for me an Echinacea herbal beverage with Vitamin C, which he knew I'd appreciate, and I did. I worked as an alternative physician and often suggested use of Echinacea to my patients.

Tom and Christina dated for about a year before she started helping him at the store. She described the store as not having a lot of direction—with a jumbled assortment of merchandise. Christina was helping out part-time at iMi JiMi while going to school. She said Tom became discouraged at one point, and he was ready to quit because the store was not bringing in very much income. During this time she worked with Anthony and Julian Martinez for a short while to keep the store going.

iMi JiMi—The Place to Go

Since Tom and Christina were a bit older and more mature than many of their customers, they represented solid, grounded, accepting, dependable figures in the lives of some of the regular punkers, who frequented iMi JiMi. They were the adults that kids' parents might have been, and they were steeped in traditional values. They were very kind to those who frequented their store.

Tom and Christina bought black and white T-shirts with punk themes of skulls, bony rib-cages, skeletons, tears, holes, scars, and spattered blood. They displayed them on hangers covering the walls of the store in layers reaching nearly to the ceiling with extra stock on racks on the floor. Now the punk seemed more lighthearted at iMi JiMi.

Tom's original leather items: studded headbands, collars, wristbands, and belts sold easily. They sold cheap handcuffs, which fit with the SM and bondage themes of punk.

Mannequins in the windows facing 13th Avenue wore spiked punk hairstyles, punk clothing and tattoos covering arms and legs, across foreheads, sometimes extending patterns started in the T-shirt the mannequin was wearing. Tom and Chris used some of the cracked and chipped mannequins from the basement of the store, which fit in perfectly with

iMi JiMi employees, Dan Dhonau (left) and Danica Brown (right)

the punk theme of damaged people. Sometimes in the red dental chair they positioned a mannequin—wearing net stockings, T shirt, black and white face paint, stiletto heels.

Tom's Vintage Cars

Tom's Dodge convertible

Tom had two old pale-blue Dodge cars, which he'd bought from a junkyard and restored. He bought his red-and-white period Dodge convertible at an auction. Tom's vintage cars were parked in the first row of parking spaces adjacent to the Shana Marie apartment building on Corona where Tom lived. Tom eventually rented a garage along the alley behind the apartment, storage for one car.

Tom surrounded himself with wheels, much as he had done while growing up in Flushing. In his apartment were roller skates and skate boards; outside, he had three vintage Dodges and one Cadillac, and a BMW motorcycle. He also had a bicycle, which he kept in the spare bedroom of his apartment.

FreshJive, 1989

Tom had things in common with his contemporary, Rich Klotz who founded FreshJive in Los Angeles in 1989. FreshJive is a California brand of streetwear. Tom may have been attracted to FreshJive due to Klotz's skateboard background.

iMi JiMi Store Break In, 1989

In September, Tom and Christina were working hard at iMi JiMi with inventory of army-surplus drab taupe suits—all the same size—for a short, fat man, and lots of cheap panty hose or tights in various colors. This was in addition to all the baseball caps, T-shirts, and sunglasses. Actually some of the tall punkers liked the look of a suit that didn't fit-requiring suspenders, but sales were slow. They were paying off Martha's interest in the store with monthly payments, and were up-to-date in their payments. Martha had disavowed having any interest in iMi JiMi. Tom and Chris used the last of the money in the store's checking account to buy a shipment of leather jackets—badly needed new inventory.

But they had not bothered to change locks on the store after Martha left.

The morning after the new leather jackets arrived, when Tom tried to unlock the door, his key didn't work. He and Christina had attached a bike lock to the front door, but this had been cut and removed. Turns out, the store had been entered, and all of the inventory, including the new leather jackets, was gone.

CHAPTER 24: PHONE CALL FROM TOM

HOWARD AND I REMEMBER the phone call from Tom after the store was literally cleaned out, leaving no inventory whatsoever. Like many emotional events, Howard remembers where he was in traffic on his way home after work. We loaned Tom $5,000 to buy new inventory and get started again. We had loaned him money before, which he'd repaid in small installments, but when you loan money to a child, you don't always expect to get it back. I recall my phone call from Tom about the robbery, which I took in the kitchen. He was deeply hurt and betrayed at this violation; he could not conceive of someone being so nasty, beyond just a desire to sell the merchandise for money, motives were in the category of trying to cause personal pain and serious financial damage.

After the break-in, Tom and Chris were very angry. This gave them energy and resolve to carry on. Christina said they had been running the store with little stock, but from that moment on, with excitement from arrival of new inventory, the store just kept doing better and better. By this time, iMi JiMi had moved from punk to streetwear lines of clothing. Christina, a beautiful, petite blonde with long hair and big, brown eyes, was a perfect model for the streetwear they sold. She could show off the tiny, postage-stamp miniskirts, thick-soled shoes, and vests as she worked to sell these same fashions to customers.

By 1991, iMi JiMi was doing very well. Christina believes it was a good thing they'd gotten a fresh start, since they had so many bits and pieces before. Now they could focus on what they really wanted to sell. The two of them together had the dynamic energy to spot trends and run with them. Streetwear was perfect for them, far better than punk clothing. This was about the same time that rave parties were beginning in Denver.

Tom liked the eclectic pulled-together, very casual clothing of streetwear, which broke all establishment fashion rules that things had to match or "go with" each other. Besides T-shirts, they ordered cotton button-front or snap-front western-style shirts for men, and belts. They sold iMi JiMi T shirts and baseball caps in black and white.

Tom started buying worn jeans from rummage sales or used-clothing stores. The more faded or worn, the better. On visits home, he'd ask his Michigan friends to sell him their old jeans and leather jackets. He'd drive back to Denver with perhaps six or seven pairs of jeans and a leather jacket or two to sell. His Michigan friends did not understand why Tom would want their old jeans.

Now that iMi JiMi was making money, Tom could expand his inventory. He was attracted to the thick-soled or high-heeled platform shoes that he believed would sell along with the jeans. He inventoried and sold Creepers and Vans shoes, both acid-washed and regular. About this time, he ordered Doc Martens shoes, which he'd first seen in a UK magazine. He credited himself with introducing Doc Martens shoes to Denver.

Newsweek

In a March 31, 1997 *Newsweek* article "The Kids Know Cool," Gregory Beals and Leslie Kaufman wrote: "In 1990 Rick Klotz was just another cool West Hollywood twenty-something, spending his free time skateboarding and listening to hip-hop music at clubs. Then he got a cool idea: suppose he jazzed up the sort of clothes he wore on his skateboard so people could go clubbing in them, too. With $5,000 he'd borrowed from two buddies, he started making loose-fitting jeans in lightweight denim and shirts with bold stripes down the front and arms… The clothes had a 'good vibe that created a great wave.' Last year, Klotz's company, FreshJive, grossed $11 million.

"His innovations were so popular that the look is now almost passe. Worse, some of the big manufacturers he used to make fun of, such as Levi Strauss, have recently come out with designs like his. 'Now that they've caught on,' Klotz mourns, 'it's not cool anymore.' Rich Klotz, 29, is one of an emerging generation of young entrepreneurs whose rebellious, streetwise companies are shaking up fashion and related industries. These purveyors of hip 'street style' have had an impact on retailing far beyond their own sales. They are the masters of cool … who define the next hot trend. Corporate labels are out, and quirky individualism is in. Nowadays the more far out you are, the cooler you are."

This 1997 article about Rich Klotz, his FreshJive clothing, and his cool, seemed to me to describe what was happening with Tom and Chris and iMi JiMi.

Political Messages

The T-shirts from FreshJive had social and political commentary printed on them, including issues dealing with the counterculture community, perfect for the iMi JiMi crowd. Some T-shirts simply had a large print of bright red lips; one said, "Cocaine and caviar," a reference to cocaine use by older well-off community members. FreshJive baggy jeans were very popular, and their T-shirts were often seen at rave parties.

Chapter 25: A Good Year, 1991

I N 1991, WELLINGTON WEBB, Denver's First Black Mayor, was elected. Successfully capturing the Hispanic and black vote as well as 44% of the white vote, Wellington worked for what was best for Denver: promoting business and economic development, creating jobs and a tax base. He also strongly supported major projects like the new airport, Coors Field, and the new convention center, which had been started by his predecessor, Mayor Pena.

A Day At iMi JiMi 1991

One day at iMi JiMi, Tom brought in a lot of old 45 RPM records he'd bought. He spread them on the floor so people who came in had to walk on the records, breaking them and sliding around, which created surprise and excitement. He thought this was very funny, and he laughed and joked with customers. After a while, Eric Gonzalez, Tom, and Christina spent time rolling records out the front door, across the sidewalk, into the traffic on 13th Avenue, trying to roll them between cars. Eric was a good friend, an artist, and an employee of iMi JiMi.

Tom had developed into a true entrepreneur. His usual day started with making a fresh strawberry-yogurt smoothie for breakfast, along with good, strong, hot coffee. He'd take his vitamins and supplements, which he kept in the kitchen on one of the wide, white-painted window sills. Then he'd take a quick shower, dress and drive the short distance to open iMi JiMi. He'd check around the store to see where stock needed to be replaced or hanging items needed to be straightened out. He made notes for future ordering. Of course, Christina was there with him. He'd direct Josh Chapman and Eric Gonzales in jobs to do while waiting for customers. Nothing started very early at iMi Jimi. Best crowds of customers came in the afternoon.

Tom would ask Eric and Josh to clean the glass on display cabinets, the front door, the windows. He kept rags and a bottle of Windex® just under the cash register. Josh and Eric usually ended up throwing the damp rag at each other and making a game of it. Tom asked them to sweep the doorstep and in front of the store as often

Inside iMi JiMi

there were cigarette butts on the sidewalk. Tom knew the value of a neat and clean store. He even went so far as to make a "List of Things To Do When You Think You Don't Have Anything To Do." By this time, he'd covered the painted floor with fourteen-inch-square vinyl tiles in a random pattern of several colors.

Important to him was a full and neatly arranged display of sunglasses, featuring Wayfarers.

When customers tried on clothing and did not replace the garments properly on hangers, Tom asked his staff to do this, so they looked fresh. Christina was quite a seamstress and would mend small gaps in seams or sew on a button. She was fussy about keeping all of one kind of clothing together.

Shoes were in the back left part of the store with chairs and a bench to sit on while trying on the Doc Martens or thick-soled Creepers. The storeroom behind had walls covered with shelves of shoe boxes nearly to the ceiling. Tom's desk in this room held a big black phone, ordering catalogues, files of business and tax information, and a rotary file of business cards.

Above the desk, a bulletin board displayed photos, cards and promotions of interest. Here were family photos, lots of cat photos, clippings of things going on in Denver from Westword or Seed or rave cards. Always a few four-inch-square metallic red, green, yellow, blue or black-and-white iMi JiMi stickers were there on Tom's bulletin board. He kept boxes of these stickers, which he liked to put on lamp posts or parking meters wherever he went.

Tom had developed into a responsible, proud business owner, who paid his rent and taxes on time and knew the value of doing things right. He participated in community efforts to benefit others. Despite his lack of interest in following other family members to college and professional careers, he'd developed and embraced a core of integrity, and was successfully employed in his own creative business.

Tom Drove Us to Larimer

One sunny afternoon in September when Margaret and I visited Denver, Tom drove us around town in his vintage, red-and-white Dodge convertible. We parked on Larimer Street, which had colorful waving flags strung overhead. We went to The Market for a cup of coffee and a snack. This was a happy day. Tom was smiling, for he really enjoyed showing us around. This was the real Tom reflecting his truest self: proud

Margaret and Tom in his Dodge convertible on Larimer

of what he had done on his own, including his hip vintage convertible, his successful store, his popularity with his peers, and his upcoming wedding to the woman of his dreams.

Christina, Nedra, Tom, Margaret in March 1992 in Denver

Chapter 26: Another Good Year, 1992

TOM AND CHRIS DECIDED to marry. They set out to figure out all the wedding details and to pay for the wedding themselves. And in March, Margaret and I flew to Denver to meet Christina's mother, Gloria, and her stepfather, Al Berger. (Her biological father had died in a car accident when she was quite young.) We enjoyed a leisurely Sunday brunch at The Oxford Hotel, and later in the day Tom drove us to Red Rocks where we all climbed around this scenic spot just outside Denver.

For a wedding venue, Tom and Chris looked at various locations, including the Ice House on Wynkoop. They finally decided to rent an elegant Victorian estate on three acres: The Richards-Hart Estate in northwestern Denver in the Wheat Ridge neighborhood. The estate had flower gardens and a fountain surrounded by tall trees, a lovely setting for wedding guests to mingle for a July wedding.

Inside were rooms large enough for chairs for the service and the catered dinner after the wedding. Upstairs were a bride's room and a groom's room, each with a full-length mirror. Tom and Chris planned the details of the wedding cake, menu, drinks, and the disc jockey: K-Nee Hamblin II, who showed up in his black-and-white zebra-painted VW.

On a beautiful summer evening, gentle breezes moved through the crowd of guests drinking champagne on the lawn.

Christina was stunningly beautiful in her long white wedding gown with its sweetheart neckline that framed her face, as she moved from one group to another, chatting with guests. She kept the long train out of the way by holding a small wristlet that lifted it so she could walk easily.

Tom, handsome in his black tuxedo, white shirt and a red rose boutonniere, was likewise making his guests feel welcome. Their pride and happiness was glowing around them that night. The sun settled slowly the perfect night of the wedding, so wedding guests had pleasant twilight during the reception after the ceremony. Some guests brought their dinner outside, settling on a bench or a chair on the porch. Music was playing softly in the background from K-Nee's discs including: "Hold On My Heart," "Real Love," "That's What Love Is For," "Just Take My Heart," "I'll Be There," "When A Man Loves A Woman," and others.

Tom and Christina Hollar at their wedding, July 18, 1992

Gloria was petite and very pretty in a palest pink summer suit with white lace bodice, wearing her corsage of red roses, with Al, handsome and distinguished beside her in his black tuxedo. They were flanked by their three sons: Michael, Gregory, and Daniel Schneider, a strong and good-looking group of Christina's family.

The Milnors of San Antonio

were all there—Nicholas Newnam, flirting with all the girls and Daniel doing his best to be on good behavior and not embarrass his parents. Sarah was lovely with her long black hair, wearing a black tiered skirt with flowers, which was reminiscent of the Southwest where she is from. John and Cara were very happy that Tom had found a wonderful wife and was moving on with his life. They'd always been close.

Before the wedding, Laura, Margaret, and I had had our hair done at the Aveda Salon next to The Oxford Hotel. The girls chose simple, tailored navy blue dresses with white collars.

Tom's sisters were impressed with the beautiful wedding their brother and his wife had put to-

Laura, Tom, and Margaret at Tom and Christina's wedding, July 18, 1992

gether. It was fun from the beginning when we were all getting ready in our separate rooms at The Oxford Hotel, including Tom. There was some running down the hallway to other rooms. Tom asked his father to tie his necktie for him. He and Mitts clowned around and punched each other playfully, both grinning. I had chosen a black silk dress with tiny white polka dots, which displayed well the red rose corsage Tom and Chris gave me to wear.

Edward S Hollar, DDS and Thomas Edward Hollar, father and son

Chapter 27: Tom & Christina's Wedding
July 18, 1992

I WAS ESPECIALLY PLEASED with the excellent food at the reception, including crab cakes, which I am fond of, and the three-tiered wedding cake with real flowers that Tom and Chris cut together in one alcove of the dining area with double-hung Victorian windows behind them. The couple offered a symbolic bite of the cake to each other. Both of the newlyweds were radiantly happy as they cut the cake. It was a joy to see my son so poised and happy in his black tuxedo, on this, the biggest day of his life.

He'd gone around greeting and chatting with his guests, shaking hands with the men, and hugging or kissing the women during the reception, trying to be sure he included everyone.

Christina and Tom Hollar at their wedding, July 18, 1992

One scene that flashes in my mind of the wedding reception was Pete Flye, Mitts Lee, Tom, and Greg Schneider puffing on big black cigars standing outside near the porch of the Richards-Hart Estate. They all looked as if they might get sick from it.

Tom had wanted to drive his vintage red-and-white convertible, but after he, Mitts, Dan, and Kris washed it in Washington Park the afternoon before the wedding, it wouldn't start. So he and Christina left after the beautiful ceremony and wonderful reception in the black Honda dragging empty cans from the back bumper, with "Newlyweds" painted on the rear window.

✦

At that time, we each had a beautifully decorated room at The Oxford Hotel on the second floor facing 17th Street. Each room was decorated with antique furniture. Heavy drapery on tall casement windows matched the carpeted floors and upholstered chairs. The many prints and paintings of railroads, mining, cattle, cowboys, and stagecoaches depicting settling of the West gave us a sense of sharing the history of The Oxford Hotel and Denver. This oldest historic hotel in Denver opened in 1891.

Originally built to house travelers arriving by rail, The Oxford Hotel stands just one block from Union Station, the city's large railroad hub. The hotel was designed by the same architect as the Brown Palace, another historic Denver Hotel, and became a prominent, popular destination. When The Oxford Hotel opened, with its elegant interior but unassuming plain red-brick exterior, it had carpeted or marble flooring, oil paintings, mirrors, the latest in room-fixtures and furnishings, its own dining room, barbershop, library, saloon, elevator, Western Union office, and stables.

The Rehearsal Dinner

For their rehearsal dinner the night before the wedding, Tom and Christina chose a long-and-narrow room in The Oxford Hotel. It had stained-glass murals and mirrored walls above dark-wooden wainscoting panels, a marble floor, and crystal-and-silver chandeliers. This beautiful room is next to the Cruise Room and behind The Oxford Bar.

The Oxford Hotel was remodeled in 2012 or 2013 and this room now holds dining tables, as an extension of the dining room of McCormick's Fish House and Bar.

That memorable evening in July, 1992, family members on both sides got to know each other a little. Notably present were: Christina's mother, Gloria, and her step-father Al, as well as her three brothers: Dan Schneider from New York City, an editor at New York Times; Greg, a graphic designer, and Michael Schneider, an architect, from Los Angeles; Tom's sisters, Laura and Margaret; his aunt and uncle from San Antonio, John and Cara Milnor and the cousins Tom grew up with: Nicholas, Sarah, and Daniel Milnor.

Gloria and Al also hosted a backyard picnic at their home in Arvada before the wedding, an informal gathering where the wedding party mingled, had a beer or glass of wine, and had a good time.

Tom's Cholesterol

Tom called from Denver in 1992 because he'd had a checkup required to get a marriage license. The doctor discovered his cholesterol was 436, and wanted Tom to take a drug. (Average cholesterol then for a man his age was 179 mg/dl. Normal cholesterol was considered to be 240 or lower, 200-239 mg/dl was considered borderline high.) Tom wanted to know what to do. This was the beginning of his interest in eating a good diet.

Penny Miller of Pegasus Restaurant on 13th Avenue across the street from iMi JiMi noted the difference. She said Tom wanted salads, soups, and things that were good for him, a big change from his preference for vending-machine junk food and pizza from Gina's in Flushing.

When I next went to Denver, he proudly took me for lunch at Green, where we had organic salads with crunchy seaweed on top. Howard and I liked Green, and went back even after they moved to a new location further south near Washington Park.

Thanksgiving, 1992

In 1992, Tom and Chris came home to Michigan for Thanksgiving, and we had our usual roasted turkey with sage and celery dressing, fresh cranberry, apple, and orange relish, pumpkin pie, root vegetables and green beans, red wine, etc., but I left on Sunday afternoon to fly to Kansas City for a conference with the American Academy of Environmental Medicine. I was sorry I'd planned to travel on this precious weekend when Tom and Chris had traveled all the way from Denver to stay with us for the long weekend. Soon after I left Michigan, the newlyweds flew back to Denver.

The November 1992 Issue of *The Seed*

An article entitled, "Wear It's At! Over Five Years of Keepin' the Cool Clad" by Lisa S featured iMi JiMi. The article carried a photo of Tom and Chris, told the history of the store starting in 1987 as a skateboard shop, then as an all-black clothing store with spiked leather, selling to an ever-increasing number of customers. The article reported that for the last year, iMi JiMi had been selling streetwear, and it had been selling well.

Tom and Christina were quoted as saying they believed that streetwear would be around for a while. When asked to describe his typical customer, Tom said, "Age-wise, we get people in here from 15-35 years old. It's really a mixed bag. There are a lot of high school kids and a lot of college kids that come in here regularly, but we also get men wearing suits and ties. It's a pretty even distribution of men and women."

Christina added, "When I first started working here, when skateboarding

152

was so popular, I would see kids come in here with absolutely no money and try to bargain and haggle with me over the price of a 25-cent item. That doesn't happen anymore."

Asked how clothing lines were chosen for the store, Tom replied, "Well, we go to trade shows two or three times a year, and sometimes people come to us. If we know another store is going to one show, we'll go somewhere else so that what we have will still be unique."

Christina replied, "People think that going out of town to a show is like a vacation, but it's not. It's exhausting. To try to choose what other people will like is really difficult, especially from the huge variety of things that they have at these shows. There's a lot of risk involved."

The interviewer wanted to hear what it was like to run a clothing store, and Tom said, "It's ten times the amount of work that people think. It's twelve-hour days, six days a week. We have to work really hard to find the lines that we have, and it's always a risk to carry something new because most people have never heard of it. We have to advertise and sell things before other stores get to it. That's how we make our money. We want to keep on the edge of what's happening, and that's part of what keeps the job interesting. Everything is always changing."

Christina replied, "From the surface, a clothing store looks like it would be nothing but fun, but it's so much more work than that. If the alarm goes off in the middle of the night, you have to go down and check it out. If something goes wrong on your day off—tough. It's your store, and you have to make it work."

When asked, "What do you like best about owning your own clothing store?" Tom said, "I can work and have a good time. Like right now I'm really excited about some of the things we're getting in next year. I can't tell you what they are; it's a secret. But I will say that they are great. I'm always interested to see the way that the scene will change. The raves this year have completely changed the nightlife of Denver. And to me, that is exciting."

Christina said, "Of course it's fun to sit in there and listen to music and meet people. But I think the best part is when we get a new line in. We try something new, and people like it. It makes you feel so good—like you did the right thing."

I have always had the notion that sooner or later iMi JiMi would have started repairing jeans with suede or leather patches with the trademark wiggly letters of iMi JiMi, copying Tom's Grandma Hall's GHJ logo patches. Christina was an accomplished seamstress, although she most likely did not have time for something like this.

Chapter 28: Changes & Rave Parties, 1993

TOM CALLED TODAY to wish me a happy birthday. He was in good spirits and said iMi JiMi was doing well. He told me of a party he and Chris had helped make successful by distributing party maps from their store.

Rave maps were colorful cards printed with a phone number to call for location of the next party. These cards were vague, so that it was not immediately apparent what the card was for. Tom was talking about a rave party held at an arena. Since iMi JiMi sold rave-type clothes, the parties helped sales at the store.

Raves

A rave was an all-night carefree party where people danced to a rhythmic beat, with free expression, not necessarily with partners. Bright lights or strobe lights lit the room. Often works of art decorated the dance hall, which usually was an abandoned warehouse or building not in use.

Raves were part of the youth culture. Adults generally did not approve of them. Promoters worked secretly to find locations and publicize them. That's where iMi JiMi came in; they distributed rave-party cards, which held links to the locations.

Rave parties were popular in cities all over the country. Young people went to raves to have fun. There was a sense of unity and caring among those who attended, at least in the early days, and of getting away with something. Smoking and alcohol were a part of these parties, but some also offered energy drinks with herbs and vitamins.

Early on, the letters PLUR were used to describe rave parties. This stood for, "Peace, Love, Unity, Respect." Ravers could spend $5.00 for a ticket, which was good for all night.

Owners of buildings or warehouses where rave parties were held typically didn't know about the parties, so felt no responsibility. Promoters found ways to enter the empty buildings and warehouses. Rave promoters paid no taxes, obtained no permits. They did hire exciting DJs—a must for a successful rave party, and good DJs were in demand.

Early on, ravers cleaned up the location when the party was over. They didn't leave litter and empty cans. There were no fights, no trouble, no bouncers. Early rave parties were for fun, and there was a sense of goodwill, but drugs increasingly became a part of them, leading to the downfall of raves, as partygoers lost their sense of unity and caring.

Some of those on drugs became ugly and paranoid, so others didn't have so much fun. When security was required, off-duty police officers were hired to guard entrances.

Rave parties are no more, having become main stream. As of 2013 the new night-life sensations were called EDM parties (electronic dance music) and featured a DJ with a laptop and little other equipment.

Tom's Phone Calls

Tom often called home on Sunday evening about 6:30 Michigan time, which would have been 4:30 in Denver. At the time, we didn't have caller identification on our phone. I'd answer, and no voice would reply, but I'd hear a resounding belch. I'd know it was Tom. He had perfected his ability to belch at will and was really good at it. I always laughed that he'd kept this talent from his childhood.

During this phone time, Tom sometimes told me how hard he and Christina were working and about the stress related to choosing stock for the store and not knowing whether it would sell or not. Opening a store or a business doesn't guarantee success. I think it was Tom and Chris's spirit and upbeat approach to life that kept iMi JiMi going and doing so well. Tom never once mentioned the store next door, Fashionation, which was their big competition during the punk days, but less so after iMi JiMi began to sell streetwear.

The Last Time I Saw Tom Alive, May 1993

Tom and Christina came to Michigan for Margaret's graduation from Michigan State University's College of Osteopathic Medicine in May, 1993. During the ceremony, (since I had graduated from the same college in 1986,) I was able to "hood" Margaret on stage at Wharton Center, signifying that she'd received her D.O. degree. We received a nice round of applause since mother-daughter teams were not common, although father-son teams appeared regularly.

We all—Laura, Margaret, Ed, Tom, Chris, Howard and I—attended a reception on the lawn near Wharton Center in East Lansing, and then had fun during lunch at Pinocchio's in East Lansing after the ceremony.

Tom had rented a Jeep station wagon to take Christina the next day to northern Michigan, where he'd gone as a child to Pictured Rocks and Tahquamenon Falls. That was the last time I saw Tom alive.

They were happy, having fun, and Tom was proud to show her this part of his life, although Christina was basically a city girl.

While staying with us, Tom and Christina hiked our rolling backyard hills. Christina wore my old brown felt hat, and he wore the old white motorcycle helmet with the peace sign on it, which was humorous since it was out of style and nerdy.

Tom lived before the days of smart phones. Now I am sure he would have the app called, "Yo!" on his phone. Apparently this app only sends one message, "Yo!" Tom used this often, and would have seen the humor in a phone app called "Yo!"

Tom and Christina wearing her mortarboard when she graduated from college in May, 1993

Christina graduated from Metropolitan College of Denver, May 1993, with a degree in Sociology.

Anne Hollar's Visit to Tom and Chris, July 13, 1993

Anne Hollar, Tom's half-sister, arrived at Stapleton Airport where Christina picked her up in their silver Mitsubishi pickup truck. Christina drove to an REI store in LoDo, where Tom met them in the red-and-white Dodge convertible. Tom drove Annie around LoDo in the convertible and had a good time showing off Denver, especially some of the bronze statues in the park above the bus terminal.

Anne lived in Colorado Springs, where she worked at Dale House as a counselor. Her friend Christie also flew into Denver Stapleton and stayed with her at Tom and Chris's apartment in the spare bedroom.

Each day they went to iMi JiMi where Tom was installing a ceiling light fixture—a metal one with long wiggly metal arms extending from a central plate on the ceiling like an octopus. At the end of each metal arm was a light. No fluorescent tube lights for Tom!

The first night, Tom and Chris took their guests to Benny's Mexican Restaurant. Anne said Tom and Chris were fun to be with. They had three cats: Annie, Speedboat and Spider.

The last thing before Anne and Christie left to catch a bus to Creed, Colorado where they were attending a camp, Tom took Anne for a ride around Washington Park and Capitol Hill on his big, black, 1972 BMW R75/5 motorcycle. What joy he had in doing this—showing off his bike to his sister, while summer breezes cooled them after a hot summer day in Denver.

Wedding Album Prescience

Our family has a history of making funny albums for other family members about important events like weddings. On Saturday, July 17, 1993, I took my packets of wedding photos from July 1992 to make an album for Tom and Christina as a gift for their first wedding anniversary. I worked feverishly as ideas kept coming to me, and by afternoon I was still in my nightgown and robe, working on the album on the dining room table. I had worked very hard to come up with a fictional story and put the wedding photos into its context.

In the wedding-album story, Tom and Chris had planned to marry, but Tom was afraid of the commitment, so he had run to the hills. Literally.

Still a thread connected the two. In the made-up story for the album, Chris had had a tough past in which she had been a gang member herself, and Tom had saved her and brought her to a better place. (When I did the album, I was not fully aware of how terrible gangs actually are.)

In the story, Tom came back from the hills to save her again. One photo in the album was of Sarah, the San Antonio cousin, aiming a gun. All the Milnors know how to shoot guns. I had introduced guns into the wedding album and gangs

Chrisistina and Tom Hollar in their Corona apartment before their trip to California

without knowing what was to come in the early hours of July 23, 1993. I shipped the album to arrive quickly in Denver. Friends said that when Tom viewed the album, he laughed and showed it to others.

Anniversary Trip, July 19, 1993

In mid-July Tom and Chris visited friends and family in California and stopped in Las Vegas, Nevada on the way back to Denver.

Tom had booked a luxury suite at The Venetian, where he and Christina enjoyed a Wolfgang Puck dinner to celebrate their anniversary. They scheduled massages at the spa and had fun on a private two-passenger gondola ride both outdoors and indoors.

Tom and Christina just after returning from anniversary trip

I have photos of the happy, smiling couple having a good time during this trip. I received a post card in Tom's handwriting: "Sitting on the beach in Santa Barbara, having a good time, Love, Tom and Chris."

July 21, 1993 Wednesday

Laura talked with Tom on July 21, and he was in good spirits. He said they had had lots of company this summer; he and Chris had been on vacation or had had company all the time. He mentioned that Annie had stopped to stay with them. He told Laura that they'd had a great time in California and were burned out from all the travel and entertaining, although they'd loved every minute of it.

Chapter 29: The Last Night
July 22, 1993, Thursday

TOM AND PETE FLYE had been friends for years. When Tom married Christina, he no longer goofed off with Pete, so on the night of Thursday, July 22, 1993, Tom went to the Rockies' game at Mile High Stadium with Pete for old times' sake.

Margaret was working as an intern at a Grand Rapids hospital that night and on a whim, decided to call Tom. She caught him just before he left his apartment to meet Pete.

She could not tell me about her phone conversation with Tom until two years later, since memory of it was so intense and sorrowful, yet she was glad she had talked to him just before he died.

Party at Rock Island

After the Rockies game, Tom picked up Christina, who was dressed for a party and looked especially beautiful. One of their clothing suppliers at iMi JiMi was sponsoring a party for Tom, Chris, their friends and employees, held at Rock Island, a nightclub at 15th and Wazee in LoDo. Pete had found another way to get home after the game.

GOODBYE NOW DEAR MARGARET

Goodbye now, dear Margaret.
Can't talk any longer—
I'm going to the Rockies' game.

I'm going with Pete—
Old friend tried and true—
And we'll have a wonderful time:

We'll laugh and we'll cheer
We'll have a few beers—
Good times like we used to know.

Gotta go now, dear Margaret.
I'll call you tomorrow—
We'll pick up where we left off

Stay well now dear Margaret
I'll talk to you soon.
But **above all**, dear Maggie, **have fun**!

Chapter 30: Just Past Midnight
July 23, 1993

AT ABOUT 12:55 AM on July 22, 1993, Tom and Christina Hollar pulled up in their 1988 black Honda Accord to park in their usual space across Corona Street from the busy King Soopers Market on the corner of Corona St. and 9th Avenue. They parked in the first space in the second row, their usual spot.

In the Parking Lot—Almost Home

They were very tired. They'd left the party early because they had to work the next day. They were still sweaty from having had a vodka tonic and from fast dancing. Tom turned off the ignition, leaned over to give Chris a kiss on the cheek, and said, "I really want to get those FreshJive T-shirts in the window tomorrow."

"Yes," said Chris, "And maybe the new black high-top Vans we just got in. They'd look good on the second tattooed silver mannequin with the green hair."

They noticed two men walking through the parking lot toward their car, which was not unusual in the busy King Soopers lot. Tom shifted in his seat, planning to get out of the Honda, when the two men approached quickly and yelled at him to get out. As this was happening, Christina got out of her side of the car, planning to go to the trunk to retrieve her purse as she normally did. One man opened Tom's door and, with a muscular, tattooed arm, grabbed him by the shoulder and dragged him out of the car.

Everything happened fast with no time to realize its significance.

Tom said to Christina, "Just ignore them," something he'd learned from his father. Sometimes if you go on about your business and don't look your aggressor in the eye, nothing bad happens. But this time, the non-confrontational approach didn't work.

"Gimme your money and your keys!" shouted one man.

Tom, car keys still in his hand, slammed them down on the asphalt, and was walking away, hoping this would be the end of it.

But one of the men pulled a gun from a black shoulder holster, pointed it at him, and shouted, "We're takin' her."

Tom turned, panicked beyond his control, not knowing what to do, terrified that Christina might be hurt, powerless to do anything about it, screamed, "No way! Not her! You're not taking her!"

The man named Steve approached fast and shot Tom at close range on his left side, obviously aiming for his heart. Steve was using hollow point 0.38 caliber bullets in his snub-nosed Smith & Wesson revolver.

Just after the shot, the other man hit Christina. She fell face down on the asphalt. She hadn't realized at first that one of the men had walked around the car to where she was. He then started hitting and kicking her.

Tom cried out, "Arrrgh!" grabbed at his chest, staggered toward his home not far away, and fell to the pavement scraping the right side of his face on the rough cement sidewalk.

The gunman walked to where Tom lay and fired a second shot point blank, intended to go through his head, but it hit Tom's upper left shoulder instead and traveled down through his lungs. The first shot was probably a fatal one, since it severed Tom's thoracic aorta causing forceful blood flow into his lungs and chest cavity with each heartbeat. (Records show that the shooting was at 12:56 AM on July 22, 1993.) The gunman bent over, and went through Tom's pockets, removing his wallet.

Christina still lay face-down on the asphalt when she heard the second shot. The men then screamed at her to get back into the car. Then they lifted her to her feet and shoved her into the back seat.

The gunman drove the black Honda while the other man, in the back seat, beat Christina repeatedly on the face and head with a hard object, possibly the car phone from the front seat. She temporarily lost consciousness, but kept coming back into awareness of what was happening before lapsing again into a daze. Her head hurt terribly.

She remembered her attackers very well. She said, "They were awful, awful people. They were shouting and wild, screaming in loud shrill voices. They sort of freaked out at what they had done." At this point, she did not know all of what they had done.

Big Men

"Hey, bro,
How come you grievin' that Holla
man?
He had a GOOD LIFE,
so what's the fuss?"

They are big men who shot my son.
That night their weird energy
met his.

jangled nerves
firing hot
sizzling blood
drugged rage
loaded envy
out for prey

WHITE SKIN TROPHY!

BLONDE PRIZE!

stabbing jealousy
instant hate

WE CAN'T HAVE IT

NEITHER CAN YOU!

After the Shooting

Tom's black Honda, with Steve at the wheel, sped off out of the King Sooper's parking lot, squealing its tires, turning right onto Corona and headed south.

Denver Police Reassigned to Section 2

Later, two veteran Denver Police officers on duty in Section 3 were reassigned to Section 2 when the regular officer, John Brinkers, had been moved to Denver General Hospital duty. They were looking for the black Honda, since the crime was on police radios all over the city. One of the policemen suggested they go street, alley, street, alley, and cover all of Section 2.

Christina Found

By chance and the Grace of God, police officers Vince Lombardi and Scott Hartvigson spotted the black Honda in an alley in the 2100 block of Lafayette Street early in their search. Officer Hartvigson, riding passenger, noticed a shiny gleam in the rearview mirror as they passed the dark alley. They made a hasty U-turn, squealing their tires.

The murderers heard it and fled the vehicle on foot. This may have saved Christina's life. A resident reported hearing two men run between her house and the next one at about that time of night. She could hear them talking.

When police officers found Christina at 1:25 A.M. in the black Honda, she had been badly beaten. At first they thought she might have been shot and that she was dead, since there was so much blood spattered all over the windows and interior of the car. But when she moved her head, Vince Lombardi said, "Jesus, Scott, call an ambulance, Code 10."

Christina was rushed to the hospital, and soon skilled professionals worked to stabilize her at Denver General Hospital, a Level One Trauma Center.

At Denver General Hospital, John Brinkers described her beating: front teeth were knocked out, facial bones and nose broken, lacerations on her face. He said that two or three times, she'd asked if he'd seen Tom. Christina later said that her mother, brothers, and friends had saved her with all their love and prayers.

Months of Treatment

Indeed, Chris's mother Gloria found the best surgeons and dentists and coordinated the extensive procedures Christina went through during ensuing months.

CHAPTER 31: CALL IN THE NIGHT

SOUND ASLEEP in our comfortable bed with its summer duvet and the dog asleep in her bed nearby, the chilling ring of the phone awakened us about 5 o'clock the morning of July 23, 1993.

Howard answered and said, "It's Laura. She needs to talk to you."

Awake now, I answered the phone.

Laura said, "Mom, Tom's been shot. A man named Gary called from Denver General Hospital. He wants you to call him; he wouldn't tell me anything." She gave me the 303 number he'd given her, which I wrote down.

The phone seemed to ring too many times before a man's voice answered. I said, "This is Nedra Downing, Tom Hollar's mother. I am calling to talk to Gary."

"This is Gary," the voice said.

"What happened?" I asked.

"Your son's been shot," he said. The call was strange, to someone who identified himself only as Gary.

"How? Why? What happened?" I shrieked.

Gary added only that Tom didn't or wouldn't make it, and my brain refused to register what that meant.

Shaking, I told Howard, "We need to go to Denver, NOW!"

I called the Denver General Hospital number and told them who I was. After what seemed like too long, I was put through to an emergency-room doctor, who said Tom had been in asystole (no heartbeat) when he'd reached the hospital. The doctor said the first shot went through his aorta and into a lung, and that he died quickly. He said Chris had been abducted, assaulted, and beaten. She was being attended by the trauma team. He said her X-Ray was OK (probably of her cervical spine, meaning her neck was not broken), and she was going to CT scan at 5:30 AM.

Now what had happened started to penetrate into my conscious mind—my son was dead! Christina was badly beaten!

Sometime during the early morning, we spoke with Bill Buckley, whom we thought was with Denver Police Homicide Division. He told us briefly what had happened. He said the event was a random-pattern robbery: killers took money, ordered him out of the car, her back into the car. He argued, and they shot him. They beat her severely, lots of trauma. The car was found in an alley with Christina in it, a bloody T-shirt and her purse were in the alley. There were eyewitnesses to the murder. Chris and Tom had been at Rock Island Club earlier. The two men had come from across the street.

At the time, some details about things found in the car were almost an annoyance—they had nothing to do with Tom or Christina, or so it seemed then. These important details helped Denver detectives and police officers figure out who had done this savage attack on two innocent people, but were information overload for me at the time. Then, I just needed to get close to what had happened to my son. How had it been for him at the end?

Tom's Sisters Cope

Howard immediately got on the telephone with Northwest Airlines about our emergency. Airlines are quite accommodating for such situations, and they found seats for us on a flight out of Detroit around 9:00 AM.

Cara and John Milnor and Sarah called from San Antonio. I don't know who called them. Howard talked with his father and his sister, Gail.

We hastily put things into a suitcase, ate something, although neither of us was hungry, and were on our way to the Detroit airport, an hour and a half away when there is no traffic. We must have gotten a dog sitter, although I don't remember doing this. Sue Robbins, our friend and girl-Friday, probably offered to do this. She was very fond of our black standard poodle, Jodi, and knew our cats quite well.

Laura was in her first year of medical school and had a final exam the next week. She decided to stay in Michigan to be with Ed in Flushing. He planned to go to work as usual, needing the routine of his life to help him get through. Laura changed her mind and was able to delay taking her final for two weeks. She most likely got a lower grade on this delayed final than if she'd taken it on time. She traveled to Denver, arriving with Margaret.

Margaret, an intern, had just completed her night shift. She said the resident and the other interns would cover for her for the last seven nights she was scheduled at a Grand Rapids hospital. This was an extremely kind thing for them to do, since working twelve-hour shifts is exhausting, and the other doctors were already tired before taking on additional night shifts. Margaret now had a week off her hospital duty and wanted to come to Denver as soon as possible. She first went to our home in Holly, took a nap, petted Kalamazoo, Tom's former dorm-room cat, and her cat, Atilla, who napped with her. Then Marge and Laura flew to Denver.

I wrote in my journal, "There is nothing anyone can do now; my son is dead. All we can do is to keep his memory alive in our thoughts and to honor and respect the life he lived, to be glad for the happiness and successes he had."

Sirens

Sirens screamed
in the black of the night
as they rushed to the scene of the crime.

The sky was red
the night he died
sunset spilled all over the west.

I remember when
my son was young
the dirt and the sand and the fun.

How wrong for him
to die like this,
bleeding to death on the ground.

Chapter 32: Flight To Denver

WE'D FLOWN WEST so many times, but never like this. Announcements on the plane were too loud, irritating; everything was unimportant, in the way, trivial; people were slow-moving, annoying. The flight lasted forever, and the whole time I sat seat-belted in place, holding back tears and screams. These people had no clue, nor should they, about our awful dilemma.

Where would I find him? Where had he died? Why was he shot? He didn't deal with guns, drugs, or aggression. He avoided confrontations and had always been well-liked and fair. Who could have shot him? Was there some awful, giant mistake?

✦

Circling Denver, I looked down, dreading what was to come. No longer able to hold back tears, I left the plane sobbing with my husband at my elbow. He had his arm around me to steady me and guide me through the crowds toward baggage pickup. I was only distantly aware of people staring, for we were in some other place that was on a separate clock; time was measured only by the events that unfolded.

Coincidences followed us. In the Denver airport, pulling our bags toward National Car Rental, we met Lisa and Loren, part of Howard's extended family. Loren taught pottery in Aurora, Colorado, at a junior college, and they were newlyweds. They'd heard about Tom.

Where should we go first? We stopped by iMi JiMi. We chose this probably out of habit, a touchstone for being in Denver, and it was on our way to Tom and Christina's apartment and the hospital. A few young men there waved angry fists at us when we got out to read the sign posted on the door: "Closed due to death of Tom Hollar and the beating of Christina." Once they knew who we were, we were glad-handed and hugged.

Later we learned that one man there was a gang member, who counted Tom as a friend and who'd frequented the store.

Mannequins in the windows facing 13th Avenue were stylishly dressed with black-net stockings, Doc Martens, tattoos, bright-red lipstick and nails, trendy postage-stamp-sized skirts, and long strings of beads. This looked like business-as-usual at iMi JiMi, quite normal before the event. I felt proud that Tom's store pulled off this much style and attitude, and that he had been a part of it.

Denver General

I didn't remember how we knew, but by this time, we knew that Christina was alive.

We'd checked into The Oxford Hotel, so maybe we learned it from a newspaper or television, and I suppose William Buckley had told us. We knew we must go to Denver General Hospital on Bannock Street, a Level One Trauma Center. We'd navigated Denver streets often, but never before to this part of town. We found the place and parked. I was shaking and very tense as we walked across the asphalt, not knowing what we'd find inside.

In the large front entrance, we got Christina's room number from the receptionist and saw Pete, one of Tom's old friends, staring at the floor and

174

pacing in some sort of a daze. He could only stammer that they wouldn't let him see Christina.

ICU

We were not prepared for what we found in ICU. Police guards were outside Christina's room. Two of her brothers, Greg and Michael Schneider, her mother, Gloria Berger, and her stepfather, Al Berger, were at her bedside. Her face was bruised and swollen, with heavy bandages over much of her face. Her mouth, partially open, showed dark dried blood. Her front teeth were missing. Her left ankle, which had been sprained, was now in a plaster cast suspended in a sling.

What kind of hateful, vicious person would inflict this kind of destruction on a tiny, helpless young woman? Despite her injuries, plus heavy doses of sedatives and pain killers, Christina managed a tiny smile when she roused enough to know we were there. Later, she said she kept wondering where Tom was. She was terrified that her attackers might find her, so—to reassure her—her brothers spent the night trying to sleep on the floor of her room in ICU.

When Laura and Margaret arrived early on July 24, they spent time rubbing Traumeel cream on Christina's bruises. She was dazed, not knowing the whole story of what had happened. We were all shocked at the extent of her injuries.

I took poignant photos of her in ICU with the girls. I recall upon leaving her room, seeing the police guards and dietary carts with trays for patients. I was appalled that they were serving dry-looking lunch meat sandwiches on white bread and green Jello. Patients were to get well on this kind of fare? Christina couldn't eat it anyhow.

Morgue

William Buckley from the Prosecutor's Office came to politely ask if I would identify my son. Procedures required a next-of-kin for this job, and I was the first on the scene. I asked whether I could examine the body; he said he'd see to it. We were escorted most graciously down to the basement morgue, where things changed abruptly.

The woman at the counter, behind bulletproof glass, told us curtly that we'd have to wait "over there." She motioned us toward a maroon vinyl settee with chrome arm rests in the small room. I had an awful feeling of anguish and disbelief, when I realized Tom was no longer my son, but a numbered piece of property, evidence, belonging to the Homicide Department. I sobbed silently while waiting in the cold room with Howard's arm around me for comfort.

Our feelings were not a consideration to these people, who dealt with murders as a daily part of their jobs. We were outsiders. They had no time to cater to us; they had work to do. After a very long time sitting in the tiny office, they called us to a small room where just Tom's face and neck were on display behind glass, but very close.

The police officer on duty shrugged and said it was not possible for me to view any more of my son—no matter that I was a physician and had worked with cadavers and had touched death before.

"Maybe at the funeral home later," he said.

I believe now that the pathologist was in the middle of her autopsy when we arrived, and that Tom was all cut open so that even an official from the Prosecutor's Office didn't have authority to allow us to see him during the process. Autopsies are conducted following strict guidelines, much like surgery. Outsiders could not easily be allowed to be present since they could introduce or pick up germs, pathogens, and it was not possible to have them go through the process of scrubbing and donning sterile gowns necessary at an autopsy.

We continued to get information from William Buckley about what was going on, information that we heard later in 1994 at the trial. Carol Malezija, our victim's assistant, once she was assigned to our case a few months later, also kept us informed.

Alfalfa's Market

We left the hospital sometime later—totally unaware of time. I knew we needed to eat, so we headed for Alfalfa's Market on 11th Avenue (now a Whole Food Market), where Tom had taken us many times. Enjoying black bean soup and veggie pita sandwiches, we realized that we were hungry as we sat on high stools around a small round table listening to hip-hop music. But I was still in stunned disbelief that this day was actually happening.

The place was full of Capitol Hill residents of many ages: from tanned bicyclers with tattoos and tight, black cycler pants and purple or orange hair to white-haired residents with mesh shopping bags who were taking their time, carefully choosing a bunch of greens to purchase or eating a sandwich, and other fit-looking young men and women in running shorts and sneakers sipping tea or mineral water. Bicycle racks outside were full; bikes were well-chained in place or a wheel had been removed.

9th and Corona on July 23, 1993

We had yet to go to the scene of the crime, dreading being so close to the horror of just a few hours prior. We parked in the King Soopers' parking lot next to where Tom and Chris lived at The Shana Marie.

Howard steadied me as we walked to the place and saw the pool of Tom's dark blood dried on the sidewalk under the locust tree where he'd died. I can't put words to my feelings, only that it wasn't-couldn't-be real. I stood there crying, staring, hands folded over my heart, in a gesture of

Kris Baehre, Mike Evans, Nedra, Steve Simmons standing by hearse, July 23, 1993

great pain to that chakra, wondering just what had happened to my son Tom, wanting to comfort him somehow. It was still daylight. Tom's silver Mitsubishi pickup truck was parked next to his vintage convertible in the row of cars next to the apartment building. In this same row, in the first parking space closest to the sidewalk along Corona was Tom's 1940 black Cadillac hearse, looking good and nicely restored. He died within six feet of the hearse, almost as if it had been staged in some macabre way.

At first, Howard and I, Kris Baehre, Danica Brown, Steve Simmons, Danica Darling, Karl Waechter, Mary and Emily Frembling, and Christina's brothers were the only ones there.

But during the afternoon, as we stood near the hearse, out of nowhere Mike Evans appeared—stunned, scared. Mike, a handsome, curly brown-haired Denver college student from Stuttgart, Germany, could hardly talk; dark circles under his eyes revealed his lack of sleep. He didn't immediately tell his story, but it came to us in bits—some later from others who knew him well. We had a phone number where we could reach him through his father, who lived in Denver. His parents were divorced, and his mother lived in Germany.

Mike's Story

Mike had been on his way to King Soopers for a late-night snack around midnight on July 23, walking on the sidewalk across Corona from the parking lot where the assault and murder took place. Mike Evans saw Tom with company. Mike did not want to bother Tom at that time of night, so he did not cross the street to say, "Hello."

Steve Antuna of The Denver Police Department's Homicide Bureau videotaped Mike Evans giving his statement at Denver Police Headquarters after Tom was shot. Mike was visibly shaken at the time of the video. He was emotionally upset, which is not surprising since he'd just witnessed the murder of his friend. Mike had been on his way to King Soopers for a late-night snack around 12:55 A.M. on July 22, walking on the sidewalk across Corona from the parking lot where the assault and murder took place.

Mike said he saw Tom Hollar get shot in the torso, cry out, "Aargh," clutch himself, stagger a few steps and then collapse on the sidewalk a few feet away. Mike was directly across the street.

He said the shooter wore a white undershirt, and described him as being very trim, with no body fat. He had no beard. Mike described the murder weapon as a handgun or revolver, not a semiautomatic.

When asked whether he could recognize the man, Mike said he could identify him. He stated that he would be able to testify that he saw Tom Hollar get shot.

After the shot, Mike was scared since he was close and afraid for his personal safety. He started running toward King Soopers. He heard the second shot, looked over his shoulder and saw the gunman bend down to go through Tom's pockets. Mike also saw the black Honda moving across the parking lot. He heard people in the car, heard a woman scream and a man's voice, but he did not see the second man.

My Son on the Evening News

After Alfalfa's and visiting the scene, we returned to our room at The Oxford Hotel, where we turned on TV in time to see a photo of Tom from an old driver's license filling the screen on the news. Even though we had been living with the event all day, seeing it on TV as other Denver viewers were seeing it at the same time made it seem distant, belonging to someone else.

But that photo of Tom with straggly hair hanging down over his face was unmistakably my Tom—a photo he had laughed about and liked all the more because it was not flattering. Later, Norm Bloom, a local photographer, who'd taken Tom and Christina's wedding photos, supplied the media with better photos.

News from Denver's TV stations, Channels 2, 4, and 9, commented that the assault was, "A senseless act of violence," and that "The level of brutality was astounding in a simple robbery, and there was no obvious reason for it in a simple robbery."

After dinner, we went back to 9th and Corona for a short time. When we returned to The Oxford Hotel later, after a short rainfall, I began to write my poem about the event on hotel stationery.

Ed, Laura, her husband Rich, and Margaret were all staying at the Radisson on Court Plaza.

Night of July 23, 1993

Thunder crashed
the night you died
lightning lit the black sky.

I stood beside
the pool of blood
on Corona the place you died—

there by the hearse
all covered with flowers
and candles that flickered in the wind.

The gods were mad
at what had gone on
showing anger and furor and might.

6:00 News

We turned on the TV
in our hotel room
down on 17th Street.

Tom's face on the screen
larger than life
a happy look on his face, *my son!*

A smiling picture of them,
then a scene of the crime
yellow tape marking off the spot

Floodlights shone
in the black of the night
a pool of dark blood on the walk, *my son!*

Their car in an alley
on the 6:00 news
the place they found Christina.

The day was more horrible
than could be imagined
how did such evil find them?

From the call in the night
the emergency flight
Christina in ICU

My son in the morgue
with blood on his teeth
so recently breathing, alive—

Now on the news
like a bad dream
not someone else this time.

Another Cadillac

In the afternoon of July 23, while we were busy at the scene of the crime, not far away, the two murderers were busy using $400 cash (about the same amount Tom and Christina had had) to buy a used Cadillac. It is chilling to think that they may have driven by while we were there, as it is said that murderers return to the scene of the crime.

Don and Nancy Dhonau

Like a strong rope to hang onto while climbing, Don and Nancy Dhonau were there for all of us. Tom and Christina had chosen Don to pull together their wedding ceremony. They had written the vows themselves with much deliberation and discussion. Rev. Dhonau knew and understood who they were, their sincerity, and their very great love for each other. He and Nancy were around in the days after the event, willing to do whatever needed to be done. Nancy in her quiet way, with her soft, comforting voice and Missouri accent, cheered us as days went by.

There at the memorial service, the burial, and countless times in the years afterward, Don and Nancy went out of their way to make us feel welcome, offering their friendship on numerous trips we made to Denver down through the years. They invited us for dinner in their gracious home in Denver; they hosted a buffet for all those who were able to attend a tenth-anniversary reunion. We all knew we could call upon Nancy and Don whenever we needed their support.

CHAPTER 33: JULY 24, 1993

"WE ALL HAD A BIG SLEEPOVER last night," Kris Baehre said. "We're sticking together." He was referring to the fact that friends of Tom and Christina slept at the murder scene in the back of Tom's Mitsubishi pickup truck on the night of July 23.

What People Said After the Murder

In a July 24, 1993 article in *Denver Post*, staff writer Tracy Seipel wrote: "Hollar owned the iMi JiMi clothing store at 609 E. 13th Ave, which sells an eclectic mix of apparel and paraphernalia to a hip, young, progressive music crowd that frequents other businesses in the neighborhood."

She quoted Steve Simmons, who said, "Nothing like this is ever supposed to happen to anybody. And now what they had is gone. For no reason, nothing gained. Nobody proved anything to anyone except that people can be cruel and inhuman."

Andy Holman, Tom and Christina's landlord at the Shana Marie Apartments said, "What do you say? He was just a good kid. A real, straight, good kid, who had his feet on the ground. He was a handyman. He loved to work on cars. He was a wonderful neon artist, and if you went by his shop, iMi JiMi, he was always changing it. He had more creativity going for him than any of those stupid downtown stores," said Holman.

William Logan, publisher of *The Seed*, a local underground magazine about underground culture, called Tom Hollar, "...a leader in the community of our generation...iMi JiMi was a business he cared about, but even more than the business, he cared about the scene. He let people hang out there," Logan said. "He was always very fair and friendly... He wasn't just a businessman trying to sell the hip clothes to the youth culture. He was a part of it and cared about it. He supported and helped people by selling tickets for various events and parties."

Penny Miller, owner of Pegasus Restaurant across 13th Avenue from iMi JiMi said, "He was a young, ambitious guy. I'd see him there at the store at all hours of the night setting up windows with his wife." Then vandals would break the windows like it was a target. He'd have something really nice in the windows, and they didn't want to pay for it."

Yannis Reger, who worked at Howard's Liquor Store next door to iMi JiMi said, "It's too bad. They were good kids and fun to be around—smiling and laughing all the time."

Neighbor David Land said, "They were probably the nicest people in the building. They were totally in love."

Outside iMi JiMi, July 24, 1993

In a July 24, 1993 *Rocky Mountain News* article entitled, "Businessman killed; wife beaten," Lynn Bartels wrote, "Ted Stathopulos owns the building where iMi JiMi is located. Tom Hollar opened the business six years ago. 'He paid his rent. He worked hard. He married a wonderful girl. I can't believe I'll never see him again.' Stathopulos said. 'He and his wife, they were just great kids.'"

The Bartels article went on, "'Tom really was the neighborhood,' said Penny Miller. 'It's a great neighborhood, and we love it, and we're really trying to get rid of the crime.' She said that Tom Hollar supported the Unsinkables, a 150-member coalition working with Denver police to combat neighborhood crime, particularly crack cocaine sales."

Bartels further wrote, "The growing crime problem in the Capitol Hill area is one reason that Steve Simmons, one of the Hollars' closest friends, moved out." She quoted the 32-year-old Simmons as saying, "'There are too many free agents running around here. There's crack activity, turf battles among gangs and gay-bashing. Tom was all about peace.'"

July 24, 1993. Margaret, Howard, and Kris Baehre, on sidewalk near where Tom died

CHAPTER 34: DENVER'S SUMMER OF VIOLENCE, SUMMER 1993

THE SUMMER OF 1993 came to be known as "Denver's Summer of Violence." "Denver's Summer of Violence," an August 8 *Denver Post* article by staff writer Steve Lipsher, noted that irrational shootings sparked fear in areas previously untouched by crime.

"A string of senseless shootings has the metro area citizens in fear of encroaching urban violence. Each incident seems more shocking than the one before it, even to a society hardened by constant barrage of tragic news from across town, around the block, or next door."

This article quoted Governor Roy Romer, "It's a random and impersonal kind of violence, and that's very scary to people." He called it "…an abandonment of our moral code."

Romer was quoted in another *Denver Post* article by Fred Brown, "Gang Fear Lurks in the Shadows." Romer said, "It's not just the number of acts… It's the increased awareness that these very young people have no code of conduct, no moral framework that teaches them to respect life."

Denver District Attorney Bill Ritter said, "The violence we are seeing has, to some extent, a random nature, and while it has a gang dynamic, we have innocent people who are not gang-involved who are being injured and killed—and that is something new."

Mr. Lipsher's above-cited article went on to note that the community's heightened sensitivity toward violence was due to its spread to the suburbs and traditionally white neighborhoods. For years, most of the crime was restricted to minority neighborhoods.

Denver Police Chief Dave Michaud said, "I don't know if we're having more innocent people murdered, but it's more high-profile cases."

"Statistics showed little change in the number of violent crimes in 1993, although   authorities agreed that prevalence of weapons among youths was at an all-time high.

"A high-intensity gang sweep by Denver Police officers in August 1993 confiscated 69 guns, mostly from teenagers."

Reverend Leon Kelly, Director of the Open Door Youth Gang Alternative program was quoted in the same article by Mr. Lipsher. "It's always been the feeling that as long as their violence is among themselves, that it's within the gang element, then that's fine. Let them kill off each other. But now that innocent people are becoming victims, it's a different ballgame. There's been a change in the mindset of some of the kids in the gangs—many of them feel they are victims of the system, and the system is run by the white establishment.

"They feel, 'If you're going to go out and do something, don't kill yourself or your race. It's a battle against the establishment.'"

The article, "Denver's Summer of Violence" also had contributions from *Denver Post* staff writers Stacey Baca, Mark Eddy, Howard Pankratz, Marilyn Robinson and Tracy Seipel.

Laura Greiner at the University of Colorado's Center for the Studies and Prevention of Violence was quoted, "Youth are calloused by the prevalence of violence around them and feel hopeless and resigned to their fates—attitudes that contribute to their violent acts. Typically, when you're young, you have this great optimistic attitude that you'll live forever," she said, citing a survey by Lou Harris, sociologist. "Kids no longer hold that attitude. They're more pessimistic. They do not think they'll live to be 30. They are definitely being impacted by the violence they are experiencing in their families, at schools, in their neighborhoods and society. It's affecting their outlook on life."

Denver Post's Steve Lipsher's article on "Denver's Summer of Violence" quoted an 18-year-old Denver gang member, "Violence is a Fact of Life." Violence prompted him to buy a hand gun. "Death puts fear in most people. You hear about it every day. You wonder every day: 'Who did that? Who got shot?' You've got to keep your eyes open and be aware."

From *Denver Post Archives*, posted June 28, 2012, "Summer of 1993 Violence in Denver" included:

May 2	Ten-month-old Ignacio Fabian Pardo was wounded by a stray bullet, while he was at the Denver Zoo. A shot that had been fired at City Park grazed his head. Denver Zoo is surrounded by City Park west of Colorado Boulevard.
June 9	Broderick Bell, age 4, was hit in the head by a stray bullet during a shootout between passengers in two cars speeding through Park Hill. He was riding in a car with his parents. His recovery gained wide publicity causing the community to focus on violent crime. Demonstrations led by his mother prompted police and public officials to crack down on gang violence. Newspaper headlines during our week in Denver from July 23, 1993 until July 30, 1993, heralded Broderick Bell's release from the hospital. Public interest in him and sympathy for Broderick was great. He still faced months of therapy, although he could walk.

June 10	A realtor was found shot to death in a garden-level apartment on E. 8th Avenue. His stolen Lincoln Continental was recovered behind the Ogden Theater on E. Colfax Street.
July 23	Tom Hollar was murdered and his wife, Christina was abducted and assaulted at 9th and Corona near the King Soopers Market.
July 26	Michael Barela, 4, was shot in the head during a drive-by shooting as he was riding in the back seat of his parents' Blazer.
July 27	Andrew Cordova, 3, was hit in the arm by a bullet, while on his aunt's porch in northeast Denver.
July 28	Louis Roth III, 43, was shot and killed as he was driving home on Montview Boulevard in Park Hill, less than four blocks from his home. His wife, Christina Noel-Roth, a ballerina, described him as a gentle giant. He was 6 feet, 4 inches tall. His billfold was missing, and robbery was believed to be a motive for the killing. He had several gunshot wounds in his torso.
August 2	Lori Lowe, 27, was shot and killed as she drove to a friend's apartment. She had accepted her first teaching job in Denver for the coming fall. Lori Lowe was from Michigan. Her mother and I were in touch for a while.

Actual number of murders in 1993 was 74, while in 1992, there were 95, and in 1994 and in 1995, 81. As *Denver Post* columnist Fred Brown wrote in his August 8, 1993 article "Gang Fear Lurks in the Shadows: "So in raw numbers, the 'Summer of Violence' was an exaggeration; in raw fear, it wasn't." He said that a better name would be, "Denver's Summer of Fear."

From Fred Brown's July 15, 2007 *Denver Post* on-line article "Gang Fear Lurks In Shadows:" (article appeared at different times. when you look now, you get the July 15, 2007 date which is from the Denver Post archives, while the first date of August 8, 1993 was the original date of publication.)

"Up until the special session of the Colorado legislature, Colorado had a reputation as an enlightened pioneer in its treatment of juvenile offenders. Denver had one of the first of the few juvenile courts in the country. The goal was to rehabilitate more than to punish."

"That changed after 1993. The goal became public safety."

Governor Roy Romer called a special session of the legislature that began on September 7, 1993 and lasted 10 days to address the problem of violence in Denver. *Rocky Mountain News* editorial page reported on Governor Romer's "Iron Fist" program. Among bills passed in this special session were:

- A ban on handgun possession by youths under age 18
- A provision for more jail space
- A law allowing 14-to-17-year-olds to be tried as adults for violent crimes
- The right for Prosecutors to 'direct file' against juveniles in adult court instead of having to submit to a transfer hearing, where a judge would determine whether the case should be moved out of juvenile court

Also noted on the editorial page was that legislators were reluctant to hold this session because they saw the proposed new laws as cosmetic, not really solving the problem, which proved to be the case.

Reported gang violence in northeast Denver in 2015 remained high. Twelve of seventeen murders in Denver were gang related as of mid-June 2015.

Reverend Leon Kelly has maintained his outreach ministry to Denver's gangs—helping to reduce gang violence and helping gang members turn their lives around—since the 1980s. He believes that as more whites are moving into parts of northeastern Denver, revitalizing neighborhoods, gangs have smaller territories and are more aggressive. As a result, some areas that are becoming more affluent are also seeing more crime.

This was reported in a Channel 9 News Story I found on-line with no information about authors. Rev. Kelly says there is great need for alternative programs for gang members to help get them off the streets.

Other programs, such as Ceasefire, are trying to reduce gang violence. In this approach, certain gang members are tapped to meet privately with police officers, community leaders, and social workers. These law enforcement and community leaders demand they stop their violence and promise strong punishment if they don't. Social workers offer them a path to reform. Results of this program are not easy to measure.

CHAPTER 35: AFTER THE MURDER

CHRISTINA—from her hospital bed at Denver General—chose to keep iMi JiMi open after the assault and murder. She didn't want any defeat at the hands of the murderers. Employees of iMi JiMi kept the store open as usual.

The Weekend: July 24 and 25 1993

Early the next day, Saturday, July 24, 1993, we went back to the parking lot, to the spot of Tom's blood on the sidewalk not far from the black Cadillac hearse. A few hours earlier this place had been cordoned off with yellow tape as police do while investigating a crime: a CSI.

I was choked with grief, but wanted to understand what had happened to Tom and to be as close as I could to what he suffered. I traced his steps from the place where he had parked his black Honda the night before and where he must have been shot the first time, and then the obvious place where he fell to the sidewalk and scraped his face, where he was shot the second time. The distance was not far, perhaps two car lengths.

Black Cadillac Hearse July 23, 24, and 25 1993

Under the locust tree, Tom's black 1940 Cadillac hearse became an icon of the whole event—the place that crowds gathered first before streaming all over the parking lot and other King Soopers parking lots and the lawn in front

Top left: Dan Dhonau and Nedra July 24, 1993. Top Right: Hearse, early July 23, 1993.
Center left: Kris Baehre, Mike Evans, Steve Simmons, July 23, 1993.
Center right: Ed Hollar lighting a candle, July 25, 1993.
Bottom left: July 26, 1993. Bottom Right: July 27, 1993

of the apartment building. The hearse was the place where Denverites came to pay tribute to Tom and Chris, to tell us they were sorry, to place flowers, candles, remembrances on its hood, roof, and bumpers, to write poems and grieving thoughts and messages to Tom on the asphalt where it was parked; they came to be a part of the scene—the hearse was the center.

Jaegermeisters bottle and flowers left on the hearse, July 24, 1993

At first there were a few candles and flowers on the hearse, but during the weekend flowers completely covered the vehicle, and candle wax was running down the sides of the old car. Someone put a small flask of Jaegermeisters on the running board.

Tom often did things because he thought they were funny or for the effect they might have on others. He loved to be a little outrageous, maybe this was part of it. Out of curiosity I tried Jaegermeisters, and I couldn't see how he could actually have liked drinking it, but what do I know? Maybe he did.

The Market

For breakfast or lunch, we often walked from The Oxford Hotel to The Market on Larimer. On July 26 or 27, as I sat outside at a small, round table with metal ice-cream-parlor chairs, with sparrows pecking crumbs left on empty tables and the ground, some woman who worked nearby recognized me and said,

Carole Malezija having coffee at Market in 1994

"How can you just be sitting here eating?" as if I should still be in shock.

I said, "Well, we have to eat." We liked the good coffee and muffins at The Market and especially their salads, sandwiches, and soup at lunch time. I liked to get a cold shrimp salad with dill, a cucumber salad, and a tuna-salad sandwich on whole grain bread with lettuce and tomato. We liked to watch the mixture of people there—professionals, hikers, bicyclers, college professors, students, street people.

Bands Played in King Sooper's Parking Lot

Denver Post reporter Bill Briggs, in the July 26 article, "Capitol Hill Mourns a Friend," wrote: "They came. They cried. They rocked. Three days after the murder of Tom Hollar, 30, a leader of Denver's alternative art scene, hundreds of friends yesterday turned his Capitol Hill street into a shrine and his name into a battle cry. Corona Street became a mixing bowl for the hip and the homespun, the old and young, the angry and sad—exactly the kind of eclectic crowd Hollar would

Band behind King Sooper's Market. Crowd in parking lot July 25, 1993

have loved. In a parking lot—just feet from the spot where Hollar collapsed early Friday after being fatally shot—friends scratched tearful messages on the pavement in shades of pink, purple and white chalk…Smoky incense hung in the air as mourners quietly transformed Hollar's 1940 black Cadillac into an altar. They sprinkled rose petals on its hood, wept on its front fender, and burned candles on its running board."

A few days after the murder, *The Denver Post* featured a poignant photo of red-haired Pete wearing a blue T-shirt, draped over the hood of the flow-er-covered hearse in a gesture of complete grief over loss of his old friend.

This was a happening. Bands played across Corona from the crime scene, behind the supermarket, one after another, including Wretched Refuse, Hip-pie Werewolves, Choosy Mothers, and Depression.

Bill Briggs wrote in the above-cited *Denver Post* article: "Tom Clonin, who played bass for the Wretched Refuse group, said, 'The best way I could say goodbye to my friend is to play my music for him.'

"'We look at it as an assassination, not a murder,' said musician Count D. 'They assassinated a peacemaker.'"

People milled about. Others sat on the lawn, often staying for hours. TV crews were there.

Bands were playing "in tribute to their friend, a man whom they called an inspiration." Tom and Chris had befriended people—students, artists, home-less in their neighborhood. They were like big brothers or parental figures to ever so many, who were slightly younger and less grounded. Tom and Chris had welcomed all and had cared about them at iMi JiMi.

Briggs quoted me as saying, "Tom was a creative, fun-loving art buff, who raved about the statues and murals in Denver. He was a 'dirty kid,' who dragged buckets of toads and sand into his childhood home and always saw

Margaret, Nedra, Emily, and Mary Frembgen near site of Tom's murder on July 24, 1993

Margaret, Andy Holman, Howard, Kris Baehre, July 24, 1993

the good in everyone." (He didn't actually bring sand into the house, since he had a huge sand box outside in the yard. He did, however, bring in a bucket of toads, which he and David Van Brocklin played with in a block castle they made with ramps for the toads to come hopping out upon.)

Briggs reported: "A crowd of about 50 sang and grooved to the music" and he reported that I said, 'We hope this kind of caring and spirit will go on. Strangers are shaking hands and hugging us over our mutual loss.'"

CHAPTER 36: PEOPLE LOVED TOM

Sidewalk Messages About Tom—The Medium JULY 25, 26, 27 1993

Sitting near the locust tree, close to the bloody spot on the sidewalk, sat a woman with long, flowing-white hair and black sunglasses. She was using pastels to sketch the hearse and—above it—a sketch of Tom with black hair and light-blue suit. She said she was in touch with Tom and that he had this message:

"It's OK here. Find someone wonderful and have a good life."

Those are words he might have used. She also said the murderers were north of this spot where the event happened, which was accurate.

She sat there in the same spot for two or three days, and she spoke at the memorial service. Someone said she was a well-known medium. I still have her pastel drawing, signed Verna K. Nahulu.

In a *Denver Post* article "Hearse

Drawing of Tom and hearse by medium
July 25, 1993

Festooned," staff writer Alan Katz reported: "The couple's antique black hearse was festooned with carnations yesterday at the Capitol Hill site where the 30-year-old man was shot to death Friday morning. All day, casually dressed wellwishers gathered by the hearse to pay respects to the owner of iMi JiMi …"The article went on to describe the gruesome ordeal.

Crowds around the hearse
July 24, 25, 26, 27 1993

In the crowd that day was Jim Boucher, an old friend from my childhood in Ohio. He came from Laramie, Wyoming where he had an established practice as an optometrist. Jim said he was at my disposal, there to lend support—an extremely generous thing for him to do since he was very busy with his practice. He also traveled extensively related to his work on the NASA space projects.

Karl Waechter was there. He was an old friend of Tom's, an employee of iMi JiMi. At that time he had blue hair. He was the one who'd gone back to the store in the middle of the night to dig out Tom's phone list so authorities could call us in Michigan to tell us about Tom's murder. Karl came to Laura's name first, hence the sequence of phone calls.

Mary and Emily Frembgen

Mary was a single mom, who was putting herself through school, and who lived at the Shana Marie apartment building with her daughter, Emily. "Tom was one of Emily's most important male role models; he was always so sweet with her," Mary said. "He'd come watch Emily's big theatrical productions in their backyard. He made this a safe and friendly place to live." Mary and Emily were among the crowds of people during this time at 9th and Corona.

Tom had befriended Mary by babysitting Emily to give her a break. He would get out board games like Clue® or Monopoly® or maybe take her skateboarding in the parking lot next door. Mary said Tom was "always a constant friendly face."

Andy Holman, Landlord of the Shana Marie Was in Crowds Around the Hearse

We also met Andy Holman, who was Tom and Christina's landlord at the Shana Marie and their friend. Shana, his pretty daughter, was there arranging fresh flowers along the porch railing of #4, where we sat part of the time. Tom and I had sat there on one of my visits when Tom enjoyed showing off by greeting many passersby, whom he knew. He was clearly happy, enjoying himself.

Charles Calloway

We chatted with Charles Calloway, one of Tom's friends from The Oxford Hotel, who had helped Tom with rooms for the wedding party in July 1992. Tom had introduced us to Charles Calloway previously, and on this weekend, it was nice to see him in the crowd.

Kris Baehre and Danica Brown

Kris and Danica, who lived together in the Shana Marie, came to talk to us. They'd been there that night, heard the loud discharge of the first, then the second shot. They were afraid, but when all seemed quiet, they ventured out to find Tom face-down on the sidewalk and bleeding. They called for help, and Kris said, "Hang on, old buddy, help is coming." Kris knelt on the sidewalk by Tom, holding him until the emergency team arrived. Kris calls this "a very difficult memory," but takes comfort in the knowledge that Tom knew he was not alone.

Danica recalled the gurgling sounds Tom was making as he breathed while blood oozed onto the ground in spurts.

"He's dead! He's dead!" Danica said, "Oh, I hope he didn't hear me say that."

Kris told Danica to go back upstairs because he felt she was not helping. Kris Baehre will always be special to me since he was comforting Tom when he died.

Emergency Medical personnel who attend such murders always say, "He died quickly," which is what I was told on the phone with Gary at Denver General. There is no way Tom died quickly. He died an agonizing and stressful death after the first shot severed the large thoracic aorta, he grabbed his chest in agony, and after he fell, his still-beating heart pumped his blood onto the sidewalk.

Pete Flye

Redheaded and almost incapacitated with shock and grief, Pete Flye mingled with the crowd spending time near the spot where Tom died.

Martha Manwaring and a friend whom I didn't know, were in the crowds for several days. I was not in the mood to talk to her.

Wellington Webb, Mayor of Denver

On Monday July 26, we were advised that Mayor Wellington Webb and his wife, Wilma, were coming to the site where Tom was murdered, and people were constantly gathered by the hearse. The Webbs arrived in the early evening, and we chatted.

Wellington was very sorry this had happened; he and Wilma were kind and gracious. They came as individuals and parents to express their condolences and had not advised the media of the visit. They didn't come for political gain or publicity. They were sincere in offer-

Howard, Wilma Webb, and Nedra at Tom's murder site

ing their sympathy, a great comfort at the time.

Later we took to his office two T-shirts, "iMi JiMi, END THE VIOLENCE" on the front, and "TOM HOLLAR, 1962-1993," on the back. Christina's brother, Greg Schneider, a graphic artist, designed these T-shirts. The T-shirts were black with white and red printing, or white, with black and red letters.

Mayor Webb with T-shirt

Pachelbel's Canon

It seemed as if everywhere we went in Denver after July 23, *Pachelbel's Canon*, written by the German Baroque composer Johann Pachelbel, was playing: at the Tattered Cover Book Store, The Oxford Hotel, on the radio, and Cherry Creek Mall, where we shopped for clothes for Howard. To this day, this beautiful music transports me back to Denver in July, 1993.

Reward Posters July 26-27

Early the next week on July 26 or 27 posters announcing a reward for information went up all over the city. In this photo, Christina was wearing her mortarboard from her college graduation in 1992. (She holds a degree in sociology.)

The poster stated: "Reward for information about the slaying of Tom Hollar and the brutal beating of Christina." The phone number for Denver Police Department was listed. One of these posters was on a telephone pole two blocks from the home of soon-to-be-suspect Shane Davis.

Karl Waechter holding a Reward Poster at iMi JiMi

Monarch Society

Part of what we had to do on July 24 and 25 was to plan a viewing, service, and burial for Tom. We chose a wooden coffin since we were not sure whether Christina might choose cremation, but in the end, she wanted a place she could go to, a cemetery plot. Christina was still in Denver General Hospital and not able to participate, except for choosing a plot at Fairmount Cemetery.

We looked at three or four funeral parlors, which all seemed too formal, too stuffy for Tom and his friends. Then Reverend Don Dhonau suggested The Monarch Society on Pearl Street, just four blocks away and around the corner from iMi JiMi in Capitol Hill.

The Monarch Society is a locally owned and operated Denver business that offers a gracious alternative to traditional funeral homes. They welcome members and non-members and serve people of all faiths.

The Monarch Society on Pearl St. in Denver

When we arrived, we knew at once that this was the right place—an older brick Victorian house painted barn-red, with white decorative trim around the double-hung windows, a friendly front porch, and rooms that seemed like home.

We arranged with them to pick up Tom from the morgue and to prepare him for viewing. They also agreed to let me examine my son at the funeral home, which I did on Monday morning, July 26. He was visible through a heavy clear plastic body bag which I pulled back. I saw the large round wound the size of a quarter rimmed with dark dried blood on his left chest below the heart and the second wound on his upper left shoulder, noting the layers of yellow fat under his skin where the pathologist had stitched him back together.

Laura remembers the Y incisions in Tom's body and the strong black sutures used by the pathologist. She dissuaded me from trying to turn Tom over to better look at the second wound. The pathologist would never have guessed that family would be viewing her handiwork. Deeply disturbing to me, with near nausea, the awful way Tom died was revealed by the gunshot wounds in his body.

Staff at Monarch Society passed out pewter butterfly pins to all of us. The card attached read: "Mitzpah Butterfly. This beautiful pewter design offers a sign of hope for those who experience the pain of grief. The butterfly is the sign of new life, representing death as a transformation, not a finality. The Mitzpah Blessing offers the hope of reunion with the person who died." The blessing is lovely, and it became the hymn: "May the Good Lord Bless and Keep You," for me. This hymn is a comfort whenever I hear it or play it on the piano.

Chapter 37: Viewing At The Monarch Society

DURING THE TIME that visitors filed through the room where Tom lay in his casket, Laura, Margaret and I spent hours in the chairs and sofa in this room. Friends and family took their turns.

Margaret and Laura viewing Tom

With Tom the Last Time

On Wednesday July 28, I sat quietly with Tom in his flower-filled casket in the viewing room at the Monarch Society. My thoughts ranged from his happy early years growing up in Flushing, Michigan to his later years in Denver with Christina and iMi JiMi— probably the happiest time of his life. He did it right: he had fun and was successful living his way; he had one great life. He had the courage to be kind and gentle; he didn't make a big deal out of things.

As I sat there, the day wore on, and the light grew dim. Nothing could stop or should have stopped my flow of tears and feelings of emptiness and

Nick Milnor and Mitts Lee with Nedra viewing Tom

Cara & Nedra, second row: Sarah, Dan, Nick, John Milnor

Mike Evans and Pete Flye at Tom's casket

Kris Baehre, Dan Dhonau, Steve Simmons by Tom's casket

profound loss. He didn't look like himself; his hair was slicked back in a way he never would have chosen.

Then I noticed a little trickle of what looked like bright red stage blood running down the corner of his mouth on the right side. This was something he used to do at home to be a little outrageous for his backyard chums. But now it came as a great surprise to me as he lay there dead. (By this time, his body had been out of the refrigerated space where they are stored at funeral homes, for quite a few hours, and materials used in the embalming process to make him look more natural and alive were starting to melt.) I have always wondered if it was some kind of prank he did from the other side to try to bring me out of my state of deep grief. Although I noted it, there was no way I could laugh about it then, but now I find it amusing.

At the Monarch Society

I sat with my son at the Monarch Society,
Alone in a room with him.
I sat with my cold, still, son.

My son lay there with his coal black hair,
A familiar bend to his nose.
My son in a different way.

I sat right there on a small wooden chair,
Alone in a room with my son.
I sat with my cold, still, son.

A chrysalis in a coffin cocoon,
He'd already morphed an adult.
This time, he'd flutter unseen.

I sat with my son as the day wore on,
As the light grew dim,
At the Monarch Society in Denver.

He'd stay right there
With his coal black hair
In his little wooden box
Forever.

Visitors at the Monarch Society

Crowds formed a steady line of visitors to see Tom as he lay in state at the Monarch Society. Most of them were young people who frequented iMi JiMi, and many wore punk attire. These friends started leaving things in Tom's casket: letters, poems, photos, flowers, small personal items—tokens of their affection for him. Kris Baehre left a mounted 8 x 10 photo of one of Tom's pale-blue vintage Dodge cars. Mitts and Doug Otero came from Michigan; the Milnors came from San Antonio. Dan Milnor, a professional photographer, took many photos.

Visitors at the Monarch Society

Messages written in the registry book at the Monarch Society included:

"We've lost a friend."

"We'll miss you Tom." "You still had so much to give. They had no right to take your life!"

"Tom, we love you very much and will miss you. Rest in peace, brother."

"Tom was a wonderful man who treated everyone well and never said a bad word about any person."

"Speedy recovery, Christina!"

"With love and respect."

"Spirit will live!"

"Remember the good times," wrote Paul Italiano of Fashionation.

Laura, Margaret, and I sat on the sofa and on chairs in the viewing room. As I sat there, Julian Martinez came in, knelt on the floor beside me, cried, and said Tom had been a father to him. Julian came from a large Hispanic family and had little attention or support from his working mother and often-absent father. He gave me a pretty heart-shaped music box that played, "Oh What A Beautiful Morning."

Howard talking to Michael and Gregory Schneider in the blue Volvo with Christina after they drove her to the Monarch Society on July 28 for a private viewing of Tom

The card with the music box was signed, "Julian Martinez, your Denver Street Kid." I keep this pretty music box in my study where I spend many hours writing or working. I play its cheerful tune every so often, but viewing

Laura viewing Tom in his flower-filled casket

it always chokes me up, and tears brim in my eyes, as they are right now.

Later Julian wanted me to give him money since he and a friend wanted to create and publish guitar music for Tom. Christina filled me in on how things were and advised me not to do it. I have lost touch with him, but Kris Baehre says he's still around 13th Avenue. I'd like to see him again when we are in Denver.

SPIRIT

The Indians say,
past the second day,
you cry no more tears for the dead.

The spirit, they say
can't fly away
as long as those tears are still shed.

So fly! My son!
to the sun and the moon
to the mountains and deserts and seas.

Blow with the wind
Sparkle in snow
Shine in the diamonds of dew.

Spirit wild and free
Come back to me
Whenever, however you can

Goodbye Old Friend

His friends put their rings
Silver coins, precious things
In the casket to go with my son.

Gestures they made
Showing their love
For Thomas, their buddy and friend.

Cara put her frog-
The pin that she wore-
On her clothes every day, until then.

The casket was full
Of the flowers they laid
With their poems and photos and notes.

No one was ready to
Let Tom go.
We wanted to hang on, somehow.

I left a kiss.
On his cold, still face
And cut off a lock of his hair.

CHAPTER 38: JULY 27, 1993

STAFF WRITERS Marilyn Robinson and Tracy Seipel of the *Denver Post* reported that the Capitol Hill killers "had cased the area for 20 minutes like wolves out looking for prey." The reporters quoted witnesses, "The two men were walking around the King Soopers' parking lot looking in nearby cars. The way they were checking out the parking lot would make us think they were looking for victims."

Lieutenant Curt Williams reported witness accounts: "They were in the area for about twenty minutes, looked like they were looking for someone to attack. They didn't single out Tom and Chris, but the couple drove up at the right time to become victims."

On this same day, Detective Dan Wycoff took a photo lineup to Christina where she was staying with her mother, Gloria, and Al in Arvada just after her release from Denver General Hospital. Christina was not able to recognize Harrington's photo, saying that he did not look familiar. Wycoff had previously shown Christina another photo lineup where she viewed a photo of Shane Davis and said that maybe he could have been involved though his hair looked too long. Wycoff noted that Christina had to hold the photos against her nose in order to see them.

Arrests

"Suspect Arrested in Hollar Slaying" July 28, 1993

Denver Post staff writers Marilyn Robinson and Tracy Seipel reported: "Shane Damone Davis was being held without bond last night in Denver City Jail for investigation of the murder of Tom Hollar and the kidnapping and assault of his wife, Christina. Also yesterday, he was sentenced to 300 days in jail for past minor crimes.

At least one other suspect is being sought for the attack that has shaken the Capitol Hill neighborhood near the King Soopers store at E. 9th Avenue and Corona Street."

The article continued, "Davis was picked up for questioning Tuesday night (July 27) in northeast Denver and was later arrested...Arrest and search warrant affidavits were sealed by a judge at the request of police and prosecutors, who fear publicity may jeopardize their case. 'There's still another killer out there, so we can't talk,' said homicide Detective Dave Neil...Davis will be advised formally this morning in another courtroom of the latest charges, and many of the Hollars' friends plan to be there...

"'If this was a wild animal—a dog or mountain lion—that had attacked Tom and Christina, it would be shot right on the spot as soon as it was found,' said Ken Hamblin Jr., a friend of the Hollars. 'I really don't think there's anything we can do to save the two gentlemen, and I don't know if it's worth the taxpayers' money to make that attempt,' he said. 'I know it's society's problem, but that doesn't excuse what they did. I can understand it to some degree, but I can't forgive it,' he said."

Rocky Mountain News carried an article on July 24, 1993, by Lynn Bartels, "*Businessman killed; wife beaten*" which stated, "The death of 30-year-old Tom Hollar and the attack on his wife, Christina, 27, stunned the Capitol Hill neighborhood where the couple lived and worked. Friends and neighbors wept openly Friday when they talked about the crime ... Andy Holman, who

218

owns the seven-unit apartment complex where the Hollars lived, called them, 'an absolutely delightful couple. They really gave a lot to Capitol Hill', he said.

A photo accompanying the article showed Kris Baehre, who lived in the

Steve Harrington, left. Photo by *Associated Press*.
Shane Davis, right. Photo by Kent Meiries *Denver Post*

same apartment building as Tom and Christina, standing in a tense posture of remorse near the spot where Tom's blood stained the sidewalk. Baehre said that "after he heard the gunshots he ran to the balcony of his apartment. He saw Tom Hollar lying on the sidewalk and the abductors leaving in the black Honda." (At that time, he didn't know that Christina was in the car, but he did actually see the black Honda leaving the parking lot.) Kris said, "I ran outside, and there was Tom. I said, 'Hang on Tom, hang on.'"

Bartels' article stated, "Tom Hollar was taken to Denver General Hospital, where he was pronounced dead at 1:25 am.

"Police on…patrol found the Hollar car in the alley between Lafayette and Marion Streets in the 2100 block. Christina Hollar was inside, bleeding and incoherent. Mathew Smith, whose backyard abuts the alley, said police woke him early Friday (July 23) to ask whether he had heard anything, but he said he had not. Smith, 70, said the car was found in a nook in the alley, hidden by large trees. He said, 'If somebody parked in there, they must be somebody who goes up and down this alley regularly and knows this area.'"

Memorial Service, Washington Park, July 27, 1993

A notice appeared in the Denver newspapers, so hundreds of Denver citizens attended the informal service we planned.

A lovely evening, Tom's Memorial Service was held on July 27, 1993 in Washington Park, which was shaded by tall trees. Mayor Webb gave a speech and said he'd asked the Denver Police Department to focus extra attention on this case. Reverend Dhonau officiated at this service, and he steadied me while I read the poem I'd written over several nights when I couldn't sleep. I'd sequestered myself in the bathroom at The Oxford Hotel so my light wouldn't bother Howard. The words just came to me, haunted me, until I wrote them down.

Nedra after reading Tom's Poem at Memorial Service

Nedra and Howard at Memorial

In Loving Memory

THOMAS EDWARD HOLLAR

Born - November 6, 1962
Died - July 23, 1993

MEMORIAL SERVICE
Washington Park
Tuesday, July 27, 1993
6:30 P.M.

OFFICIATING
Reverend Donald I. Dhonau

CONTRIBUTIONS
Tom Hollar Memorial Fund
C/O Imi Jimi
609 E. 13th Ave.
Denver, CO 80203

Arrangements by Monarch Society

Brochure for Tom's Memorial Service on
July 27, 1993

Tom's Poem

They shot my son,
My only son.
Cold bloodedly murdered my son!

My son lay dead
with a shot in his head,
my generous fun-loving son.

He is gone from this life
leaving his wife
and all of his wonderful friends.

Tom was his name
He'd gone to the game
with beautiful Christina, dear.

My son lay dead.
One year he was wed
to Christina, Christina dear.

He had a store
but it was **much** more
where many would gather around.

He loved this town
where he was gunned down:
Denver, Colorado, **my son!**

Life is not fair
that **he** should be there
July 23 at that time.

They took his life
and beat his wife
my wonderful peace-loving son.

He had no chance
as he turned to glance
at beautiful Christina dear.

No place to run,
faced with their gun,
they wantonly murdered my son.

They gunned him down.
He fell to the ground.
They shot him again in the head.

Tom was so fair,
now blood in his hair,
the lifeblood I gave him oozed out.

A person can go
a whole lifetime through
without having to do what I did.

My son lay dead
in the morgue, they said
with homicide officers there.

Who is this young man?
This handsome young man?
Lying dead, quite dead, in the morgue?

I stood with my grief
my shocked disbelief,
quietly viewing my only son.

His face inches away,
a glass in between,
I sensed those last awful moments.

Dark, dried blood on his teeth,
scrapes on his face,
swollen neck where they'd put in the tubes.

It was as if
it were a joke
and he'd wake up and talk to me.

I gave him the will
and waited until
I knew I would have to go.

The policeman there
shed a quiet tear
when I said, "It's Thomas, my son!"

"It **is** my son Tom!
My **only** son Tom!
My happy and fun-loving son!"

"God give us peace
'cause we can't make sense
of his brutal and horrible death."

They shot my son
but life must go on
my wonderful fun-loving son!

He'd want you to strive
to keep his spirit alive
and not let his death be in vain.

So do your good deed,
help someone in need
Help keep iMi JiMi alive.

He'd say to us now
what he always said,
"Have fun, dear friends, have fun!"

Chapter 39: At Tom's Memorial Service

VERNA K. NAHULU, the medium, gave a talk, and a Native American stepped out of the crowd with a flute to play "Amazing Grace," since he had heard that I liked it. The clear, simple tones of his flute playing this beautiful music in Washington Park will always be with me in memory.

A friend said, "Tom would laugh at us because to him, life was joy, not sadness."

Wellington Webb said, "Extra investigators have been added to the case," and he vowed, "We're going to do all that we can to bring the perpetrators to justice so your son can rest in peace."

After the service, a redheaded girl came forward and handed me a bouquet of white roses and gave me a hug. This is when I broke down, sobbing.

Attending the Memorial service were friends and family,

Mayor Wellington Webb speaking at Tom's Memorial Service, July 27, 1993

227

including Tom's friends, Doug Otero and Mitts Lee from Michigan; Tom's father, Ed Hollar, Tom's half-sister Anne Hollar from Colorado Springs; Laura and her husband; Richard Kovalcik from Michigan, Margaret; and Howard's father and stepmother, Howard and Irene Downing from South Carolina, as well as the couple from Aurora. My old friend, Jim Boucher, loyal and supportive, gave me a wonderful big hug after the memorial service—he was such a joy to have around, he could actually make me smile during the ordeal.

Jim Boucher of Laramie hugging Nedra after Memorial Service on July 27, 1993

Christina was released from Denver General Hospital on July 27, but was unable to attend the memorial service. She and her two brothers from California drove around Washington Park in the family's pale-blue Volvo during the ceremony, so she could hear some of it and see the crowds of people and the helium-balloon sendoff at the end.

July 28, 1993 Christina's Private Visitation at the Monarch Society

Christina came privately during a time when the Monarch Society was closed to outsiders, on Wednesday morning, July 28, 1993. She was in a wheelchair. Her brothers and a Denver police officer carried her up and down the front steps. This was the only time she had to be close to what had happened to Tom, and she was still weak and tired. She spent a few hours with Tom in his casket, the only time she had for personal grieving.

At that time, I was using a notebook-sized Franklin planner to keep notes of all that went on, so I sat on the sofa flanked by Laura and Margaret, for long hours during Monday and Tuesday. We put together the memorial service held at Washington Park, in south-central Denver, a place Tom had liked, where he and his friends had washed the red-and-white Dodge convertible before the wedding.

News Coverage of Tom's Memorial

Denver Post staff writer, Jim Kirksay, wrote in an article, "300 Bid Farewell at Tom Hollar Service," published July 28, 1993, "Through the tears, between the sobs, in a tree-shaded place in Washington Park, nearly 300 people celebrated the joy that Tom Hollar brought to them. The eclectic group of young and old, trendy and staid, tattooed ladies and conservative neck ties, all sadly remembered how much happiness Hollar brought to any occasion. They wept and told of their love for the 30-year-old Michigan transplant, who was gunned down outside his Capitol Hill home Friday. Hollar's wife, Christina, was kidnapped in the incident and severely beaten.

"The most moving testament came from Dr. Nedra Downing, Hollar's mother. She recited a poem she'd written in a Robert Service-like manner."

On July 28, 2014 Chris Newcomer quoted the mayor's speech in *The Rocky Mountain News*: "None of us can predict or understand why

Crowds at the Memorial Service

229

senseless tragedies happen the way they do, or why this summer has turned out to be quite different from any other summer we've had in Denver. It's very difficult to explain to a mother."

Chris Newcomer also reported that Don Dhonau said to the crowd, "In the last five days, you have come together. You have shown me a spirituality that comes from commitment to community. Whether you would describe yourselves that way or not, you are a people of faith." He also described Tom and Christina as "pillars of eclectic Capitol Hill."

KNUS Town Meeting in Front of King Soopers on 9th Street

July 28, 1993, I was asked to be a part of a radio program about violence on station KNUS, broadcast in front of King Soopers on 9th Avenue. I agreed, but only stayed a few minutes. Speakers began complaining and brought up issues that didn't interest me. I was still reeling from Tom's death and Christina's terrible injuries and wasn't prepared to deal with other issues. I did meet Governor Romer. Later Prosecutor Silverman told me that he had been in the audience that day.

Chapter 40: The Funeral,
July 29, 1993

THE FUNERAL BEGAN with a service at 2:00 P.M. in the small chapel near the entrance to Fairmount Cemetery followed by the graveside service and interment performed by Rev. Don Dhonau. The chapel was a low stone building surrounded by shrubs, with a spire on top like a church. Tom was in his casket in the black hearse from Fairmount and was not brought into the chapel. Christina was unable to attend the chapel service.

To me, this service was a necessary rite, but it was not very meaningful. There were no eulogies; it was a standard service. However, rituals in life are important; prayers at the service, the 23rd Psalm especially, were comforting. I found myself repeating the 23rd Psalm at home later as I walked around in the beauty of our backyard surrounded by woods and accompanied by my dog,

Tom's casket just before being lowered into the grave, with Rev. Dhonau standing beside it

letting what had happened in Denver sink in.

After the service, our cars lined up behind the black hearse holding Tom in his wooden coffin. We slowly circled around Fairmount with its tall trees and winding drives, to reach the far southwestern part where Tom's grave had been dug. A few folding chairs had been assembled under a tent, and baskets of flowers were arranged around the gravesite.

Reverend Dhonau's graveside service seemed more personal to me than the chapel service. After his words, one at a time, Dan, Karl, Danica, Kris, Margaret, Laura, Ed, Gloria, Greg, Michael, Steve, and I stepped up and threw long-stemmed red roses on Tom's brown wooden casket as it was being lowered into his grave. Christina spent a moment placing something personal in the open grave.

Christina at the funeral greeting K-Nee Hamblin, Jr. with Karl Waechter on her left

We were saying our last good-byes. The finality of seeing his casket lowered deep into the cold, dark earth was harder for me than prior events, since now he was no longer physically around, and I had no more duties related to his death.

I pictured him as I'd seen him at the Monarch Society, unchanged and unaware, his ordeal was over. I stood by the gravesite as attendants from Fairmount cemetery started shoveling the dirt on the top of Tom's casket, thus filling the opening. His final resting place. Forever.

Now my job was to grieve and move on.

Christina was able to attend the funeral service in a wheel chair and tended by her brothers and friends. She was pale and thin, her long blonde hair pulled back into a simple ponytail.

(She'd gone to iMi JiMi before the funeral and had spoken to Karl Waechter, a friend and loyal employee, about matters related to keeping the store open. She felt strongly, as I did, that iMi JiMi is where Tom's spirit lived; keeping the store alive and well would embrace him in his new life after death.)

Christina sat there, flanked by friends, crying quietly, showing little outward emotion

Chris's mother Gloria was there with a neighbor from Arvada, but Al was not with her. I had trouble being chatty and cordial to a stranger at my son's funeral, so I didn't spend much time with her. I walked ahead to be alone.

Doug Otero and Mitts Lee came to Denver for the funeral

Christina faced the loss of her life with Tom, plus procedures to repair her injuries. She was exhausted.

The funeral was over in mid-afternoon, and Christina had yet to go to a police lineup.

My Best

Brand-new black polka dot silk dress
wanted to look my best
for his big life event;
becoming who he was.

Long rustling full skirt
crisp, shiny iridescent black silk
excitement pouring from its folds
as I danced.

Joy in my soul
my son, his new wife, their magic day.
Energy, anticipation, and love;
turning a corner of life.

Then depth of pain, couldn't speak;
limp black dress long by my ankles
there by his casket that hot day
full of agony, spent energy, grief.

Now wilted polka dot silk dress
hangs in my closet, plastic cover
to seal off remembered hurt.

Occasionally, I bump the bag
releasing cloudy memories;
dull black silk dress stirs,
rustles, remembers.

That dress, my best.

Lineup July 29, 1993

While we were burying Tom and preparing for our flight back to Michigan, witnesses were viewing a lineup of suspects at the Denver Police Department.

Armedia Gordon, Head Homicide Supervisor of the Homicide Unit of Denver Police Department, chose the lineup participants from men in custody and selected those who resembled Steve Harrington, and of course, Steve Harrington himself. She allowed the participants to choose their positions in the lineup.

Supervisor Gordon said that Christina had been very sick at the time of the lineup. This didn't stop her from doing her best, and she understood what she was to do. She didn't complain, but while waiting for the lineup to begin, she lay on the floor of the police station wrapped in blankets, being too weak and sick to stand. At this time she was unable to pick Steve Harrington out of the men in the lineup. But witness Mike Evans and one other witness positively and unhesitatingly identified Steve Harrington as the attacker.

Prosecutor Silverman, who watched the event, was quite moved by Christina's efforts to look at the lineup of men when she was obviously struggling just to stand up. Since this was the same day as the funeral Christina had not been able to eat regular food nor had time to rest. She had been out of ICU fewer than two days.

Christina said she did what she had to do for Tom. The emotional strain of looking at Tom's murderer and her assailant less than a week after their brutal attack was sickening and draining.

✦

Steve Harrington had a Jeri curl. Armedia Gordon explained that the Jeri curl is a process that changes the hair, not unlike a permanent wave, so that new growth of hair is a different texture. Jeri curl makes the hair appear fuller, and it can be styled. Steve wore his hair in a bushy style for the lineup, which was the way he'd worn it on the night of the murder—a startling, savage look.

True to the Mayor's pledge, police had been working on the case around the clock, and Harrington had been formally charged early on July 28. He had been in custody since Tuesday, July 27.

Shane Davis had been arrested on Wednesday, July 28, linked to the case by a piece of a torn business card with a woman's phone number written on it, as well as a watch and a coin purse, which were found in Tom and Christina's black Honda abandoned in the alley.

From the July 29, 1993 *Denver Post* article, "Two Men Linked to Hollar Slaying," Howard Pankratz wrote: "A distraught Willie Lee Henderson, father of Harrington, refused to believe his son killed anyone…'He might swipe a car, but kill someone? … I can't see Steve killing anyone. You don't know your kids these days, but I can't see him doing that. I love him, I love him dearly,' said Henderson, near tears. 'I just don't want to believe he did that. If he was a bad kid…But he's not a bad kid.' Henderson said he has the deepest sympathy for the victims and their families. 'My heart goes out to those people,' he said."

This was the only expression of sympathy from any of either murderer's family that I am aware of. I felt that Henderson was sincere, that he loved his son, and probably did not know what went wrong.

CHAPTER 41: BACK HOME
JULY 30, 1993

FLYING BACK TO MICHIGAN on July 29, 1993, we resumed our lives after the intense week of July 23, 1993. We went back to work on Friday, July 30, 1993, and I wrote paychecks and I saw patients on this day, although it was hard to focus. The routine of the job and support of patients helped me.

This same day, in Denver, Christina began her long series of dental appointments.

I thought about how enduring painful dental procedures would not help her with her awful tiredness, but it was good that she was getting started.

I'd ordered the two Denver newspapers, *Rocky Mountain News* and *Denver Post* to be delivered to our home. Since these papers arrived several days after publication, their news was not fresh, but at least we could stay informed.

The next day, Saturday, July 31, 1993, I was glad not to have to go to work or anywhere, for that matter. So I got up about 9:30 A.M. took my morning coffee and newly-arrived Denver newspapers, sat on the deck in shade of the big oak tree, with Boris,the orange cat, purring on my lap.

I read about the arrest of a second suspect in the attack on Tom and Chris. This was a 20-year-old suspected gang member, Shane Davis, who lived not far from where Christina had been found in the black Honda in the alley. On a telephone pole near his home, someone had placed one of the posters with Tom and Christina's pictures on it offering a reward for information about the assault and murder.

We had known before we left Denver that one suspect was in custody. Now there were two. This allowed me to relax a little. Wheels were turning. Mayor Webb was true to his word—Denver Police were working hard on this case and they were

Nedra with Boris at home,
July 31, 1993

getting results. We could do nothing more in Denver. It was good to be home to get back into a new kind of normal pattern.

A few days later, I read about Shane Davis having been arrested earlier in the year for car thefts, with bail set and later reduced by another judge, and still later his being released on his own recognizance, free to walk out the door, get back on the streets, and repeat his pattern of crime. This stirred anguish and "What if?" thoughts, which I had to let go. If he hadn't been released, Tom would still be alive.

I was very tired, so I took a walk around our yard in the woods, always a pleasure, and then took a nap.

The Work of Grief

I wrote in my journal: "I don't see this period of grief as a time for hushed voices and quiet behavior, crying when needed. I see it as a time to turn sad energy into creative expressions—living, ongoing things."

I began writing poems, keeping journals, planting gardens, cooking new things, working. My loss gave me new insights into helping patients who'd had similar losses. I saw this as a time to do what Tom had been doing—putting forces together for the good.

Friends tried to be helpful with such things as books, including, *Why Bad Things Happen to Good People*, which was no help to me whatsoever. My work was my therapy, along with two patients who were counselors. I did some work with help from one of them and read the work and thoughts of Rudolph Steiner, including his book, *Life between Death and Rebirth*. I tried to do his style of meditation, but never felt I connected with higher beings. I do recall one caution from his work: once channels are ready to receive, one must train to block download from unwanted or damaging sources. A patient gave me a Bach Flower Remedy, Star of Bethlehem, for sorrow.

I read books by authors who'd studied at the Monroe Institute, where they learned techniques for allowing consciousness to leave the body to where perception came from sources in the universe, rather than the usual bodily senses. This work was quite convincing and interesting, basically a form of deep meditation. Perhaps this work led to a series of dreams I had and still remember.

Dreams

At the time of Tom's death, I awoke screaming several times. I had two memorable dreams that seemed very clear:

One. I was hovering somewhere in a curtained room, probably a hospital emergency room, where an EKG showed a flat tracing (asystole) or non-working heart pattern, rather than the normal, active heart pattern of P, QRS waves. Two doctors were attending a man on a gurney, probably Tom. I remember seeing this flat EKG and feeling deep sadness, hopelessness.

Soon after Christina was taken to ER at Denver General the night of July 23, she was curtained off in a small room at the same time Tom lay dead in another small, curtained room nearby. I don't know who told us this, nor if it is true.

Two. Two angels or heavenly helpers in a higher realm had been assigned to help Tom ascend. I could see from above something like a hole in clouds where the two were trying to help pull Tom up, but he was ready before they were prepared, so they were having difficulty and trying to hurry.

I had three or four dreams that each repeated for three or four nights: I saw bright, beautiful colors across my dream screen. Something very creative was passing through my brain during these dreams.

One night, I saw mostly blue with a little turquoise green; another night I saw lavender with hues of pink and magenta; another time, a deeper blue with shiny white spirals; and another was strong primary colors with red, yellow, orange, blue. I believe Tom sent those dreams.

He loved light and liked working with neon; he was fond of strong blues. Neon signs he'd made for a business in Castle Rock are still there, last I knew.

One time when I was in Denver, Tom and Christina took me to see these signs that looked very professional. We had dinner somewhere in Castle Rock.

When we saw a big, black motorcycle adorned with blue neon tubes along the lower part of the bike in St. John's, Newfoundland in 2014, of course I thought of Tom.

I had another recurring dream about a maze of roads going up and around a mountain, where I could see a destination city at the top as well as approaching roads and dead ends. I was outside on other roads, trying to get in, and I could see Tom in his little red car speeding up these road mazes, zigzagging around, but I could never reach him. He seemed to know I was there.

I had a dream of Tom leaving shore in a canoe while I was still on the shore. He moved across the still lake to the other side, and I struggled to find a way to join him or reach him. I had this dream more than once.

I had many dreams, night after night, in which beautiful works of art—finished paintings, tile art, tapestries, jewelry, carpets, and fabrics—kept appearing fast, one after another, each stunningly beautiful. I felt as if I were in a creative flow, a privileged place where new ideas were born, where the muse was visiting those capable of tapping in, where magical beauty filled my dream screen.

MIRED

Black glass waters
swallowing
vanishing
wake.

Clouds
enshroud
time.

Mired.

Groping
flat city maze.

Searching
emptiness.
Nowhere.

Air avalanche,
Gasping.

Never.

Emily's Near-Death Experience

A good patient and friend, Emily Rath, had severe asthma attacks. She was hospitalized with a near-death episode in 1997 and came to the office later to tell me about her experience. Her story was a great comfort to me.

Emily told this story again in January 2015, as she remembered it: She had had a severe asthma attack, was intubated, and awoke in the hospital.

She said she was gone, on the other side, that Jesus was there, and he said to her in a clear voice, "Tell Dr. Downing her son is OK. He's happy here with me in heaven." I recalled from the first time she told me of this experience in 1997 and from notes in my planner, that Tom sent a message, "Take care of Christina."

CHRISTINA

Tom had just begun
to do the things
with his life that he wanted to do.

He'd found his wife,
the love of his life,
Christina, his soul-mate and friend.

We all can see why
he chose her for
she's made of superior stuff.

They smashed her left eye
and left her to die
the night they murdered my son.

She's healing her wounds
and knitting her bones
and working each day at the store.

The scars to her soul
although they don't show
may take forever to heal.

Chapter 42: The First Full Week at Home
July 31, 1993

SITTING ON THE SIDE PORCH at home, we saw lots of Monarch butterflies. For months after Tom's death, I chose to wear the small pewter butterfly pin from the Monarch Society on my lapel every day, somehow making me feel connected to Tom.

Boris

Boris was our orange shorthair cat, which I'd spotted in the lower woods by the road one day as I was returning home. He sat glowing in a beam of sunlight coming through the dark woods.

I always said, "Hisself (Boris cat talk) was sent down on a sunbeam straight from God." That first Saturday morning at home, July 31, I sat on the deck in my nightgown and robe with morning coffee and with Boris on my lap, close and warm, purring his calming affection.

This same Saturday, iMi JiMi was very busy. This was reported to me by Karl Waechter, Josh Chapman, and Jami Behrenbrinker, who worked at the store at that time. I had notes in my Franklin planner.

August 1, 1993 Howard's Letter to Christina

Howard does not write many personal letters. He wrote the following letter to Christina on August 1, 1993 after we'd settled in upon returning from Denver:

"Chris—I'd like to say again how happy we are that Tom met you and that you had a couple of good years together. Not everyone is so privileged.

All of us were totally unprepared for the outpouring of love and anguish from your friends and acquaintances. We came to Denver expecting a lonely funeral and ended up hugging and crying with half of Denver. It was a unique experience, which I will carry with me the rest of my life.

Many of your friends used phrases like "He was a father to me," or, "He was like a big brother." More than one person said Tom helped them get off the streets. One woman told me how Tom had befriended her after she was raped in the alley a few doors from your apartment. It apparently made a big difference to her. We had no idea that Tom had this sort of effect on so many people's lives. We are very proud of him.

I think you have the strength necessary to get on with your life. It will be painful, but if you hold on to the good things from the past and look forward to good things in the future, you'll make it.

Nedra and I really do consider you one of our daughters—we would love to hear from you, or see you, anytime.

Please have the strength to avoid making any major changes in your life for a while. Your friends at the apartment and the business love you and will protect you—they are eager to. Looking out for you will help them with their grief.

God bless you—keep in touch.

Love, Howard

August 3, 1993

Howard was sitting in his brown leather chair with a cup of morning coffee in our kitchen facing the back woods when William Buckley called with an update about a neighbor, who'd heard two men between the houses talking the night of the murder. Police had no fingerprints yet.

Grave Marker, August 1993

Christina chose a simple grave marker for Tom's grave, which wouldn't be ready to be placed there for several months. The grave marker was a rectangular slab of light gray marble with black letters carved into its face: "Thomas Edward Hollar, November 6, 1962-July 23, 1993. Beloved husband, son, brother, friend, forever in our hearts."

Christina stayed in Arvada with her mother and Al while recuperating. She had ongoing expenses for her medical and dental care; and she spent time in therapy for what amounted to Post-Traumatic Stress Disorder (PTSD). She felt that the Emotional Freedom Technique (EFT) helped. In EFT the victim taps on acupuncture points while saying affirmations related to getting over the stressor. Trained therapists teach EFT techniques to patients. Others close to the event, some residents of Shana Marie, suffered PTSD for years after the event.

Tom's Grave Marker

Christina reported that the whole event seemed unreal to her—far away, long ago—but the surgeries and dental work were exhausting, stressful, and painful, very real and happening now. She said she still expected to see Tom appear.

Chris's mother Gloria said, "Chris is such a dream; it makes it easy to want to do things for her." Gloria and Al's Arvada home was quiet and lovely with its antiques and tasteful furnishings, a perfect place for Christina to feel safe and be comfortable during her recovery.

Chapter 43: The Beginning of the Trial Process

HE ARRAIGNMENT WAS HELD August 5, 1993. I had not been aware of the processes that must happen for suspects to be brought to trial, but now an organized series of steps started to unfold, which would lead to a jury trial in May and June, 1994.

An arraignment is the formal reading in a courtroom to inform a defendant of the criminal charges against him or her. Arraignment of Steve Harrington and Shane Davis was held on August 5, 1993.

Social Information About Steve Harrington, the Man Who Murdered My Son

The following material was quoted directly from a Pre-Sentence Courtroom 16 Document:

> First felony conviction: Reno, Nevada. Conspiracy to commit robbery, sentenced to three years in prison in Carson City, Nevada. He was released June 2, 1993.
>
> Steven Harrington, aka Henderson, was born April 11, 1972, in Monroe, Louisiana, to Katie Washington and Willie Henderson. According to the

defendant, his parents were not married at the time of his birth. He advised that at age six months both parents moved to Denver. They were married approximately a year and a half later. Mr. Harrington's family constellation consists of one brother and one sister. He was born second of his mother's three children. According to Mr. Harrington, his parents divorced when he was age three or four. Shortly thereafter, he, his mother, and brother moved to Reno, Nevada, and his father remained in Denver. At age six or seven, his mother married Sylvester Washington, with whom she later had one daughter. Mr. Harrington, his mother, and stepfather later returned to Denver.

The defendant stated he attended Cheltenham Elementary School, Samuels Elementary School, and Hamilton Elementary School. He stated he obtained good grades when he wanted to while in school. In Jr. High School, he failed all courses. He advised that he failed the seventh grade due to behavior problems. He was suspended from elementary school once, but frequently was suspended in Jr. High. He attended Thomas Jefferson High School for one semester. During this period he played sports. He stated he discontinued his formal education at Thomas Jefferson during his freshman year.

The defendant advised that after dropping out of Thomas Jefferson High School, he, his mother, and brother moved to Monroe, Louisiana, due to his mother and stepfather's separation. He advised that it was at this time he became affiliated with gangs. The defendant advised that six months later the family moved to Reno,

Nevada. It was then he learned that his mother had been diagnosed with AIDS as a result of a blood transfusion she received during the birth of her youngest child.

Mr. Harrington stated he received a three-year sentence in Reno, Nevada. Upon his release on June 2, 1993, he immediately returned to Denver. He had resided in Denver for approximately two months prior to his arrest for the latest offenses.

The defendant advised that initially he had a good relationship with his father. The relationship deteriorated following his parents' divorce. As a juvenile, some question existed regarding his welfare. On August 31, 1989, it was determined that his immediate welfare required attention. Therefore, the Court determined he should be placed in detention until further notice. He was released from detention on February 22, 1990.

When questioned about his companions, Mr. Harrington related that he has a mixture of friends, the majority of which are gang members.

About the Prosecutor

Craig Silverman graduated from George Washington High School in 1974 where he finished in the top twenty academically, while lettering seven times in varsity sports. He graduated in 1978 from Colorado College, where he graduated with academic honors after setting a single season scoring record in basketball and pitching undefeated in baseball during his senior year. Craig was among the top twenty in his class when he graduated from law school from the University of Colorado. He became a lawyer in 1981.

CHAPTER 44: ROCK ISLAND CLUB BENEFITS

ROCK ISLAND HELD TWO BENEFITS for Tom and Christina in August, 1993. (Christina was unable to attend since she was still weak and in the process of having dental procedures and surgeries, each of which caused pain and took days to recover from.) One of these events was named, "A Celebration of Life in Honor of Tom Hollar." It pleased me to know that people in Denver were moved to support these benefits, and that Tom was being remembered at a venue he would have liked. Tom and Christina regularly went to Rock Island to dance.

These events drew crowds of hundreds from the greater Denver area. All kinds of people paid $5.00 to show their support for Christina. In the article dated 8/6/93 in the Denver Post, 'Club backs Hollar's widow,' by Stacey Baca, she wrote, "It's real important to be here to show his wife that people still care," said a woman from Golden, Colorado, "A lot of people are here because they are sick of the violence. It's just good to know that people really do care and are there for you."

Many teenagers in the crowd were wearing clothes from iMi JiMi, like FreshJive oversized blue jeans or Creepers platform shoes, which they very likely had bought from Tom, while others wore ordinary blue jeans and white tee shirts.

Young and old were on the small dance floor at Rock Island, grooving to the loud hip-hop music in the smoke-filled club with bright colored lights around the walls of the room. Tom would have loved the energy of the place, and the mixture of people.

CHAPTER 45: AUGUST 7, 1993

I SAT ON THE SIDE PORCH in the morning after a night of rain. A gronky black bug with big round eyes landed on my sleeve and stared at me. Was it Tom saying, "Hello?"

My cat Boris settled on my lap after having been out all night. A shrill bird sang from the woods. I sat there meditating, focusing on Tom to try to tap into his energy. I was seeking guidance about what direction I should take. Hummingbirds darted to the feeder, chasing each other. Howard turned on Max Ferguson on Canadian FM for his Celtic music.

We had been playing Patsy Cline records, which immediately took me back to 951 Corona, Denver, where Kris Baehre and Dan Dhonau had played her records from their porches so that we could hear them from the parking lot.

Ed Hollar came to plant forget-me-nots in our gardens, a loving gesture from Tom's father. I regret not being more sensitive to his anguish during the time after the murder. I was wrapped up in my own ordeal and didn't extend as much support to him as I wish I had done. His daughters Laura, Anne, and Margaret were with him, and he was close to them. I was reassured that he didn't spend time alone.

In Michigan August 7, 1993

On Saturday, August 7, Gloria called from Arvada, Colorado to tell me that she was thinking of me and that she and her friends were praying for me. She said that no words could express her upset and feelings of great, great loss.

Gloria said that she and her friends and church members were very impressed with Tom and his relationships. She had been focused on Christina, and now her grief for Tom was just beginning. She and her friends sent wonderful cards with notes in them sending their good wishes and condolences. One cannot measure help and energy coming from prayer.

Gloria, Christina's mother, in her home in Arvada

Insurance

Meanwhile, Al was trying to find some insurance that would help Christina pay her medical bills. Christina's hospital bills were already substantial and there was a good deal of reconstructive surgery yet to follow. Tom's medical insurance paid a very small death benefit. Howard and I paid funeral expenses.

Since Howard was an insurance agent, he agreed to see if any coverage for Christina's medical bills could be found in the insurance policy covering the automobile. Colorado has a modified "no-fault" automobile insurance system which provides medical and lost income coverage to people injured in an "accident" arising out of the use or operation of an auto. Initially, Farmers' Insurance was reluctant to apply coverage to Christina's medical bills, questioning whether her injuries were the result of "the use or operation" of the auto, or merely took place within the auto.

Howard contacted a number of insurance people in Colorado who were fellow members of an insurance society he belonged to. They graciously provided a substantial amount of information about Colorado automobile insurance and court cases interpreting the policies. There was substantial agreement among them that the Personal Injury Protection portion of the policy should be able to pay Christina's medical bills up to $50,000, plus some modest lost income reimbursement. If that argument failed with Farmers' insurance, it was a possibility that the Uninsured Motorist Coverage might apply, as the muggers certainly were not "insured" under the policy.

On September 22, 1993 a woman in the Denver City Attorney's office told us that the city would pay for all of Christina's hospital bills at Denver General Hospital. Howard talked to the adjusters at Farmers' Insurance a number of times, pointing out legal precedents which would make it possible for them to cover Christina's bills. After a period of resistance, they agreed on October 5, 1993 that they would apply the Personal Injury Protection portion of the policy and pay Christina's medical bills up to $50,000. Christina's health insurance from her college days had lapsed.

The insurance claim for damage to the car itself was handled in a routine manner. According to the investigators and the adjusters, the interior of the car was covered in blood. Farmers' paid $3000 to the lessor (GMAC) for this repair. Since the balance due on the lease exceeded this figure, GMAC took the car to cover the residual amount owed.

August Denver News: Urban Violence

On August 7, 1993, the *Denver Post* featured articles by Mark Obmascik and Al Knight "Urban Violence: First a Diagnosis, Then a Cure."

From the articles: "Experts are scrambling to figure out the causes of this summer's streak of well-publicized violent crimes.

"Many people blame it on gangs, drugs, and handguns. Others take a more philosophical approach and cite breakdown of the American family. Some point a finger at poverty and declining quality of public schools.

"Another significant factor behind the front- page crimes is the factor of growth and development, dubbed 'big is bad.' In the past five years, metro (Denver) voters decided to turn Denver into a big city. We approved a giant new international airport; we built a major convention center and signed on for a series of public works projects such as E-470 beltway that will forever change the quality of life along the Front Range.

"For a while, the metro area basked in the advantages of growth: home prices rose, unemployment dropped, and downtown Denver, especially LoDo, became a vibrant center of culture and nightlife. Sure, there was talk that bigness might lead to more smog, traffic and maybe more crime. But the new airport jobs were now, and crime was only an abstract threat."

The article listed the individuals shot during the summer. "Now we are forced to deal with the ugly side of the big city life that metro Denver has chosen. Although news media imply we're in the middle of a dramatic crime wave, statistics indicate otherwise: In 1987, 191 murders were committed in Colorado; in 1992, 213, a 11.5% increase but Colorado gained nearly 100,000 new residents in the same five years so the murder rate has stayed steady."

Al Knight, Denver Post perspective Editor wrote, "The 'big is bad' argument has merit in that population growth may produce unwanted social effects including crime and violence. The current problem of violence perpetrated by urban youth, however, seems to be not so much a result of how many people live here, but how they live. The problem in the recent round of shootings and killings is not that they are more numerous than other years, statistics may be the same. What's different is:

> The perception that shootings and killings are more random,
>
> The geographic area of violence is spread out, suggesting that anyone can be the next victim.
>
> Past impressions have been that victims of gangs were likely to be from the same geographic area as their attackers and most likely to

be of the same racial or ethnic group. Importantly, three of the most recent shooting victims have been white, and the suspects described as black.

There have been widely reported speculations that not only were gang members involved in the shooting of Lori Lowe, 27-year-old school teacher, but that gang initiation may have been a factor. This kind of talk scares people.

Residents had fled the inner city violence for safety in the suburbs. The recent random violence, racially motivated in part, reached the suburbs. Governor Ray Romer brought about legislation for short-term measures to curb violence. Fixing the underlying problem is more difficult, because it includes single parent families, drug use among young people, and poverty. Such solutions as socialized child rearing, better day care, revised work rules, increased welfare to aid child rearing, more jobs, more educational opportunities for children, more family intervention, and parental screening have been suggested. Failures in child-rearing suggest that state efforts are required and that child rearing should be a collective effort.

"People in outlying areas left the inner city and do not want to spend time and energy on problems they left, but more prisons and law enforcement are OK, as are more gated properties, more alarms, more high security fences.

August 7 News: Second Murder Suspect Jailed

On Saturday, August 7, 1993, *Rocky Mountain News* Charlie Brennan wrote the article "Second Murder Suspect Jailed."

Brennan listed a chronology of events beginning with Tom telling Christina, "Just ignore them," and ending with the two suspects being in custody.

Police arrested Steven Dwayne Harrington, 21, Thursday night. He had just left Arapahoe County Jail, where he'd been held since Tuesday on an outstanding theft warrant."

On July 27, 1993, Denver Police Detectives Wycoff and Neil were driving and saw Steve Harrington walking. The detectives pulled over and said, "We want to talk to you." Steve Harrington got into the squad car without any resistance and never left police custody. (This was told to me at the 20th anniversary of the event, July 23, 2013, at a luncheon at The Oxford Hotel. I didn't get further details at that time.)

Continuing from Brennan's article of 8/7/93: "A combination of cooperative witnesses and a classic blunder by the perpetrators led police to Harrington and Davis."

"Arrest affidavits allege that a coin purse found in Hollar's car contained a torn business card bearing a pager number. Through that number, investigators found a 21-year-old Denver woman, who said she had traded telephone numbers a few hours before the shooting with Davis after he approached her at an east-side gas station for a date."

"Police believed the presence of that torn business card in Hollar's car undeniably linked Davis to the crime. Focusing on Davis led them to his friend, Harrington, and witnesses subsequently placed Harrington at the scene of the crime."

"Harrington, identified by a witness as the triggerman, was advised of his rights by Judge Robert B. Crew." Information is from August 7, 1993 Rocky Mountain News article, "Second Murder Suspect Jailed" listing chronology by Charles Brennan.

Harrington was ordered held without bond for investigation of first-degree murder, first-degree assault, and first-degree kidnapping. Both suspects had multiple aliases and lengthy criminal records. They are both suspected gang members. Harrington sported a 'Crazy Crip' tattoo on his left arm and two tattooed teardrops on his face."

"These are two vicious individuals, who perpetrated this crime at random," said Detective David Metzler.

Harrington's father, Willie Lee Henderson said, "The witnesses may be wrong."

Henderson and Harrington's brother, sister, and girlfriend were on hand Friday for his arraignment. Henderson continued, "My son is a very brilliant kid. He's very athletic. He wasn't in no gangs. They were just little run-around friends of his. Not everyone with their britches down is in a gang."

"'Charges filed against both men are likely to include two murder counts—first-degree murder after deliberation and first-degree murder while committing a felony and car theft,' said Chief Deputy District Attorney Craig Silverman."

Rocky Mountain News staff writer, Katie Kerwin wrote about the pager number on the torn card that led to Davis's arrest. "The woman had given Davis her number at about 9 P.M. on July 22 outside a gas station when he and his friends tried to pick her up.

'He approached me like any other young man would,' said the woman, who asked that her name not be used. 'Davis and his friends were very friendly,' she said, 'But talked like gang members.'"

"The woman told police about the incident when they came to her home four days later and asked her about the torn business card found in the coin purse in Hollar's car. She explained the encounter, and then got the other half of the card, which was still in her car.

She identified both Shane Davis and Steve Harrington in photo lineups as two of the men outside a Conoco gas station at E. 34th and Colorado Boulevard that night. Police believe it was just about four hours after she saw them, that the two of them shot Thomas Hollar and beat Christina."

CHAPTER 46: AUGUST 21, 1993

CHRISTINA AND I CORRESPONDED regularly. In a letter I wrote to her dated August 21, 1993, I wrote, "It is a perfect day here—72 degrees, sunshine and a slight breeze. There is mixed shade from the oaks and maples in our yard. We have birds, butterflies, and dragonflies. Boris killed a bat outside last night. Jazz is playing on the radio. Two cats are asleep on the porch catching their rays; the third cat, Kalamazoo, is asleep in Margaret's bed. She was Tom's cat when he attended Western Michigan University, and she prefers country living to dorm life.

"'Mood Indigo' just played, reminding me of a beautiful deep blue that Tom loved, used, remembered, and commented about when he was young. I had worn a corduroy robe in this color when Tom was a baby.

"The metal frog birdbath Tom made has several cute little frogs in it. He would be pleased.

"Doug Otero, Tom's childhood friend, who made the trip to Denver for Tom's funeral, said he had to pull over on his way home from work because he was crying so hard the other day.

"You have in iMi JiMi an extended family, providing caring and acceptance for many people. You and Tom were serving as the 'rock' or base for this family, like parents—truly a great thing you were doing there.

"I talked to a man from Puerto Rico, who is working with young Hispanics in north Detroit. He is trying to do what the two of you were doing—giving day-to-day support they might not be getting at home. He liked the story about Julian Martinez. Although it may be difficult for you to continue these contacts, they may help you in the grieving process.

"I feel almost disloyal getting ready to go to Switzerland. Should I be allowed to have a good time now? The tickets are all in place, so we'll go. We're staying in Wengen, which is one mile high, like Denver.

"We will visit Mike Evans's mother in Stuttgart on our way to Switzerland, and take a photo of him for her. Dan Milnor took some very good photos—one of your black dining room table with Annie, the grey cat on it, with the tiled fireplace behind—a prize-winner.

"Creativity ran in our family, too. Tom's Aunt Jan was a weaver and worked as a teacher at Toledo Art Museum, where she had works on display. She also worked in Santa Fe in a weaving shop on Canyon Lane.

"I have been creative all my life, have taken painting and drawing classes at DePauw University and Flint Institute of Arts. When I retire I'll spend more time drawing, doing watercolors, and writing. I'm collecting stories about Tom and may do something with it.

"At work, I am able to forget while I am involved with patients, but in between and all the rest of the time, it's constantly in my thoughts. I am having dreams related to what happened. This means my subconscious is trying to deal with it.

"Marge and Laura want to come see you and are working on it. If you want a reprieve from Denver, please come visit. It is nice here, and we have room for you and would love to have you.

"Signed, Nedra and three cats."

Chapter 47: September, 1993

MONTHS AFTER the high-profile murder, after Christina's many surgeries and dental procedures began, the hearse stood like a lonely sentinel to all that had happened there. Cleaned of its dripped candle wax and dried flowers, the face of the black Cadillac was embedded in the memories of all who had been a part of the tragedy and the days following it.

Lonely hearse, fall 1993

Information About the Trial

William Buckley from the Prosecutor's Office and (later) Carole Malezija, our Victim's Assistant, kept us informed. September 27, 1993, the case was assigned judges and a courtroom. Prosecutors would present evidence in a preliminary trial to be sure there was enough to warrant a full trial, so the case would be bound to District Court. I was advised that I could be there and that hearsay is allowed in a preliminary trial, but not an actual trial.

Defendants usually do not say much in a preliminary trial since it could be damaging later. The judge sets dates for the defendants to enter their pleas, which most likely would be, "Not guilty." Two to four defense counselors were expected to be assigned.

The judge sets trial dates for fewer than six months from the date of defendants' pleas, but the trial may not actually be held on this date because of continuances or delays.

WE ARE PROUD

Goodbye, my dear son
we shall have fun
as you always told us to.

We are proud, my son
for what you've done—

made sad children laugh,
knew how to reach
hurt child inside,
Heard their plea
Felt their loneliness.
Two souls sharing a joke and a smile.

Battered souls
Tattooed rose
Studded nose
Scarred skin
Shaved hair
Masochistic
Macabre
Community
Agape
Acceptance.
Your life was very valuable.
You changed the world
All around you.
We're proud of who you were.

POMC

One of my patients, who had lost a child, suggested I join Parents of Murdered Children. This group provides support for those mourning the loss of a murdered child. Since I usually worked late, was very tired, and felt I was working through the pain of my loss on a daily basis, I chose not to drive to evening meetings of POMC. However, I have supported the group and added Tom's photo and story to their memory wall.

Vacation

On our trip to the foot of the Alps, we stopped to see Mike Evan's mother, Helga Engle in the Stuttgart Airport. She told me that had it been her son who had been murdered, she could not be sitting there where I was, on vacation. While I was suffering through grief, I was not incapacitated, and was able to go on, even though the terrible events of Tom's murder were never far away in my mind.

We regretted not having time to go with Helga to her home, where she wanted to serve tea. We had reservations and a long drive through the Black Forest to our night's lodgings. We had planned so we could arrive at Wengen, Switzerland to meet our group of hikers on time.

As it turned out, I was in no shape to take this trip, and simply leaving the country didn't stop my mind from returning to Tom's death and Christina's beating. I was not acclimatized, and I have short legs, so I had trouble keeping up with the other hikers, who'd already been hiking together for two weeks. At times, I could not help crying, but I didn't want to take the time to explain to total strangers who were on holiday. It was stressful for me, and we had to chat with strangers at dinner.

But we loved the Alps and the Swiss trains, which are very punctual. I recall trips we made to various hiking spots where we had just two or three minutes between trains and had to run down the tracks to catch the next train. On one of our hikes, for we had left the group and decided upon our own hikes, we met a small group of Swiss Army men who were out for a day on the trails. My mother was Swiss, so it was especially nice to be in this picturesque country with its rolling countryside, colorful chalets, grazing sheep, and Mercedes tucked away in garages.

CHAPTER 48: OCTOBER, 1993

HOWARD, WHO WAS THEN a partner in Security First Insurance in Flint, Michigan, was finally able to make headway on the issue of Christina's black Honda. Howard spent time on the phone with adjusters from GMAC and Farmers Insurance.

At that time, Christina thought she wanted to drive the black Honda since she said it has been a good car, but in the end, the condition of the car—and probably the memories associated with it—dissuaded her.

Visit To Fairmount Cemetery Grave Site

I went back to visit Tom's grave for the first time on October 7, 1993, and periodically thereafter. Whenever I flew west and had an opportunity to stop over in Denver, even for a few hours, I visited Tom's grave.

In May of 2000 I stopped in Denver for a few hours on a trip to California for a medical conference. Don and Nancy Dhonau graciously met me at DIA, drove me to the gravesite, provided a delicious picnic lunch, and then returned me to the airport to catch my next plane.

When I visited Denver for a few days in 1996, Noel and Suzanne Waechter met me in LoDo for lunch at an Indian restaurant, which was a very nice thing for them to do, providing a pleasant break from eating alone.

The grave at my first visit in October, 1993

The Grave

It was cold and gray
had rained all day
first time I went back to his grave.

Sculptured hedges
hiding death
in mossy vaults—
its proper place.

His plot was all bare
no marker there
Dead grass grown over the mound.

Fall leaves, one by one
spiraled to the ground.
Wet gold 'neath my shiny black boots.

Shivering in the chill wind
trying to grasp forever
My grief welled up, burst out!

"God with your might
It is not right
That my son lies here in this place!

So still and drab
with cold marble slabs
in row after row after row

He is not here!
He can't be here.
He is too wild and too full of life!"

Life Is So Cheap

Life is so cheap
when you live by the gun
you don't see any old men.
Expecting to die
by age 30 or so,
They watch friends die
every day.
No hope, stuck there,
get what you can.

October 7, 1993

You play it out
the best you can
when faced with death of your son.

No day goes by
without the thought
that you'll never see him again.

I See My Son

I see my son in everyone,
the faces go by in the crowd.

The young man there
with greased black hair,
and earrings in one of his ears—

It could be Tom,
my only son,
or maybe that man over there.

I see his black car go here and there
It passes by without a wave.

The driver there
looks just like my son Tom,
but he obviously doesn't know me.

Visit to the Apartment October, 1993

Christina and I drove from her mother's home in Arvada, where Chris was recuperating and keeping appointments with her doctors and dentists, to the apartment on Corona, which she had continued to rent.

It was extremely difficult for her to go back—the first time since the event. We were both overcome with emotion and the enormity of what had happened. Here, life had stopped July 22, 1993.

CAMELOT

We went back, she and I
to the place where
they'd lived and loved
not so long ago,

951 Corona, Number 4.
A strange silence now—
but for their orange cat—
still living there, wild and afraid.

Things as they'd left them:
1950s curved rose sofa
he'd loved so much.

As a child he created
with sand, mud, clay;
His sense of style now in these rooms.

Partly done crossword puzzle,
home mortgage rates circled
in a folded newspaper
on the glass globed coffee table.

Wedding photo there;
smiling one of him, one of her.
Vitamins on the kitchen windowsill.
Far Side Calendar showing July 22, 1993

Last photo of him there on the mantle:
Tom and the sea and the setting sun;
my grown son as he was
at the end.

Crazy art deco chandelier in the dining room
above the shiny black table
where Annie, the gray cat, liked to sleep.

The black entertainment center,
with a spider plant
and an Andy Warhol print.

The bicycle wheel sculpture
he'd made as a child,
bookcases full of books:
one on top, bookmark in place.

Antique wooden wardrobe by the front door
with his old-style white motorcycle helmet
he saw humor in wearing

Imi Jimi jackets and hats and T-shirts,
a good-looking brown leather jacket,
two pairs of rollerblades there by the chest.

The Colorado wool ski logo blanket
I'd given him on his 30th birthday, his last,
I shared with Tom and Christina in Colorado
Springs.

Clean polished oak floors.
A bright oil painting they'd just bought
on a two-week trip to California
visiting old friends, as if to say goodbye.

His card to me said, "Hi, Mom!
We're having a great time
sitting on the beach in Santa Barbara.
Love, Tom and Chris"
Happy times, so happy they were!

We went back, she and I
to this place they'd lived-
His touch, his things everywhere-
This last bit of him here in these rooms.

He'd moved on, my son
to a world I didn't know-
his life out here, out west.

Now I tried to touch it
to see who he had been-
this son of mine grown up,
now gone.

Filled with things he chose,
This quiet space, his last statement.
My son's life, his world, here in these rooms.

She stood alone in their room
with the window facing the street,
the room they'd shared
not so long ago.

I tried to know him,
my son who'd grown up and away,
by standing silently in these rooms
full of his things.

We couldn't disturb anything-
that way it might not be true,
things might be as they were before.

We stood so quietly-
two women who loved him
at the beginning and end

I knew him so well then;
she knew him best now.
we didn't speak.

They were happy here, life was so good:
Camelot couple, my son and his wife
sparkled brilliantly for the short time they had.

Christina and I went back
for one last look around.

The Preliminary Trial

On October 21, 1993, the preliminary trial was held before Denver County Judge Larry Bohning to determine if there was enough evidence to proceed with a full jury trial. Christina went with a police escort. Friends and relatives of Steve Harrington and Shane Davis were all over outside the courtroom and attended the preliminary trial.

Steve and Shane appeared in handcuffs and leg restraints. Their families and friends shouted racial accusations outside the courtroom, as if this trial were to be a white-versus-black trial.

"You ain't gonna git no niggers this time," Steve Harrington's sister cried out.

Laughing in Court

Those are her words,
    they are not mine.
    We want the one
    who shot my son.

They took Tom's life
    and beat his wife,
    and now they are
    laughing in court!

They made it seem
    like a racial thing,
    not our idea or plan.

We only want the guilty man.

Christina's Testimony

In an October 22nd article, *Rocky Mountain News* reporter Sue Lindsay wrote: "Widow Identifies Two Suspects in Capitol Hill Slaying."

Lindsay quoted Christina's testimony at the preliminary hearing: "We had parked the car in the King Sooper's parking lot at 9th and Corona after midnight when two men approached the car... I had gotten out to get my purse from the trunk. I ... remember getting up from the asphalt."

Christina recalled that one attacker had a gun and that the men pushed her into the car. "They were beating me on the side of the head. The next thing I remember is waking up in the back seat of the car and trying to lift my head up."

Lindsay wrote, "She was calm, but choked up over details of her injuries—broken nose, facial fractures, torn cheek, cuts and bruises over her entire face. She said she doesn't remember her hospital stay or statements she gave to police."

Asked by a defense attorney about how the District Attorney had told her to testify, Christina said, "They told me to tell the truth."

The defense attorneys asked her many questions about what she saw, what she remembered, who did what when. (The defense attorneys would later try to use her answers to discredit her as a witness.)

She further testified that the two men approached on the driver's side of the Honda. "I was hit in the face immediately after the first shot; I was down on the ground. I do remember hearing the next shot." She remembered details of the two men: acne spots (pitting) on Shane Davis's face, and that the man with the gun was lighter than the other.

While standing at the back of the car, she saw the man with the gun for a split second. He wore a white T-shirt. The man in the T-shirt drove; the man in the plaid shirt got into the back seat. The man who got into the back seat she identified by pointing at Shane Davis.

"Denver Police officer Vince Lombardi testified that he found Hollar in her Honda Accord in an alley at the 2100 block of Lafayette St. at 1:24 AM … He saw blood spattered on the windows and a person sitting in the car whose head was two times the size of a normal head. 'The victim turned and looked at me. It startled me. I thought for sure she was dead. There was blood all over the place. There was so much blood, I asked her if she was shot.'"

Another Woman's Testimony

A woman who lives in the 9th-and-Corona neighborhood testified at the preliminary hearing, saying the men walked toward her car as she left King Sooper's store, but she was able to leave the parking lot. "She said she was '100% sure' that Steve Harrington was one of those men. "I recognize that same glare," she said, referring to the evil glare he had in court as he stared down various witnesses.

Steve has prominent eyes that seem to bulge a little, and a way of puckering his mouth and twisting his face that was especially threatening when focused on you.

Witness Intimidated in Court

Danica Darling, who lived at the Shana Marie Apartment Building, was arriving home from work at the time Shane Davis and Steve Harrington were in the parking lot on July 23, 1993. She got a good look at them and identified them.

But when she testified during the preliminary hearing, she found it difficult to concentrate because of the abusive glaring and obscene

Steve Harrington's glare in the courtroom.
Photo by George Kochaniec Jr.
Rocky Mountain News

hand gestures one of the defendants directed at her. She said Steve Harrington flipped her off while she was on the stand, and "…it made me feel very nervous and upset and disgusted and scared."

Danica Brown told a reporter that "Harrington said to her in the hallway as people lined up outside the courtroom, 'You punk-assed bitch, I can get you. These shackles don't mean shit.'

Later, when Danica told of this episode in court, Harrington laughed.

From an October 22, 1993 *Denver Post* article by George Lane: "Two to be Tried in the Murder of Shop Owner:" "Yesterday, October 21, 1993, Denver County Judge Larry Bohning ordered Steven Harrington and Shane Davis to stand trial in the slaying of Tom Hollar and the beating of Christina Hollar."

"Judge Larry Bohning found that the presumption is great that Steve Harrington and Shane Davis would be found guilty; i.e., We have a case."

Shane Davis and Steve Harrington will enter pleas on November 15 before District Judge Paul Markson. If convicted, they will be sentenced to life in prison without parole or death by lethal injection.

GUILTY, OCTOBER 21, 1993

How do you feel
about today
Oct. 21, the pretrial?

Must you relive
what happened that night?
The fear, the horror, and pain?

"Not guilty," they said
smirking on the stand,
Steve gave the finger to Kris.

They were cocky and rude
and so were the brood
of sisters and brothers and friends.

They called Danica names:
"White bitch," they said.
No remorse for what they'd done.

Christina went alone
to take the stand
the day of the preliminary trial.

She faced the judge
her voice was calm
"They did it, Your Honor," she said.

Carole Malezija

In October, 1993, we were introduced to Carole Malezija from the Prosecutor's Office, who was our Victim's Assistant.

Her job was to keep us informed about what was happening: where we were to be, to explain or assist us in any way that she could. Carole is one of those people who truly found her niche in life, for she is the kind of compassionate, caring person perfectly suited for this job of helping victims get through very stressful and emotional events with calm reassurance. I believe she is at least part angel.

Carole went on in her job to help victims of Columbine murders and many others. She has received professional acclaim from her peers, and is now teaching others in her field. We feel very fortunate to have had Carole with her beautiful, sunny Czechoslovakian face, blonde bangs, wide smile, and sparkling blue eyes there for us. I can picture her wearing traditional Czech dirndl skirts and dancing.

Carole and I became friends and met for lunch, dinner, or coffee down through the years when I was in Denver. She was supportive to the point of bringing flowers to Tom's grave at Fairmount one time when I was there—not easy since she continued to work full time, and this was at a distance for her.

CHAPTER 49: NOVEMBER & DECEMBER 1993

O N NOVEMBER 15, 1993 two defendants entered pleas of "Not Guilty" on the charges against them before Judge Paul Markson. They were held without bond. Trial was originally set for March 7, 1994 in Denver District Court.

Thanksgiving 1993

"Christina and Greg flew to Detroit and then drove to our home in the country for Thanksgiving dinner. As usual, we were also celebrating Laura's birthday, which is November 25.

Laura and Richard Kovalcik with her birthday cake, Thanksgiving 1993

Ed Hollar with Christina Hollar and Greg Schneider looking at photos, Thanksgiving 1993

While they were here, we put Christmas lights on outside ever-green trees, which is much easier to do before snow falls. We did the spoon-on-the-nose trick and found that Greg's nose was especially suit-ed to holding a spoon, since it has a bend at just the right place.

Greg Schneider winning the "Spoon on the Nose Contest," Thanksgiving, 1993

December 5, 1993 in Denver

In a *Denver Post* article entitled, "Gangs by the Number," Christopher Lopez reported that Denver police released details of their "gang list." It held 6,567 names, with more than 93 percent of the names representing black or Hispanic people.

Apparently, this large number of names did not actually represent true gang members. The article continued, "Police administrators say hard-core gang members in Denver account for no more than 250 to 300 people. Coun-cilman Hiawatha Davis said the list is evidence that Denver's war on gangs has degenerated into a blanket persecution of minorities. ...

"In addition to the list, Davis is angry about a crackdown on alleged gang members by special police Impact Units. Officers on this gang detail have made thousands of misdemeanor arrests during the past four months…This is something on the order of an official policy of harassment on certain groups of citizens.

"Mayor Wellington Webb had authorized the Impact Units in response to a public outcry over gang violence, drug dealing, and other street crime."

Letter from Mayor Wellington Webb December 13, 1993

Mayor Webb sent a seasonal letter of comfort and understanding as our first holiday season without Tom approached. He sent assurances that Denver will continue to work to reduce violence with quick law enforcement and long-term prevention.

This sincere expression from Mayor Webb was above and beyond any duty he had. He and Wilma felt our loss on a very personal level, and related as parents, knowing that holidays magnify the sadness of loss.

We received a Christmas postcard from Mike Evans in Stuttgart. He was spending time with his mom there, saying that she was doing well and that things were slowly becoming normal again. He sent his love and best wishes for our happiness and good luck in 1994.

December 18, 1993

Howard and I usually plan a weekend away or a short vacation at the time of our wedding anniversary, December 16. One year we went to Denver, stayed at The Oxford Hotel, and bought tickets to a Russian ballet.

In 1993, we drove to the Homestead on Lake Michigan, where we'd taken the children a number of times. We often cross-country skied, or they played on ice formations on the lake or walked trails through the woods. This trip, while driving home through beautiful forested country around many lakes of Leelanau County, a snowstorm started.

Heavy Snow

Dizzying white blizzard
blasts pellets of snow
at our car
as we go…

It's a good night
to go to bed
and cover your head
'neath the down.

The headlights shine
on a graveyard there—
stones being covered
by drifting snow.

My son, who's dead
Won't go to bed—
He's lying so cold and so still

He's in his wood box
his hand on his chest
and his black and white shoes on his feet.

Christmas 1993

For Christmas in 1993, Glenda Hanley, my Office Manager, chose a music box that plays Pachelbel's Canon as my gift from the staff, something I will always treasure and play now and then, but the flood of memories and emotions that go with hearing this music is upsetting even now. This box is the place I keep the lock of Tom's hair I cut off while he was in his casket at the Monarch Society.

Lights

Christmas tree lights
glimmer bright in the night—
wonderfully cheerful sight.

The glowing moon
lights up the clouds,
silver strands floating above—

You're there somewhere
in the sparkle, the glow—
a part of the magical show—
bright light of the moon
then sun's glow on the snow.

Christmas will be
rough this year
without my fun-loving son.

We always looked forward
to his coming home,
his mirth and twist to the day.

Fix Me Up

"Fix me up, doc,
my son's coming home,"
said my patient
on December 22.

"I can't be sick
for his rare visit—
he seldom
comes home
anymore."

"I'll help you get well
as best I can—"
Pangs of sadness,
I held back tears.

I felt his joy
anticipating a visit
from his son,
didn't burden him
with my loss.

Chapter 50: January, 1994

Rocky Mountain News recapped the year 1993, by noting events: "Colorado Rockies at Mile High Stadium brought in good scores and high attendance at games: 3-93, Rockies beat the A's; 5 - 9 3 , Rockies hit the one-million attendance mark....

"Teen violence caught the news: 3-19, 15-year-old gang member arrested for killing another teenager in drive-by shooting. 5-93, stray bullet hit a boy at Denver zoo."

The News reported that "Denver is on the road to becoming a major league city with the new DIA and entry into National League's Western Division. Pope John Paul II and President Clinton's meeting in August, part of World Youth Day, related to Violence, brought the national spotlight to Denver related to discussions of violence. Denver wanted to be included in the big leagues, but not in their violence."

Lori Lowe's Mother's Letter January, 1994
Lori Lowe was murdered in Denver on August 2,1993, less than one month after Tom, and gang members were suspected of being the murderers. Lori Lowe, like Tom, was from Michigan. I had contacted her mother at that time, since we had shared this unlikely tragedy.

An article in *Rocky Mountain News*, October 4, 1993 by Lynn Bartels, was titled: "Couple Laments Loss of Woman Who Was 'Gift To Whole Family.'"

Bartels wrote, "Marjorie Lowe was 38 years old; she and her husband, Don, already had three sons, ages 10-15 when Lori Anne was born on June 6, 1966. Marjorie Lowe was quoted as saying, 'When Lori Anne arrived…we were thrilled to death, just thrilled to death. She was a gift to the whole family.'

"'Lori was three-and-a-half when her father died. She made such a difference in my life," said Marjorie, a registered nurse.

Marjorie, in a letter to me said, "When Lori was eight, her older brothers had largely left home, so she and I were very close."

Later, Charles Gentry, an engineer colleague of Don Lowe's, lost his wife and then he and Marjorie married in 1988. They described Lori as giving the "impression that she was gentle and needed some protection, but she was tough" and determined. "Once she decided to do something, she did it."

The Lynn Bartels article quoted Marjorie Lowe as saying about Lori, "She loved her life in Colorado. I told a friend of mine last summer, I don't think she'd ever come back to Michigan."

From an article in the *Gazette Telegraph* by D'Arcy Fallon sent to me by Marjorie Gentry with the dateline cut off, but I assume it was from August 1993, "There are many things people remember about Lori Anne Lowe. That she had a radiant smile. That she was shy, but could empathize with young children. That she agonized about the decision to move from Avon to Denver to take a teaching job, but she took it in the end because it was too good to pass up.

"But most of all, they remember her kindness, her sweetness. Early Monday morning, Lowe became another statistic in Denver's rising crime wave, fatally shot as she sat in a rented car, trying to find an acquaintance's home in an unfamiliar Arapahoe County apartment complex.

"She was shot about 1 AM outside an apartment complex just off South Quebec Street at East Arkansas Avenue. … Lowe, 27, … after graduating from Colorado College two years ago, had been preparing to start a new job at Whiteman Elementary School in Denver, where she'd been hired to teach a bilingual class for third-graders.

"The job at Whiteman was to be her first full-time teaching job, and she was 'ecstatic' about getting it, said friends in Colorado Springs.

"After graduating from CC's prestigious Elementary Education Master's Program, Lowe had been working as a substitute teacher in Vail and wanted to stay in that area. ...Permanent jobs were hard to come by in Vail.

"When Lowe was offered the job at Whiteman, she worried about the crime in Denver, but thought she could handle it, said a friend who described Lowe as a city girl at heart with a liking for skiing and jazz and the arts."

In my letter from Marjorie Gentry of January 16, 1994, she said, "We share a common grief and deep loss in the deaths of dear children. We were notified on August 23 of the death of the young man, a sixteen-year-old, whom police officers felt was Lori's murderer. I admit to some satisfaction in his death for myself and for Lori's brothers."

"We travelled to Colorado in September to attend two memorial services for Lori, where we visited with friends and fellow students from Colorado College in Colorado Springs, as well as students she had taught and their parents from Vail and co-teachers at Vail Ski School where Lori taught three to six-year-olds to ski."

"At the second memorial service at Douglass Valley Elementary School at the U.S.A.F. Academy in Colorado Springs, where Lori had done her student teaching, children sang songs, spoke of remembrances of Miss Lowe, and helped plant two evergreen trees at the school in her memory."

During this trip when Marjorie visited with investigative officers of the Arapahoe Sheriff's Department, she said that the officers "felt they knew all four young men involved in Lori's case." One gunman had been killed, but there was insufficient evidence for arrests of the others at that time. She was "impressed with the kindness shown us and the professionalism of the police team."

Later, two of the four men thought to be Lori's murderers were arraigned for trial. Marjorie Lowe's letter continued, "I always said that the death of a child must be the worst of tragedies. I still believe that. I, like you, will never outlive the overwhelming sadness the death of a child brings."

Shane Davis Accused In Another Shooting

In a March 26, 1994 *Denver Post* article Howard Pankratz reported: "Man says he was shot by alleged Hollar assailant. Donald Morrell claimed that one of the men who allegedly murdered Capitol Hill businessman Tom Hollar last July tried to kill him five weeks before Hollar's death…"

"By all odds, Morrell should be dead. He was shot twice at point-blank range in the back of his head in a Denver alley. He still carries a bullet in his head. Doctors told him the only reason he survived was because the shooter was too close to him and used the wrong type of bullet. Had hollow points been used, he would be dead."

Hollow-point bullets are hollowed out at the tip, limiting penetration, but allowing expansion upon entering the target, thus causing more tissue damage, shock, and blood loss in the victim. Solid point bullets travel further before stopping. Hollow points do more immediate damage to the victim.

In court, Morrell looked directly at Shane Davis and said to the defendant, "What's up, Punkin?"

In a March 2, 1994 *Rocky Mountain News* article, Ann Carnahan reported that Davis was charged with attempted first-degree murder, first-degree assault, aggravated robbery and mandatory sentencing for violent crimes. Bond was set at $1 million."

I'M SORRY

I'm sorry
Katie Washington
what happened to your son.

For if he'd
turned out better,
he wouldn't have shot my Tom.

I'm sorry
Mrs. Davis
that you have lost your son.

For you've lost him
sure as I
to drugs and gangs and guns.

April 1994

During April, 1994 hearings, prosecutors reported evidence: finding a hair on the bloody T-shirt found in the alley near the black Honda. This hair matched the hair of Steve Harrington, and the blood on the T-shirt matched that of Christina Hollar.

Mother's Day, May 8, 1994

Christina visited us in Michigan for Mothers' Day. On Saturday night, we started looking at albums I had kept from July 1993: photos of crowds around Shana Marie, photos of the hearse covered with flowers, and photos of the memorial service and poems I'd written related to Tom's murder and her assault.

She wanted to look at this part of her life she had not seen before—a part that she had lived through but had not really participated in. She was so weak at the time, in the hospital sedated, couldn't read newspapers since she would be a witness and was kept uninformed. She didn't know the furor in the city of Denver at the time.

Christina became absorbed in the albums, looking at my photos. The hour grew late. She still wasn't done. She was trying to put it all together in her poor, tired brain: this tragic event in her life. She was seeing it for the first time: the murder, the beating, the horror of the night in a different perspective. She looked at each picture for a while, including some of her battered face in the hospital, but she wanted to see the ones of Tom as he lay dead, her face close to the photos of Tom at the funeral home in his coffin.

She rubbed her hand over his face. She tried to make sense, to understand what had happened. She tried to feel how it was for him. She'd not seen him since the funeral when she was still in pain, shock, and sedated.

She said, "You know, you could get all wrapped up in this." She spent a long time. She needed to know the enormity of it all: a piece of her life being put back in so she could close the chapter and move on. These were things she needed to know, to internalize, to absorb.

In my photo albums were some of the two of them happy and in love during their trip to California just days before Tom was killed. She told me about each one of them in the wee hours of the morning of Mothers' Day 1994.

This was a very different Mothers' Day. I stayed up very late with Christina; I no longer had a son to send me a silly card or to come home for a visit. It was a kind thing for her to do, to come to try to fill in the gap in my life and hers.

Chapter 51: Before the Trial

MAY 15, 1994

In *Rocky Mountain News* Ann Carnahan called Tom's death "a symbol of last year's summer of violence." She reported that the trial would begin on Monday May 15, 1994 in Denver District Court and noted, "The case is largely built on testimony, not so much on physical evidence, and the defense has attacked this."

Death Penalty

In a March 5, 1994 *Denver Post* article Howard Pankratz reported that District Attorney William Ritter said it was a difficult decision for him not to seek the death penalty in Tom Hollar's murder trial.

In Colorado, the death penalty can only be sought when aggravating factors exist, which they did in this case. Ritter said the death penalty is not a deterrent for crime, and it takes a long time to move such cases through the criminal justice system.

"Obtaining the death penalty in Denver is difficult," and Ritter said he wouldn't seek it unless he was reasonably sure a jury would sentence the accused to death. He said that Denver juries in the past 15 years usually had turned down the DA's attempts to obtain the death penalty. Since the 1970s, the death penalty had been sought nine times, and only once did a jury sentence a murderer to die.

He asked himself: "Am I reasonably certain a jury is going to convict? Am I reasonably certain a jury is going to sentence the accused to die?" If he doesn't feel reasonably certain of conviction, he will not file charges. If he is not reasonably certain of a death penalty sentence, he doesn't seek the death penalty.

He said many phone calls to his office provided negative feedback for Ritter's decision not to seek the death penalty for Shane Davis and Steve Harrington. "Jurors are more comfortable with an alternate sentence of life in prison without chance of parole," Ritter said.

An editorial at the *Rocky Mountain News* on March 13, 1994 read, "The death penalty is popular, but not always with juries. The main reason Ritter didn't seek the death penalty for Steve Harrington and Shane Davis is that he didn't think he could get it, and seeking the death penalty requires a big investment of the District Attorney's office resources."

Commentators on Court TV noted they were surprised the death penalty was not sought since this was a death-penalty case with strong aggravating factors.

A letter from Jan Lee, Mitts's mother, written in July 1993 at the time of Tom's murder said, "We are all mad and angry at the terrible violence of Tom's death and hope that his murderers are caught and that they in turn face a cruel death, too!"

Pre-Trial Motions, April 1994

In an April 15, 1994 *Rocky Mountain News* article, Charlie Brennan wrote: "Judge denies bid for separate trials for slaying suspects. Lawyers for Steve Harrington lost a bid Thursday to try him separately from his co-defendant in the murder of Capitol Hill boutique-owner Tom Hollar. Lawyers for Harrington, 22, argued that jurors could improperly interpret evidence introduced against Davis as applicable to their client. But Chief Deputy District Attorney Craig Silverman said such concern is unfounded. 'We would be presenting the exact same evidence if there were separate trials,' Silverman said."

In a similar article, Ann Carnahan wrote: "Witness Testimony Key in Hollar case." At a hearing in April 1994, pretrial motions were presented and agreed upon. One such motion from the defense was to not allow references to the defendants' gang membership or appearance that tied them to gangs. Judge Paul Markson decided that evidence and descriptions of the two defendants as gang members most likely would help prove the accuracy of their identification by witnesses.

Both Harrington and Davis had gang tattoos that show they belonged to a subset of a large national street gang, Crips. One witness at a gas station said they were "talking gang slang" and sagging, which is wearing pants below the hips, common among gang members.

In an April 13, 1994 *The Denver Post* article, Howard Pankratz reported: "Prosecutor Silverman said that gang connections were critical evidence, important for this homicide trial. He said that Steve Harrington is a gang member and proud of it, wearing the tattooed name of a Los Angeles-based gang on his left forearm.

The *Denver Post's* policy is to refrain from identifying specific gangs, but Silverman himself referred to the gang by name: Crips. Most of the witnesses to this transaction said the two men looked, acted, and talked like gang members.

Silverman also mentioned the coincidence that just hours after Tom and Christina were robbed of $400.00 cash, two apparent gang members bought a used Cadillac for $400 at a Clarkson Street address not far from the murder scene.

Other evidence was presented that on July 26, 1993, the Administrator of Titles issued two certified copies of the title to a 1975 Cadillac Coupe

Deville—purchased on July 23—to Steve Harrington. This was the first day her offices were open after the purchase. She produced the documents during the trial and a handwriting expert stated that the writing was that of Steve Harrington.

Defense attorneys had wanted all gang references and testimony about the Cadillac prohibited at the trial, but the judge allowed this evidence to be presented.

Further, Silverman noted that "just hours before the Hollars were attacked, a young woman met Davis at a gas station at E. 34th and Colorado Boulevard. She thought he and his companions were gang members based on their sagging pants, their demeanor and their gang slang.

"Very important," said Silverman, "is that Davis, Harrington's close friend, gave the woman a business card. The card later was torn with the woman keeping a piece. The other piece was recovered from the Hollars' car."

Silverman also said that three King Soopers employees got a long look at the attackers and described them as gang members.

Judge Paul Markson said, "The only major issue in the case is identification. Harrington and Davis claim they not only weren't at 951 Corona last July 23 when Hollar was shot, but weren't even together that night.

He said, "There are eyewitnesses who place the men together that night, and witnesses who identified Harrington as the man who fired two shots into Hollar." Markson said, "The thing the witnesses remember most about the two suspects—and the reason they focused such attention on them—is because they walked, talked, and dressed like gang members."

Markson said, "The court is personally aware of the impact gangs have actually had in the city and the potential impact it may have on jurors.

"If this were a case where the prosecution had fingerprints, a video recording of the crime or confessions of both defendants, the value of this gang evidence wouldn't be so overwhelming."

Witness List Approved

An article by Howard Pankratz in the *Denver Post* with the above title, reported: "The witness list was approved by the court. The list allowed witnesses who say Steve Harrington killed Tom Hollar and that Shane Davis and Steve Harrington were together in the early morning hours of July 23, 1993."

Witness Intimidation

Rocky Mountain News carried an article, "Intimidation plagues gang cases," on Monday, Dec. 27, 1993, by Burt Hubbard. The article began with examples: "A gang member shows up in court to testify in a murder trial with his mouth wired shut after a beating with a baseball bat.

"A 13-year-old boy and his 4-year-old sister flee a firebomb tossed into their home two days after their sister cooperates with police as a witness to a gang shooting.

"A woman gets a harassing call at work from a gang member in jail accused of shooting her son.

"Witness intimidation plagues police and District Attorneys in the Denver area who are trying to prosecute gang members for slayings, shootings, and assaults."

The article said that witnesses were scared, believing that they were targeted; some recanted on the stand, and others fled the state during the trial. Some potential witnesses refused to testify.

A photo with the article showed a sheriff's deputy using a handheld metal detector to search people entering the courtroom.

During the trial of Steve Harrington and Shane Davis for Tom's murder and the assault on Christina, witnesses testified that Harrington or his family members tried to intimidate them. Judge Markson banned one of Steve Harrington's brothers from the courthouse after the man flashed gang signs at a witness while a female family member verbally assaulted the woman. During the trial, Harrington continually tried to stare down various witnesses, including Christina.

Jury Selection

In an article in *Rocky Mountain News* May 15, 1994, Ann Carnahan reported, "Jury selection begins Monday, May 16 from a pool of more than 200 people, who began filling out questionnaires on Friday, May 13, 1994. Opening arguments are expected Wednesday or Thursday."

In a *The Denver Post* article on Tuesday, May 17, 1994, Howard Pankratz wrote: "Court closed to public, press in Hollar case. In a highly unusual move, a Denver judge yesterday ordered the public and the press barred from his courtroom while jurors are selected. District Judge Paul Markson yesterday prohibited anyone but potential jurors, sheriff's deputies and lawyers from entering his courtroom during jury selection.

"Prospective jurors were seated in the courtroom and then brought into Markson's chambers for individual questioning. Clerk Glenda Gibson said the judge didn't want the courtroom open to the public because of the fear that outsiders might taint the jury panel."

She added that there was no room in the judge's chambers for the public or the press. Jury selection almost always is open to the public. Security has been a concern because of the defendants' alleged gang affiliations.

Security was beefed-up during pre-trial hearings in April when family and friends of Davis and Harington crowded around a number of deputy sheriffs escorting the men from court. Subsequently, the number of deputies was doubled, and varying routes were used to bring the defendants to the courtroom.

In a May 19, 1994 *Rocky Mountain News* article, Ann Carnahan wrote, "Defense attorneys accused prosecutors of racial bias because they dismissed a disproportionate number of minority people during jury selection." Skeet Johnson, Defense Attorney for Shane Davis brought the accusation, and Prosecuting Attorneys Craig Silverman and Tom Clinton said the prospective jurors were excused for reasons other than race. Later they were able to explain these decisions to the satisfaction of the court.

Denver Post carried an article on May 20, 1994 entitled, "Jury Seated," by H. Park, and *Rocky Mountain News* carried an article with the same title by Ann Carnahan. It is clear the jury-selection process has ended, and the court is ready to proceed.

Judge Paul Markson said, "A clear demonstration that the system is working is that the composition of the jury clearly reflects the racial composition of the community." Legal experts indicated it was typical for accusations to be made during jury selection, but it's atypical for a judge to direct prosecutors to explain their decisions.

CHAPTER 52: THE TRIAL BEGINS
MAY, 1994

CLIMBING THE WHITE marble steps of the Denver District Courthouse became a daily event during the month-long trial, which began in May, 1994 and ended June 10, 1994. We stayed at The Oxford Hotel on the fifth floor.

Every trial day, we walked down Wazee Street from 17th Avenue to pick up the 16th Street Free MallRide bus. In a monotone, the driver called out the street names as we crossed them: "Blake, Market, Larimer, Lawrence, Arapahoe, Curtis, Champa, Stout, California, Welton, Glenarm, and Tremont."

There we got out and walked across busy Colfax Avenue a short distance to the Denver District Courthouse at 1437 Bannock Street.

No cameras were allowed in the courtroom, but an artist sketched in pastels a courtroom scene, which appeared in all the Denver

Margaret, Nedra, and Laura sitting beside front steps to the courthouse in Denver

newspapers. I still have the original, which showed Christina on the stand, Craig Silverman and the two defendants.

We had to go through security at the Courthouse, not unlike the airport, and once done, we walked the marble hallways and climbed the marble steps to Judge Markson's courtroom on the fourth floor.

Inside we found a traditional courtroom with dark wooden seats like church pews for spectators. Seats for the jury were on the right side perpendicular to the spectator seats. The judge sat on a higher level behind a large wooden desk at the front facing the spectators, attorneys, and defendants, perpendicular to the jury seats.

The two prosecuting attorneys sat at a wooden table centered in the courtroom in front of spectators, facing the judge with their backs to the spectators. The two defendants with their attorneys sat at tables off to the left. Each day they were led into the courtroom in handcuffs.

Their advisors had cleaned them up; they had neat hairstyles, wore regular shirts and trousers, no longer the sagging pants and tank tops, which revealed their tattoos. I found myself staring at them, trying to pick up a sense of who they were, a sense of how they could have done the inhuman acts they were accused of doing.

Steve Harrington's mother wandered around the courtroom. The story was that she was dying of AIDS from a blood transfusion after the birth of her last child. When proceedings began, officers made her sit down or leave. On several occasions, police came into the courtroom to search for hidden weapons in the spectator-seating areas.

The courtroom filled early, so we knew we had to be really early to get seats in the front. Special front-row seats were reserved for the press.

Dominating the courtroom each day was the towering figure of Craig Silverman, Assistant Prosecuting Attorney for Denver. He was more than six-feet-tall, broad-shouldered, and athletic. He wore nicely tailored suits, white shirts, and ties each day, and he looked the part of a competent prosecuting attorney. He was meticulously prepared each day for the job of presenting evidence to prosecute this crime: the murder of my son, Thomas Hollar and the brutal beating of Christina.

The trial began with opening statements.

Opening Statements

During the opening statements, Steve Harrington wore his hair neatly braided and pulled back tightly on his head. He turned in his chair to stare coldly at spectators, but Shane Davis sat quietly.

The Prosecutor's Opening Statement

Like an actor portraying a scene from a play, Prosecutor Craig Silverman set the stage, introduced the characters, added bits of information, filled in the details, thus leading his audience in the courtroom to feelings of certainty about who the killers were and what had happened.

In Silverman's opening statement, he presented a synopsis of the crime and told what happened the night Tom Hollar was murdered and Christina was beaten.

Complete with visual aids, Silverman planted a scenario in the minds of the jury that they could keep with them during the trial. He wanted to get to the jury with prosecution evidence before the defense had a chance to present a different perspective. He referred to "the execution of Tom Hollar," thus setting the stage for the jury to think of *execution* or the *death penalty*, which was available in Colorado cases like this with strong aggravating factors.

Silverman told about the night of July 22 and early morning hours of July 23, 1993: "Tom had gone to the Rockies' game at Mile High Stadium that night with an old friend Pete Flye and still carried exuberance from the Rocky's win as he drove to the Shana Marie Apartment building on Corona to pick up his wife Christina, who was getting ready for a party. One of their clothing suppliers was sponsoring a party at Rock Island for Tom and

Christina, their friends and employees, and they were looking forward to a good time."

Silverman asked permission to show photos of Christina before she was beaten, and when the judge agreed, Craig held up wedding photos of Tom and Christina. He said, "You can see she is a natural beauty."

He went on telling the story: "Christina Schneider married Thomas Hollar in July of 1992. They moved into a two-bedroom unit in the small apartment building, the Shana Marie on Corona, which had six units with a carriage house behind where another tenant lived."

Then Silverman brought in the facts about Danica Darling, who was an early witness in the trial. "Danica Darling worked the late shift at Racine's, a popular restaurant, and finished work at midnight when she drove home to the Shana Marie. Normally, she felt safe parking in the Shana Marie parking lot, one of King Soopers' parking lots across Corona from the store and adjacent to the apartment building, which had bright overhead lighting.

"But this was not the case in the early morning of July 23 about 12:30 AM, because Steve Harrington and Shane Davis were there, acting hostile and aggressive. Danica Darling pulled into the parking lot, and pulled out again. She wanted no part of these guys." She finally reached her apartment about 12:40 AM after having circled from Corona to 9th to the alley, and then around again until the two men were no longer there.

Silverman then described Dennis Whiteman arriving home about 12:45 AM, where he had to find on-street parking, which he did at 9th and Marion, one-half block from his home. He noticed the two men in his mirror and the way they were crouching.

Craig Silverman then told of three King Soopers' employees on break outside the store at 12:45 AM. "These employees saw Shane Davis and Steve Harrington and could describe them. They were walking west into the King Soopers lot and wore gang-style sagging pants. One had a black pouch over his shoulder and under his arm. The two men made no move to go into the

318

store, which was unusual since people who enter the parking lot at night usually go into the store. The King Soopers employees watched the two men until about 10 of 1:00 AM on July 23, 1993."

Silverman described a King Soopers' customer, Rena Wakabayashi, who was alone on her way home after work when she stopped at King Soopers and went inside. "When she returned and headed for her car, two men approached her fast. Rena, who was attractive, felt she was going to be attacked. They were close to her when a King Soopers' employee called out to her about her pretty dress. Rena was a regular customer known to the employees of the store. The two men stopped approaching her, but continued to look into parked cars in the lot. Rena lived just a few blocks away and noted the time when she reached the underground parking lot of her apartment: 12:57 AM."

Silverman then described Tom and Christina Hollar's returning to their apartment at Shana Marie. He said, "Security was not on the minds of Tom and Christina Hollar when they left the party early because they had to work the next day. There was no underground parking for Shana Marie residents."

They pulled up into their normal parking spot, parked, and Christina got out. She was dressed up and looking great. These two defendants rushed the car. They wanted two things: the valuables, including the car, and they wanted Christina.

They could have the valuables, but Tom Hollar could not let them have his wife. He yelled, hoping neighbors would come out and scare the men away. His Shana Marie home was only about twenty steps away when Steve pulled out his gun.

Tom was yelling and pleading for their lives, backing away, when Steve Harrington made a decision. He pulled out his 0.38 caliber snub-nosed Smith and Wesson revolver from his black shoulder holster, pointed in at Tom Hollar's heart, and "Bang!" in a nearly perfect shot, a hollow-point extra deadly bullet tore into Tom's left chest. He grabbed his chest, cried out in pain, staggered, and fell on his right side on the sidewalk. But Steve Harrington was not done yet. He walked to the fallen man and shot again, "Bang!" This bullet ripped through Tom's upper left shoulder at point-blank range.

Then Steve reached down and took Tom's wallet and went through his pockets.

Silverman said that Shane Davis was not just standing around while Steve was shooting Tom. He'd gone to the passenger side of the Honda where Christina was standing near the trunk, and "Pow!" Silverman made a gesture of his closed fist punching his other open hand. He hit Christina and knocked her to the pavement.

Craig Silverman described Tom Hollar dying trying to protect his wife. He claimed that Steve and Shane were members of a branch of a Denver street gang that had a reputation for going out and aggressively pursuing attractive young women like Christina.

Silverman noted that Tom Hollar was not around to tell what happened, so how do we know? Fate gave eyewitnesses to Steve Harrington's execution of Tom Hollar.

Michael Evans, a friend of Tom Hollar's, saw the whole thing from across the street.

Silverman presented the Prosecution's trump cards: the coin purse containing the torn business card with a pager number written on it, and the watch with a scratched face, both belonging to Shane Davis, which were found in the black Honda Accord where they found Christina, as well as the Colorado Rockies base-

Outside the courtroom during the trial. Craig Silverman, Nedra, and Howard with friends and family

ball cap with a tag still on it.

Silverman presented the bloody T-shirt recovered from the alley near the Honda, which had a hair on it. Hair-analysis experts identified the hair as most likely belonging to Steve Harrington. The blood on the T-shirt was the same type as Christina Hollar's blood. Silverman also introduced the 0.38 spent shell casings found in Shane Davis's home as being trophies of the crime, and noted that they were the size that fit bullets recovered from Tom's body. Silverman pointed out that shell casings are usually thrown away, but in this case, it seemed as if Shane and Steve wanted to show them off. Objections by Defense Attorneys were overruled.

Defense Team Opening Statements

Defense attorneys are not required to make opening statements, but may if they so choose. Steve Harrington was represented by Fred Torres and David Miller; Shane Davis's Public Defenders were Skeet Johnson and Kim Grogan.

Public Defender Kim Grogan made a case for another black man being with Steve Harrington that night, not Shane Davis. Michael Evans saw one man, Steve Harrington. Danica Darling identified Steve Harrington. She presented information about height differences between Shane and Steve as given by witnesses. Christina was the only witness who said they were the same height, which they are. Kim Grogan tried to use perceived height difference to defend her client, and she was trying to make a case for Shane not being with Steve that night.

Defense Attorney David Miller (for Steve Harrington) pointed out that Christina could not pick Steve out of a lineup at the police department less than a week after the crime, July 29, 1993.

T.C. Clinton, Prosecutor, had spent twelve years on the Denver gang prosecution unit. He did a lot of work on prosecution preparation for the trial, and efficiently questioned Sergeant Spenard on the stand. Spenard was able to show to those in the courtroom some gang tattoos on the two defendants.

"ECC" on the left hand of Shane Davis, and "CRIPS ECG 118" on the left forearm of Steve Harrington were gang identification.

"ECC" and "ECG" stand for East Coast Crips or East Coast Gang, which comes from the location of Los Angeles Crips gangs east of Harbor Freeway. The 118 refers to the house number where ECC in LA began.

CHAPTER 53: CHRISTINA ON THE STAND

T HE FIRST WITNESS called to testify was Christina.

On the stand, defense attorneys pounded Christina with repetitive questions about the preliminary hearing. It was tiring just to listen to it, let alone respond to it.

But Christina held a steady gaze, was poised, articulate, and believable. I noticed an occasional twitch below her left eye, where she'd had five surgeries to repair her battered facial bones. How could anyone remember all the questions she'd been asked and answers she'd given seven months before at the stressful preliminary hearing?

David Miller asked, "Do you remember going to the physical lineup on July 29, 1993?"

Christina said, "I was very sick."

Miller: "Do you recall going to the courtroom on Oct. 21, 1993?"

Christina: "I recall testifying on what happened on July 23. My memory becomes clearer as time goes on."

On May 23, 1994, during the trial, Defense Attorney Kim Grogan fired at Christina repetitive questions about the preliminary hearing: "Do you recall when Craig Silverman asked if you recognized the two men in court on October 21?"

"Yes."

"They were the right age, the right hair?" said Grogan.

"Yes."

Asked by Grogan to further recall her testimony of October 21, Grogan said, "Where were you when the men approached?"

"Still in and getting out of the car." Christina recalled replying this on October 21.

On October 21 when Christina was asked if Tom got out of the car, she had replied, "I don't recall."

When asked when she first saw the gun, she said, "It was pointing at Tom."

"Do you recall being asked on October 21 when the shots were fired, and saying, 'I don't recall?'"

"The first shot was fired before I fell; the second shot after," Christina replied.

"Do you recall that on October 21 being asked who pulled you up and pushed you into the car, saying, "I don't recall. It was very chaotic. I don't recall."

"I don't know; I don't recall saying that." Christina remained composed, doing her best.

"Do you recall speaking to Lieutenant Williams?"

"No. I don't remember a lot of the hospital."

"Do you know who struck you?"

"That man right there." Christina pointed at Shane Davis.

When asked if she recalled saying in October in response to a question, "Did you see the gunman?" Christina replied, "Yes, for a split second, and I did see his face another time."

"Do you recall in October saying, 'I did see their faces?' Do you recall being asked, 'Did both men push you into the car?' in October, and replying then, 'I don't recall?'"

When asked if she was on her own in October, she said, "No. I was with my parents for months after."

During the trial, on May 23, 1994, Christina was asked how her memory was then compared to October 21, 1993. She replied, "At that time, I had just had my second surgery on my face." This implied that she was still recovering at the time of the preliminary hearing and probably still on pain medications.

Defense Attorney David Miller (for Steve Harrington) pointed out that Christina could not pick Steve out of a lineup at the police department less than a week after the crime (July 29, 1993).

Steve Harrington denied being with Shane Davis the night of July 22. The gas station owner didn't see them together, but his daughter was able to identify Harrington because of the teardrop tattooed below his left eye. She saw Davis and Harrington together.

Davis's girlfriend, Lanica Jones, identified his wristwatch and the zipper pouch as being his, and so did his brother. Shane Davis said they were not his. His girlfriend knew there was a chip in the watch crystal. Later she denied having made this identification.

Christina Identified the Defendants

In an article in the *Rocky Mountain News* on May 24,1994, Ann Carnahan wrote: "Hollar's widow identified the defendants. The victim can't recall her stay in the hospital."

Christina had been medicated during her hospital stay with painkillers including narcotics and sedatives, central nervous system depressants, so it didn't surprise me that she didn't remember her hospital stay. She was intentionally kept subdued to help her get through painful and stressful events necessary for her to recover.

Christina wore an appropriate gray suit. She was described by Court TV staff as an "excellent witness. She was poised, composed, and certain in her identification of the defendants. She gave solid testimony."

It was obvious to me that her wide-eyed, intent, and sincere face showed that she was doing her very best to tell the truth and to remember what happened, so she could help put away the two perpetrators of the horrible crime against her and Tom. She was a totally believable witness, holding up while Prosecutor Silverman presented evidence that was emotionally charged.

She sat calmly, legs crossed, hands clasped over her left knee, while viewing and answering questions about wedding photos, and photos of Tom at iMi JiMi, identifying Tom's watch, his blue cutoff jeans, his underwear, his jacket, and his thick-soled lace-up black boots—probably Doc Martens.

Sitting there in the courtroom crying quietly, I had a more emotional response to seeing Tom's boots than I had expected. My son wore those boots when he was murdered!

Prosecutor Silverman led Christina through a series of questions to establish her credibility and to paint a word picture about her life with Tom.

She described Tom as a businessman who owned the clothing store iMi JiMi, where she had worked for six years. She said that she and Tom opened the store at the beginning of a workday and closed the store at the end of the day. Christina managed several smiles when she was talking about Tom and herself.

At Silverman's prompting, she told about their two-bedroom apartment at the Shana Marie, named after the landlord's daughter, where their neighbors were friendly, and they had three cats. She described Tom as intelligent, caring, giving, charismatic and a wonderful husband.

T.C. Clinton holding his iMi JiMi End the Violence tee shirt designed by Greg Schneider

She described their automobiles: four cars (black 1988 Honda Accord

LX 2-door, vintage red-and-white Dodge convertible, and two other vintage Dodges), a silver Mitsubishi pickup truck, and the 1940 black Cadillac hearse. When Silverman asked Christina about neatness, she smiled and said the black Honda was messy, that Tom tossed used tissues or wrappers into the back seat. She also described driving the black Honda to take trips, to carry friends and merchandise.

Christina testified that she and Tom were relaxed, having a good time at Rock Island on the night of July 22, 1993; they'd talked to friends, had a vodka tonic, danced. She said they left the party early, at a quarter to 1:00 AM, because they had to work the next day. She said Tom was in a "great mood," describing the Rockies game as the "best game he'd ever seen."

When asked by Prosecutor Silverman, Christina described what she was wearing that night: black shorts, black boots, fishnet stockings and a halter-top.

While on the stand, Christina sat attentively with her face near the microphone, occasionally sipping water.

Steven Harrington stared incessantly at Christina, occasionally shifting in his seat. His eyes seem to bulge a little, and he pursed his lips, making his glare seem more menacing, which added to the stress Christina was enduring.

She said that when Tom parked the Honda in the first space in the second row away from the Shana Marie, they saw two men in the parking lot, but did not pay any attention since there were usually lots of people in the parking lot, which Shana Marie residents shared with King Soopers shoppers. Then she described the scene where she saw Steve Harrington with the gun pointed at Tom, heard the first shot, was hit and knocked down, and then heard the second shot while her face was on the asphalt paving of the parking lot.

Seeing her bravely describing this horrible incident, doing her best to be a good witness without showing emotions she must have felt, was extremely moving, arousing empathy among those who saw her.

Silverman asked, "Did you see the faces of the men who attacked you?"

"Yes," replied Christina.

"Do you see those faces in the court room?"

"Yes, that man in the brown shirt, and this man right here in the blue shirt," she said, pointing first at Shane Davis and then at Steve Harrington.

To add drama to the courtroom testimony, with permission from the judge, Silverman walked toward Christina on the stand, asking her to stop him when he was as close to her as Shane Davis, and then Steve Harrington had been that night. When she held up her hand to stop him only a few feet away, this made the confrontation seem more real, and Christina's intimidation by the two six-feet-tall men even more frightening.

During the trial, Christina testified that Steve Harrington was the man with the gun, which he aimed at Tom and that the gun went off twice. When asked to describe the gun, she said that it was metal.

Items Found in Black Honda

On May 23, 1994, Craig Silverman presented People's evidence #47—a dark baseball cap with the cardboard price tag still hanging from it. The hat was found to be the same as those sold at many King Soopers Markets across Denver.

Armedia Gordon, Head Homicide Supervisor of the Homicide Unit of the Denver Police Department, compared two hats. She said the one found in the Honda was like one that police officers recovered from Shane Davis's home.

Christina was on the stand. "Do you recognize this Colorado Rockies' cap?" he said.

"No," replied Christina.

"Is it yours?"

"No."

"Was it Tom's?"

"No."

"Did Tom wear caps with the tags still on them?"

"No."

"Did you sell such caps at iMi JiMi?"

"No."

"Do you know how this cap ended up in the Honda?"

"No."

During the trial, a witness described Shane Davis as wearing such a cap with the tag still on it the night of the murder.

Silverman then presented to Christina People's Evidence #48—a pair of sunglasses.

"Do you recognize these?"

"Yes."

"What are they?"

"My sunglasses," she said.

"Were they in the car?"

"Yes."

Silverman was demonstrating that Christina was a reliable witness who could identify items in the car that belonged to her and Tom versus items left behind by Shane Davis and Steve Harrington. She identified their car phone, which "definitely was used in the car."

When asked, "Did they beat you with the phone?"

She replied, "I don't know."

Defense Attorney Miller commented that Steve Harrington's footprints, fingerprints, and blood were not found at the crime scene.

CHAPTER 54: MORE TESTIMONY

DURING THE TRIAL, Mike Evans told his story calmly and slowly with no German accent. Mike said he did not know the men he saw with Tom that night. He said lighting in the parking lot was good, that Tom was two or three yards from his car when the gunman pulled a gun, pointed it at Tom, and shot. He then saw Tom stumbling away from the car holding his left chest, crying out, "Arrgh!"

Mike was scared and did not want to get shot himself, so he started running down Corona, looking back as he reached the corner of King Soopers market. He saw the gunman walk to where Tom had fallen to the sidewalk, and then heard the second shot. He said the gunman was very close to Tom. Mike said he heard screams, a female voice, coming from Tom's car. He did not see who was in the car. Then he saw the black Honda being driven out of the parking lot. Things happened fast.

Mike Evans on the stand.
From *Rocky Mountain News,* May 25, 1994.
Photo by George Kochaniec Jr.

Lanica Jones

The night of the attack, when Police Officers Hartvigson and Lombardi found the black Honda in the 2100 block alley between Lafayette and Marion, the most incriminating evidence found was Shane Davis's watch and his coin purse containing the torn business card. The piece in the coin purse had a pager number scrawled on it. Investigators discovered it belonged to a 21-year-old Denver woman, who said she had traded telephone numbers a few hours before the shooting with Davis. She still had the other piece of the business card in her car.

In 1993 in a video-recorded statement at Denver Police Headquarters, Lanica Jones had identified this brown-striped coin purse with a broken zipper and a Casio sports watch to be the property of her boyfriend Shane Davis. But on May 26, 1994, during The People vs Davis and Harrington trial, Ms. Jones denied that Shane Davis owned the coin purse and Casio watch. "Also, at various instances during her testimony, Ms. Jones denied she had been shown, or that she had previously identified either (item) as belonging to Mr. Davis.

"On the following day, Detective Calvin Hemphill testified that she had, in fact, identified these items."

This information is from a Courtroom 11 pre-sentencing document supplied to me by Craig Silverman.

Lanica had also said Shane Davis had been hanging out with Steve Harrington in July 1993. She had said, "Shane hung out with Steve every night."

Steve Harrington had said he was not with Shane Davis that night. Shane Davis had said that, "No, he was not with Steve Harrington that night."

Craig pulled all of us through the painstaking revelation of details, evidence gathered by Denver Police Detectives Dave Neil and Dan Wycoff, and Rob Gomez from the Prosecutor's Office, and others, tying the bits and pieces together into a believable and accurate rendition of what happened just after midnight of July 22, 1993.

During the trial, two jurors were dismissed because they were talking about the case, discussing Jeri curl. Judge Markson had asked them not to discuss the case.

Tom's Things That Night

Silverman led us through a description of the Black Honda Accord with used tissues under the seat on the driver's side where Tom had tossed them and a small wooden baseball bat in the console where he kept it "just in case;" a little joke he and I had when I used to caution him to be careful, as mothers the world over are wont to do.

He'd show me the small bat and say, "Don't worry." The small wooden bat was from an early promotion of the Denver Rockies team that began in 1993.

Tom had audiotapes in the car, which presumably he listened to while driving. I still have some of the tapes, which I carefully listened to back then. One especially moved me with the words: "…and you'll never…see…me…again."

During the presentation of evidence, Silverman again held up wedding photos of the smiling couple, and this time showed a Polaroid photo taken of the badly beaten Christina as she was found in the Honda that night. He showed photos of her swollen, bruised and cut face when she was in the hospital, which I had given him. He used some theatrical techniques to keep his audience, especially the jury, attentive. As he was describing the night of the crime, he shouted, "The gun went, 'Bang, bang!' and Tom Hollar lay dead," as already mentioned above.

This got everyone's attention; the courtroom was very quiet, as if the audience collectively held its breath for a moment.

Silverman Added Meaning to Some of the Evidence

Silverman was quoted in *Rocky Mountain News* on June 9, 1994, in an Ann Carnahan article. "Shell casings [were] called 'trophies of killing.'

"Blow after blow was inflicted on Christina Hollar's left eye," Silverman said. He also noted that Davis has a deformed left eye. "The defendant who inflicted this on Christina Hollar was in a rage, in a frenzy of violence toward her left eye. Who in this courtroom is sensitive to his left eye?"

Christina was "sequestered," not allowed to attend the first part of the trial until after she testified, so evidence presented by others wouldn't influence her testimony. One time later, when she came to sit in the audience during a break in the trial, she and Laura got the giggles. Steve Harrington's sister, who was sitting across the aisle, turned around and signaled them to be quiet.

She shouted, "Don't you know, that's *my* brother up there being tried for murder?"

Laura didn't want to cause a scene, but she wanted to say, "Oh yeah? It was MY brother that he killed."

Alibi

An upsetting turn of events came when Delores Mercado, (also known as Dee Baker) gave Steve Harrington an alibi. She said he was with her having sex that entire night of the murder, July 22, 1993 and into the early morning hours of July 23, in the basement of Steve's mother's Montebello home.

Delores Mercado (Dee Baker), age 35, mother of two, lived around the corner from Harrington's mother. She had worked as a dental assistant. As she confidently strode down from the witness stand after her testimony, past the defense table, Steve gave her appreciative nods and looks.

Craig was able to discredit her very convincingly and to place her as a gang member herself with a criminal record. Baker had three social security numbers, none of which was hers, two birth certificates, and four driver's licenses with different names.

Rocky Mountain News' feature "Digest of the News" on June 8, 1994 reported, "Credibility of witness questioned."

"A woman who claims Steven Harrington couldn't have killed Tom Hollar because Harrington was having sex with her that night has a history of lying, witnesses say. For example, Delores Mercado has used at least three social security numbers, which don't belong to her, said Orlando Valdez, a federal agent."

Delores (Baker) Mercado didn't want her children, ages 12 and 14, to appear in court, so she had been sequestering them, not letting them go to school. They were subpoenaed by the Prosecutors, but didn't show up.

Delores Mercado lied about other things besides the alibi. She said she had to work the morning of July 23, 1993, but her boss said this was not true.

Craig had done unusual work above and beyond what he had to do when he went to her home and played basketball with her sons to try to pick up information or clues. This was a risky thing for him to do, but his passion for excellence led him there.

Silverman talked about when Harrington was first questioned by police. "He [Harrington] said he was home with his mother," Silverman said. "Steve Harrington never mentioned Delores Mercado. If he had an alibi, why didn't he tell police right then?"

Where the Gun Came From

As reported by Marilyn Robinson of *The Denver Post* and Lynn Bartels of *Rocky Mountain News* on June 16, 1994: For $125, Rodney Lewis, (also known as Rodney Davis), brother of Shane Davis, sold the revolver used to kill Tom Hollar. The sale was made shortly after the murder in July 1993. Denver Police Department recovered the gun just before the conviction of Shane Davis and Steve Harrington on June 10, 1994.

A phone call came to Detectives Wycoff and Neil from a man who said he was watching the trial on Court TV and that he had just realized that he might have bought the murder weapon. Shell casings from his gun matched those found in Shane's home, and bullets matched those recovered from Tom's body.

The gun buyer had known Shane and Rodney Davis from childhood. He said he asked Rodney whether this revolver was involved in the case with his brother, and Rodney Davis replied, "No."

Rodney Davis was arrested on June 15 and held in Denver City Jail. The charge was accessory to first-degree murder after the fact, a felony.

Rodney Lewis said he was not an acquaintance or friend of Steve Harrington, yet he visited Steve when he was in Denver County Jail.

Police records showed that Rodney used a dozen names, had three different social security numbers, and four different dates of birth on record. Prosecutors were considering perjury charges against him.

Tattoos

On June 3, Sergeant Steve Spenard, gang specialist with the Denver Police Department's Gang Bureau, was allowed by the judge to approach Steve Harrington and Shane Davis in the courtroom. Sgt. Spenard was able to show gang tattoos on their arms and hands to members of the jury and those in the courtroom. Spenard believed that Shane and Steve were the only two Denver members of a branch of the Los Angeles Crips gang.

Shane Davis had *118* tattooed on his hand. Steve Harrington had CRIPS tattooed on his right forearm.

Steve Harrington had a teardrop tattoo under his left eye. The teardrop tattoo originated in the 1990s and is an old prison-gang tattoo. It can be a symbol that the wearer has killed someone or has lost a loved one, or it can relate to the number of years in prison. The teardrop tattoo indicates the wearer has sorrow for some reason.

Harrington Disrupts Trial

In *Denver Post's* May 28 article, "Suspect disrupts slay (sic) trial, Deputy taunted in Hollar case," Howard Pankratz wrote: "As Steven Harrington was being led without handcuffs toward his Denver Courthouse cell yesterday, the muscular, six-foot-tall suspect in Tom Hollar's murder walked directly into a deputy and raised his fist, prompting several deputies to subdue him before he could strike," said Sheriff's Sgt. Phil Deeds.

"The deputies carried the 175-pound leg-shackled Harrington into his cell where he was very upset, threatening, and emotional," Deeds said. "Twice, Denver District Judge Paul Markson sent Defense Attorneys David Miller and Fred Torres to the cell to calm their client. The altercation happened during an afternoon recess—just minutes before Clifford Johnson was to testify against his former friends, Harrington and Davis."

A similar *Rocky Mountain News* article, reported: "After the scuffle, the Judge dismissed the jury for the long weekend, asking them to return at 8:30 A.M. Tuesday." This was Memorial Day weekend, and everyone was ready for a break.

Clifford Johnson

Clifford Johnson, 15, was a younger black male, who liked to hang out at Shane Davis's house. He testified that shortly after the crime, when he phoned Shane to ask if he could come over, Shane Davis told him, "Steve and I did something really bad. You do not want to be around when the heat comes down."

In a *Denver Post* article on Wednesday, June 1, 1994, Howard Pankratz wrote: "Johnson described in detail how the two suspects hung out together last summer, both carrying weapons and proudly displaying them to acquaintances. Johnson said Davis had three revolvers: a .22, a .38, and a .45, and Harrington had a .38-caliber snub-nosed revolver. Johnson said he photographed Harrington in front of Davis's home posing with the silver 0.38…" (This is an extremely disgusting image for me, upsetting me even after all these years have passed.)

"In a search of Davis's home, police seized photos of Harrington and Davis posing outside the house, as well as pictures of Davis at various locations, flashing gang signs."

Defendants Choose Not to Testify

Judge Markson clearly stated that the defendants had the right to testify or to remain silent, and that it would not be held against them if they chose not to testify. He made it clear that it should be their decision.

When asked, "Do you wish to testify?"

Steve Harrington replied, "I remain silent." Shane Davis also declined to testify.

Court TV

The trial was carried on Court TV with very high viewer numbers, allegedly drawing more viewers than Oprah.

In a *Denver Post* article on June 6, 1994, "Nation tunes in local trial, Court TV provides seat at Hollar slay (sic) case," Peter G. Chronis wrote: Court TV is a "cable channel that takes viewers into the courtroom of high-profile cases and provides expert commentators, who dissect lawyers' strategy and critique their effectiveness. ...The court network, launched in July 1991 and now boasting 15 million viewers, has two considerations in picking trials. The first...is getting and holding viewer interest. ...The second is focusing on trials that connect to a larger issue, in this case, urban violence. ...The lawyers on Court TV appear as expert commentators and are more than a little reminiscent of TV sports reporters, who illuminate what's happening on the field."

CHAPTER 55: LIVING THROUGH THE TRIAL

THE TRIAL WAS EXHAUSTING. We were told not to make noise or create scenes. So when lunchtime came the first day, with relief, we all hurried down to the courthouse cafeteria to talk about what had happened.

The San Antonio group was there. They are all talkers and gesturers; everyone was talking at once. The Los Angeles brothers were there, and we made jokes about how the courtroom, if in Hollywood, would have Ionic pillars of Styrofoam, rather than marble.

Most days we walked from the courthouse to a local restaurant for lunch. We went to Dozens, Jamzz, Pints Pub, Cherokee Street Grill, and the Denver Art Museum, where we ate outdoors at umbrella-topped tables. On at least two occasions, a Denver police officer accompanied us as we walked to and from lunch.

We were allowed one and one-half hours for lunch, and we could not be late, for when

Al and Gloria Berger at lunch during the trial

the case resumed, spectators were not allowed into the courtroom.

Defense attorneys made a big issue out of our talkativeness that first day during lunch, saying it could hurt the defendants and bias jurors. We were also told not to talk in the lavatories or make any contact with jurors.

One time I recall being in a lavatory at the same time as a juror. I was careful not to pay any attention to her, and I tried not to look at her. But it was unavoidable; our eyes met in a mirror, and she gave me a big, glowing smile as if to say, "I understand."

Victims' Assistant Carole Malezija had interesting observations that she remembered from the trial. She had a different view of things since she worked as our victims's assistant, an insider and employee of the District Attorney's office. She said that Prosecutor Silverman, when talking about the case during breaks in the trial, referred to Tom and Christina's car as, "The black Hollar Honda," which had a ring to it. She said it was part of her job to keep witnesses from being shown on TV. She also noticed Tom Clinton, a Muslim, moving prayer beads on his tesbih while sitting at the Prosecution table during the trial.

"Trial a "Living Hell" for Christina"

The heading above is the title of an article, which appeared in the *Denver Post* on June 10, 1994. Howard Pankratz wrote: "Both defendants are 6-feet-tall and muscular. The petite Hollar at 5-feet-5, weighs 110 pounds. ...Hollar appeared confident and relaxed as she pointed to Harrington as the man who shot her husband and Davis as the man who smashed her face. But yesterday, she said testifying was by far her most emotional moment in the trial. 'I was very nervous and scared, but I was there to tell the truth,' she said."

During the trial, Sunday, May 22, 1994, we had asked Christina to go along on one of our hikes in the mountains, including a lunch from Market. She declined and said it would be too much for her to do since she knew she had to testify the next day, and she had to focus her energy on that.

340

Continuing from the Pankratz article of June 10, "'I have felt determined not to be intimidated by them. It is clear to me that those are the people who committed the crimes against Tom and me. I know I'm sure because I was there and do recall certain things about it'.... Throughout the trial, Harrington has repeatedly turned to look at Hollar. ... At one point, she said she found herself in a 'big stare-down war' with the man who allegedly gunned down her unarmed husband."

When an expert testified that a hair found on a white tank-top near the abandoned Hollar car very probably came from Harrington, Harrington turned to look at Christina and mouthed the words: "Fuck you!"

"'I felt that was testimony to his guilt,' Christina said."

Reporting on this same incident in *Rocky Mountain News* on June 10, 1994, Ann Carnahan quoted Christina as saying, "That's like saying, 'I did it.' I went into the bathroom and cried."

Ann Carnahan further quoted Christina in the above-cited RMN article, when she was talking about her life with Tom before his murder and her beating. "My life was pretty well-set. We had goals; we talked about vacations we'd take. We wanted to have children and buy a house."

Carnahan also wrote, "About a week after the attack, Hollar heard that many of their friends were holding a vigil outside the couple's apartment at E. 9th Avenue and Corona Street. She asked her brother to drive her there. As they approached the apartment, memories flooded back. She threw up. ...Hollar never again lived at the apartment. She never got back the Honda where she and Tom hugged and kissed that last night. ... For six months after the attack, Hollar lived with her parents. She was bedridden for weeks. She lost twenty pounds. But slowly, she became her old self.... But sometimes she can't help thinking about that horrible night and wondering, 'Why us?'"

"'Tom would have wanted the death penalty,' she said, and so did she. But she said she understands the expense and time requirements of death-penalty cases. She's looking forward to the end of the trial and returning to some semblance of a normal life,' she said. She has thought about what she'll do July 23, the first anniversary of her husband's death. 'I will take time out to reflect on the type of person Tom was,' she said, tears welling. 'He was very fair and very giving. There was a fun air about him. He was a wonderful person.

"'It has been a 'living hell' to sit through the trial,' …but Christina Hollar said she did it for herself and her slain husband, Tom. 'I was determined to do this.'"

"Asked what she would say if she could talk to the defendants, Hollar replied, 'I *wouldn't* talk to them. I'd tell them to fuck off.'

"She said she especially remembers Davis's face as he beat her, and nothing he has done in the courtroom remotely resembles the viciousness he displayed that night. 'Throughout the trial,' she said, 'her memories of Tom have never left her. He was a very giving person and had a great personality. He was charismatic, fun, and a good businessman. I miss his companionship.'"

In Ann Carnahan's *Rocky Mountain News* article of June 19, 1994, "Trial 'hell' for young widow," she reported that Christina said she had severe headaches all through the trial and that she'd go home each day after a long day of testimony and try to unwind. She also reported that Christina said that the night before she testified in court she tossed and turned all night, finally falling asleep for two hours. Carnahan also reported, in regard to spectators remarking about Christina's composure during her testimony, that Christina had replied, 'I'm not into public displays of emotion,' and that underneath her calm appearance, she was terrified, 'But the experience was nothing compared to what she endured July 23.

"'…I don't want it to go on for years and years,' she said. 'But I'd definitely like to see them in prison for the rest of their lives.' Hollar said she did move out of Capitol Hill, but doesn't plan to leave Denver anytime soon. 'To run', she said, 'would have been like fleeing a shadow.'

"Police protection has been provided at her new home and at the Capitol Hill clothing store that she and her husband once operated together. Hollar also said she is not living in fear, doesn't know what her plans for the future are, and that she must take it one day at a time. She said she is grateful for the support of her friends and the community."

During-the-Trial Escapes

Because the long, stressful days of the trial took a toll on us, we found escapes from the tension, away from it all. During breaks in the trial, we took short hikes in the mountains with anyone who wanted to go with us.

Outside the courtroom during a break. Family and friends.

We liked to get lunch from The Market on Larimer to take with us while hiking near Denver on day trips. My favorite place is the Mount Goliath Natural Area on Mount Evans, where lovely wild flowers bloom in July.

We still retell the story about my sister, Cara Milnor, who chose a Crème Brule as part of her lunch to take on a hike. Lunches were all carried in Howard's backpack. The Crème Brule was put in, and by the time we arrived at the

Craig Silverman, Margaret, Steve Simmons and friend having lunch during the trial

Ed, Al and Gloria, Cara at lunch during trial

343

mountain, it had spilled all over the inside of the backpack. Cara is not really a hiker anyhow; she's a wonderful talker.

Sometimes we were caught in storms at Mt. Goliath, which is at about 10,000 feet high. I recall one time squatting under a large rock overhang while the storm dumped its rain, the lightning flashed, and thunder rumbled. Last time there, strong winds stirred up sand and pollen, which irritated my eyes terribly. We went to a more sheltered part of Mt. Goliath (there are two stops there) for a shorter-than-usual hike.

But even when we took short breaks, news of the trial continued and often dominated our thoughts.

Marijuana Found in Davis' Cell

Ann Carnihan reported in an August, 1994 *Rocky Mountain News* article: "Shane Davis was caught with a balloon filled with marijuana late Monday after a deputy spotted him swallowing another balloon at the Denver County Jail. Davis was rushed to Denver General Hospital, where he spent the night under observation in the intensive-care unit. At the hospital, he was labeled an escape risk ... A deputy had noticed Davis swallowing a pink balloon about 7 P.M.. After that, his cell was searched and another balloon was found, believed to be filled with pot ... Davis was accused of tossing a balloon down a hallway Sunday night. The substance in the balloon was tobacco, which is considered contraband at the jail, which is a smoke-free facility."

At the time, I assumed that family or friends visiting the jail had brought the balloons, the tobacco and marijuana. The incident came as no surprise, something that might have been expected from Shane Davis, still defiantly breaking the rules.

CHAPTER 56: THE TRIAL ENDS

AFTER OUR RELAXING and refreshing sojourns to the mountains, we'd get up the next morning to catch the 16th Avenue bus to go back to the courtroom dressed in our conservative courtroom clothes, rather than our hiking shoes.

Closing Statements

In a *Rocky Mountain News* article: "Hollar Murder Case Goes to Jury," Ann Carnahan quoted Craig Silverman in his closing statement: "Christina Hollar talked about this charismatic, caring, intelligent man, who had a good commodity—he was a great husband to his wife." His speech brought tears to the eyes of at least one juror and others in the courtroom.

"...Craig Silverman recapped the incident, including the coin purse containing the torn business card with the phone number on it, the watch with scratches on its face, the Rockies baseball cap with tag still on it—all found in the black Hollar Honda; the white tank top found in the alley, where Christina was found in the Honda, with a hair that matched Harrington's unusual hair type, and blood that matched Christina's blood type; the two reliable eyewitnesses to the shooting: Christina Hollar and 25-year-old Mike Evans, who got an unobstructed view and immediately picked Harrington out of a physical lineup as the triggerman."

Reported by Howard Pankratz in *The Denver Post* on June 10, 1994, "Suspect Pair left trail," he quoted Craig Silverman as he instructed the jury in his closing statement, as saying that "in one unguarded moment four days after Hollar died, Harrington made a statement that left no question that he and Davis were the men behind the attack. On July 27, Harrington turned to Detective Calvin Hemphill at police headquarters and, in reference to Davis, said, 'I bet that motherfucker is trying to lay this off on me!'"

David Miller, one of Harrington's defense attorneys, in his closing statement, as reported by Pankratz, "unleashed a bitter verbal assault on the prosecutors, claiming that they coached their witnesses and are trying to influence the trial by capitalizing on a fear of gangs, which is rampant in Denver."

Miller charged that the prosecution has blamed Davis and Harrington because they are black gang members, not because of any reliable eyewitness identification. Miller added, "More than 1,000 people in Denver dress and talk like Harrington and Davis and spend much of their time copying each other's mannerisms. They want you to make the leap that because Harrington is a gang member, he committed the crime… Why is he singled out from 1,000 or more gang members in Denver? Don't mold Mr. Harrington into something he is not. Mr. Harrington is not defined by his gang attire, his sagging pants. Don't tattoo him as murderer; the evidence doesn't fit."… Pankratz went on to write, "Miller said police unintentionally created a false memory in Christina by showing her Harrington at a physical lineup and earlier in a photo lineup."

In Pankratz's article in *The Denver Post*, he also wrote, "Skeet Johnson, Attorney for Davis, claimed that Davis wasn't present at the Hollar attack, despite the evidence found in the Hollars' car. He said police had found no fingerprints or blood linking Davis to the car."

My Statement in Court

We were told that at the end of the trial our input to the judge was welcome, and that we could say things to the judge, jury, and those present in the courtroom. Christina and I chose to speak in the courtroom at the end of the trial.

Christina gave a presentation in which she called the two defendants, "These social misfits." She presented a message based upon her training in sociology that the two defendants did not fit into the fabric of society. I did not have a copy of her statement to provide more details.

My presentation, addressing the two accused men follows:

"To the Two Defendants:

"I want to tell you something about the young man you shot. I want to tell you about Tom Hollar, even though I'm sure you don't care and would rather not listen. I want to tell you about him so he is not just another privileged white kid to you.

"No one gave Tom a lot of *things* when he was growing up; we were not wealthy. No one gave him a lot, except love, security, and a set of values. He had security of family to support him and discipline him and listen to him. He knew he was loved, and he learned the difference between right and wrong.

"Tom liked and respected people; he knew the value of good friends. He had a childhood where he could be a child, playing and creating and imagining. He still had this child in him when you killed him.

"The advantages Tom had were inside him, and you could not steal them. He didn't need a big silver gun or tattoos to feel important because *he knew* he *was* important. He could just be himself.

"If you had known Tom Hollar earlier in your lives, before you got the way you are now—vicious haters—you would have had fun together. He would have taken you with him down to the river to catch frogs or maybe toads from the window well. He would have taken you bike riding, popping wheelies and racing, to the pit to ride the dirt trails. He would have let you help build forts in the backyard, jump on the bungee cord hung from the tree, and play with dump trucks and army men in the large sand pile we had. Most of all, he would have accepted you, laughed with you, and respected you. These are things you needed badly back then when it would have made a difference for you. He may even have taught you to trust.

"When you killed Tom Hollar, you killed a free spirit—a trusting, fun-loving soul. He was a positive force, upbeat, wherever he was. People were glad when Tom arrived, for that's when the fun began. He had a good life; he was a good person. He was successful both personally and in his work.

"No one gave it to him; he worked hard for what he had. He started from scratch, and with nothing but his own initiative, he built iMi JiMi into something alive, dynamic, and exciting. I am proud of him.

"You may have destroyed his body, but not his spirit or the things he created or the people he touched while he was here. You have not destroyed the many happy memories we have of time with him. We can sit and laugh over these good times and the funny things he said and did. No one can take away these things.

"How sad and embarrassed your poor mothers must be for what you've done, for how you chose to live your lives. Don't blame others; you had choices, and *you* are responsible. I'm sure your mothers love you and would much rather be proud of you right now, instead of ashamed. It wasn't big men who killed my son, but rather empty cowards with a big gun.

"It was quick and cheap and easy for you to shoot Tom, to destroy what you didn't have. It doesn't take much to be a loser, to be negative, to destroy. But it requires a truly strong person to build and create as Tom did, to love and be positive, to be cheerful and happy and to have fun even when things are not going especially well.

"It's too late for you now, Steve and Shane; there's no going back, but perhaps you can tell others not to bother to follow in your footsteps. It's such a waste. Who knows what you might have done with all that energy you used for hatred if you'd done what Tom did: started out, chasing your dreams, doing good. Think about all this as you grow old in your jail cells, and the world forgets all about you."

Case Goes to Jury

In a *Rocky Mountain News* article: "Hollar Murder Case Goes To Jury" on June 9, 1994, Ann Carnahan reported that Craig Silverman confronted and pointed at the defendants, calling them "cowardly, coldblooded killers, who botched the crime by leaving behind an abundance of clues."

Silverman stared into the defendants' eyes as he stood towering above them at the defendants' table with their attorneys. I saw Shane Davis hunch down slightly in his chair while dropping his chin to his chest and meeting Silverman's eyes with upturned gaze that showed much of the lower white part of his eyes, a tiny bit of intimidation. But Steve Harrington met Silverman's gaze and glared back without so much as an extra blink of his big, ugly eyes.

Silverman continued, "It would have been tough for them to make more mistakes than they did. It would be laughable if it were not so serious."

Thus, Silverman presented drama in the courtroom, keeping people's attention by "getting in the faces" of Steve Harrington and Shane Davis when he walked close to them as they sat at the defendants' table with their attorneys. By pointing at them and saying, "Yes, you did this," he was, in fact, helping the jury know that they could also say that the two defendants did this.

Deliberation

On Friday afternoon, June 8, 1994, the jury left to deliberate, to weigh the evidence presented, and to come up with their decision about guilt or innocence of the two defendants. We expected that deliberation might go into the weekend and that a verdict might not be reached this same day, but after about three hours, the jury had done its job and returned to the courtroom.

The jury foreman handed Judge Markson a slip of paper with their unanimous verdict. Judge Markson then read the verdict: after reading each of the eight charges against the two defendants, he read, "Guilty."

Overflow crowds from a packed courtroom had been put into the jury commissioner's auditorium, where they watched the verdict being delivered (read by the Judge) on Court TV.

Verdict June 8, 1994

In case #93CR2915, Shane Davis and Steven Harrington were convicted on eight separate charges.

After the jury returned with the guilty verdict, the Judge read the jury's decision. Each man was found guilty of:

1. Felony first-degree murder
2. Pre-meditated first-degree murder
3. Attempted first-degree murder
4. First-degree assault
5. Second-degree kidnapping
6. Aggravated robbery
7. First-degree aggravated motor vehicle theft
8. Attempted first-degree sexual assault

The two defendants were led out of the courtroom along with their friends and families. Officers chose an alternate route, so their families wouldn't be greeted by the press and have flashbulbs and TV cameras to face.

Christina sat in the courtroom on the edge of her seat and when each "Guilty" verdict was read, she took a sigh of relief that all her efforts paid off.

Steve Harrington turned as he was leaving, raised a fist above him and shouted, "Crips forever."

This caused a pang of sadness. My son was still dead, and nothing that had happened seemed to have made any difference to his murderer. He was as defiant and unremorseful as ever.

In *The Denver Post* on August 9, 1994, Ginny McKibben wrote the article,

"Defiant killers get life" and quoted Harrington as saying, moments before the sentencing, "Fuck you all. Fuck all you cracker-ass mother fuckers; I'm still a Crip."

McKibben went on to write: "Davis blamed his conviction on a society that judged him because of his affiliation with the East Coast Gangster Crips." She quoted Davis as saying, 'We young folks get in gangs. You all found us guilty. Forty years in prison won't bring Thomas Hollar back.' ...

"'You can never make up for what you did, but death in prison is a step in the right direction,' said Christina Hollar."

Verdict Message

Rocky Mountain News in its August 1 column, "News of the Region," reported: "Tom Hollar's killers, sentenced by a judge Monday to spend the rest of their lives in prison, were defiant to the end. Steve Harrington and Shane Davis showed no remorse during the hearing. ...Harrington smirked at Hollar's widow, Christina, and shouted obscenities and racial insults to spectators packed into the courtroom."

Judge Markson read a statement from the jurors asking that they receive no media coverage, that they be allowed privacy to return to their lives. "They've done their duty."

A press conference was held immediately after the trial, with Craig Silverman, Bill Ritter, Christina, her brothers, Ed Hollar, Howard and me. Ed Hollar, Tom's father, said at this time that he was relieved the trial was over and that the guilty verdict was in place. He was still reeling in details of his son's horrible and brutal death, trying to make sense out of how it all could have happened.

Group at McCormick's bar

He said, "Nothing will bring Tom back. I guess that's something we'll learn to live with. But at least we got a conviction."

After the trial, the usual group of Tom's friends—Eric Gonzales, Danica Brown, Kris Baehre, Steve Simmons, Mike Evans—plus Christina, Michael and Gregory Schneider, Laura, Rich, Margaret, Ed, Howard and I gathered at the big round table that used to be in a back alcove at McCormick's Bar at The Oxford Hotel. (It has since been remodeled).

We talked about the case and the verdict, and all of a sudden, I was too tired to be there and just wanted quiet. I needed to reflect on it all. I was deeply sad, not only about losing Tom so tragically, but also about the incredibly awful experiences Christina had endured and about the terrible disruption to her life and the physical challenges she had had to go through. These were still not entirely over. I needed to cry.

I was also upset about the terrible lives of the murderers. I was relieved the ordeal of the trial was over, but there was no joy in its outcome, just sadness.

I went upstairs to our room on the fifth floor of The Oxford Hotel and lay down for a rest. Pretty soon there was a knock at the door. Christina had come to see how I was doing.

The Oxford Hotel sent a complimentary bottle of champagne to help us celebrate the end of the ordeal, the guilty-on-all-counts judgment, and the fact that the perpetrators were off the streets permanently.

The cork on a bottle of Moet and Chandon champagne flew across the room when we popped it. We then poured champagne into two champagne flutes that were on the tray with the bottle of champagne.

Christina and I raised a glass to toast Thomas Edward Hollar, each of us full of private thoughts. Later, when Howard, Laura, and Margaret came back to the room, each clinked glasses in a champagne toast to Tom, and to celebrate the end of the trial and the guilty verdicts.

CHAPTER 57: AFTER THE VERDICT

DISTRICT ATTORNEY RITTER said to Christina, "You're done." She was exceptionally relieved to hear these words. Feelings of freedom from the heavy ordeal now lifted from her brought one of her dazzling smiles.

In the June 11, 1994 The Denver Post article: "Convictions please Hollar friends, kin," Billie Stanton and George Lane quoted Silverman: "We're very pleased to have been able to do justice in this case."

He praised all the witnesses who came forward to testify despite intimidation by the defendants. He continued, "My goal is that these individuals never get out of prison and receive consecutive time on top of the life-sentences so that some governor 40 years from now understands the incredible violence of these crimes....when I saw Christina Hollar at the physical lineup, I was personally upset that anyone could beat a woman to that extent." Silverman also said that he felt relief that the justice system is working.

In the *Denver Post* article, "Harrington, Davis face life terms," Howard Pankratz wrote that Christina was ecstatic with the verdicts and quoted her as saying, "It was an end of a chapter in my life. I am very happy to close that book. I'm tired of seeing them."

She said, "I never doubted that they were guilty. I was sitting on the edge of my seat when the verdicts were read, 'Guilty, Guilty,' over and over again."

Ken Hamblin, Jr., a friend of Tom and Christina's, said, "Now Christina can get on with her life." (Ken, or K-Nee was the disc jockey at Tom and Christina's wedding.)

In another June 11, 1994 *Denver Post* article, Tracy Seipel reported on the verdict. She noted that the convictions of Shane Davis and Steve Harrington sent the message to Denver gangs: "We'll put you away for life."

Seipel also noted that Penny Miller, owner of Pegasus Bar, said the regulars had been watching Court TV for weeks and that there would be partying for Tom Hollar after the verdict came in. Tom would have loved to be there for this party!

At Wax Trax II (on the corner of Washington St. and 13th Avenue), staff watched the trial on Court TV, using a TV mounted on the counter where they worked.

Comments poured in after the verdict: Former owner Jimmy Spinelle of Seven South, an alternative-music bar that Tom and Christina frequented said, "That's what was so special about Tom; there were so many people out there who cared about him. And it looks as if Christina is doing pretty well. I have nothing but admiration for that woman."

Several Denverites commented that they felt a great sense of relief that the two men were not getting away with the crime, that the system really worked, and that the next time someone considered pulling a gun, he had better think twice.

Feelings that Steve and Shane should have received the death penalty were common. Khalif, a Ligurian immigrant who said Tom had helped him when he first came to the United States, said, "They should get the death penalty, but at least they are not going to get parole....I hope other gang members learn from this."

From the Jurors

A June 11, 1994 *Rocky Mountain News* article reported an anonymous juror saying, "It was an easy decision to convict. …It was tense at times, but we all agreed to everything. A card found in the victims' car weighed heavily. It took us to the doorstep of Shane Davis.

"We were cautious and looked at everything. We felt we went through the evidence methodically. There were so many people able to identify Harrington. The hard evidence pointed more to Davis, but more eyewitnesses solidly identified Harrington. They couldn't forget his face. The jurors believed Christina and the eyewitnesses. One juror told Channel 9 that Christina Hollar's testimony was convincing.

"Over the past several weeks we have made a conscious commitment by listening to testimony. It has been a long and, at times, exhausting process. We feel strongly that our role in the process is completed."

Mike Evans

In another June 11, 1994 *Rocky Mountain News* article, Kris Newcomer wrote, "Mike Evans's life changed the night of July 22 when he saw Steve Harrington shoot and kill his friend, Tom Hollar. He was in shock, but the event and his key role as witness consumed his life for the next year. After the verdict, Mike said he is going back to being a student."

Pegasus Bar on Capitol Hill

In a *Rocky Mountain News* article on June 11, 1994, J.R. Moehringer wrote, "Jurors in the Tom Hollar murder trial can expect free beers at Pegasus for a while. Pegasus is the bar-restaurant directly across 13th Avenue from iMi JiMi. Pegasus used to deliver cinnamon buns and coffee to the Hollars every day; Tom Hollar used to like the Bloody Marys at Pegasus; regulars at Pegasus cheered Friday afternoon as a jury convicted Shane Davis and Steve Harrington of killing Tom Hollar last July and kidnapping Christina.

"Pegasus owner, Penny Miller, said, 'It was all our ritual trial-watching that did it. Actually, it was the courage of Christina Hollar: I think it was all due to Christina and her wonderful testimony.'"

The Convicts

After the verdict, Lynn Bartels interviewed Shane Davis and Steve Harrington. In a *Rocky Mountain News* editorial, Bartels wrote: "… each professed to discern racism in his treatment by the courts. If only they'd killed a black man rather than Tom Hollar, Davis seemed to suggest (without ever admitting they killed Hollar at all) they'd be facing much less time in jail."

Harrington wrote a three-page protest poem, partly quoted in the above-mentioned *Rocky Mountain News* editorial on June 16, 1994: "We as a minority race must always see the problems we face. The justice system hates us. They want to lock us all away. They're the strongest-growing gang called the KKK."

Thus the attitude of the attackers was: "Who did this to us?" They saw themselves as victims of racism, rather than responsible for their actions and saying, "What did we do wrong?"

The editorial went on to say that "both killers have absorbed the ideology of victimhood. They see themselves not as individuals captured, tried, and convicted for a horrendous act of violence, but as members of an oppressed group that can't get a fair shake. Even as they profess to abhor the death of Hollar, their resentment against him and his wife is palpable, and their sense of grievance, rather than of personal failure all too obvious."

✦

My take on it is that Shane Davis and Steve Harrington carried terrible rage fueled by frustrations with being "stuck" in their lives without much hope of change or betterment.

They had no means to move up, no job training or experience. I think that Steve was very intelligent and could have been successful, given a better family structure and nurturing, for it seemed that his father and mother cared about him. I think Shane mostly just liked girls, and possibly could have been a family man. Their rage was targeted toward those they blamed for their situation or those that reminded them of their hopeless lot in life as gang members.

Christina

The trial had been very stressful for Christina. She said she found the strength and courage to face the two men who had killed her husband and beat her because she wanted to do it for Tom. She said she didn't even want to be in the same room with the two murderers and have to breathe the same air.

In the June 11, 1994 *Denver Post* article by Howard Pankratz, "Aftermath for victim: quiet tears and relief," he wrote, "Almost exactly an hour after District Judge Paul Markson read the 16 guilty verdicts against Shane Davis and Steven Harrington, Christina Hollar stepped out onto the wide front porch of Denver's City and County Building. Gone were the frenzied hordes of reporters, the mobs of spectators. Around her were a few close friends and family. No one else. The group sat down on the broad expanse of steps….After a few moments, Christina rose to her feet and quietly walked away from the group. She strode to the end of the steps and stopped. It was a particularly private moment. She raised her arms, then clasped her hands behind her head. Standing perfectly still, she slowly lifted her head, until her gaze fell on the windows of the fourth-floor courtroom where her husband's killers had just been convicted.

"'I can't believe how emotional I am,' she said, 'It's all over…It's been one long time for me, making sure the right verdict came down. It was a tremendous amount of stress.' When asked, Christina replied, 'No,' she wouldn't be taking a vacation. She would go to California for two days to her brother's wedding. But to take a vacation would be unfair to her employees…"

Concert, July 23, 1994

Danica Brown organized a concert honoring Tom for July 23, 1994, the one-year anniversary of the murder. She secured the Ogden Theatre on Colfax, a popular venue for such music, a friend made posters, and Danica sold tickets. However, Christina was not in favor of this concert, so Danica cancelled it.

CONCERT

Danica Brown's
planned a concert for Tom
at the Ogden Theatre on Colfax.

One year to the day
Since they blew him away
And beat up Christina so badly.

There'll be five bands
taking the stand
To play their songs for a friend.

Tom will be there
In the crowd somewhere
And he'll love every minute of it.

Chapter 58: Christina Runs iMi JiMi

〜❧〜

T OM'S CREATION, iMi JiMi, where his spirit truly lived, was mobbed with people in the days after July 23, 1993. When Christina had recuperated enough, she went back to running iMi JiMi alone for the next nine years. (Denver Police had asked her not to return to the store for at least two weeks after the murder.)

Christina's iMi JiMi business card

iMi JiMi ad during time Christina ran the store

Rumors on the street were that Denver Police were watching out for staff of iMi JiMi. Actually, I believe that returning to run the store was a healthy, but difficult thing for Christina to do. Under her guidance, the store did extremely well and kept its edge over competing retail stores in Denver.

Christina bravely went to trade shows alone, often in New York or San Diego, to select merchandise for the store. One time in the early days after the *incident*, when she was asked where Tom was, not wanting to explain, she simply said, "Well, I'm going it alone these days." Before very long, everyone associated with iMi JiMi, including all their vendors, was well aware of the whole story.

Clearing the Apartment 1994

Christina wrote that she was slowly going through things from the apartment, clearing it out, stirring up memories, which was emotionally draining for her. She sent boxes of Tom's things to us. He truly was a pack rat and had saved all sorts of little things he liked: marbles, plastic army men, baseball cards, photos, even some small clay figures he'd made as a child and kept.

Tom's Family after the Trial

Tom's father Dr. Edward Hollar returned to Michigan and continued his dental practice until retirement. He and his companion, Juanita Woolworth, liked to square dance, and they traveled all over America in their mobile home. They also had a winter home in southern Texas, where they liked to play cards with friends. He had devoted patients who were also his friends. He passed away in 2012.

Howard worked as a commercial insurance agent and was a partner in Security First Insurance in Flint, Michigan. We both worked late, often meeting for dinner at 8:00. He was at his best with complicated policies such as bank errors and omissions insurance, which allowed him to use his background in accounting and business from University of Michigan. He was forced to retire in 2000 when he was diagnosed with Stage IIb cancer at the base of his tongue, received intense treatment with high-dose intra-lesional cisplatin and IMRT radiation at the University of Iowa Medical Center in Cedar Rapids, Iowa from January until April, 2000.

I returned to my practice of alternative medicine, focusing on environmental and nutritional therapies. I was very busy, having to limit new patients to no more than two per day. I retired in 2006 to resume interests in writing, watercolors, gardening, and cooking.

Quality retirement time has been spent caring for and having fun with our two standard poodles, Jodi and then Taffy. Jodi died in 2007. Taffy, a rescue poodle, arrived in 2006. We always had cats; Atilla and Kalamazoo died in the 1990s, each receiving an honorable burial in our tulip garden, where each has a marker.

Our lives have been full, living quietly in a lovely setting in the woods, surrounded by gardens and large mowed sections where we can walk, and the dogs can run and chase squirrels. We have been able to travel—to Turkey twice, to Italy three times (once for three weeks in Tuscany), to Newfoundland, to Nova Scotia, to British Columbia twice, to Lake O'Hara Lodge in Yoho Park in the Canadian Rockies, to Vienna, Bavaria, and Slovenia, to Costa Rica Cloud Forests, and most recently to the Netherlands. Each year, we spend three weeks on a big, sandy beach on Lake Superior, where it is too cold to swim, but a wonderfully refreshing place to be to watch ships on the lake and fall-tree color changes. We sometimes travel for long weekends to such places as Quebec City, Montreal, Toronto, or New Orleans, where we are always interested in good local cuisine. Howard loves to plan trips, and now he wants to go to Galapagos Islands.

Laura Took Over My Practice

Laura, a Board Certified Internist, left a practice where she worked at the hospital every other weekend to take over my practice with no weekend work. This was a good move for both of us. Laura and her husband, Rich, spend most weekends at their resort property on the Tittabawasee River in northern Michigan. They travel each year to a warm resort area in Costa Rica or Mexico, where Laura attends a conference and Rich plays golf and deep-sea fishes.

Margaret, Neuro-Radiologist, Wife and Mother

Margaret, a neuro-radiologist, married Temel, also a radiologist, in 2004. She had John Thomas in 2006 and Katherine Suzan in 2009. The family lives near Indianapolis, Indiana. John's birthday, July 19, is the reason we stopped having candle vigils. He was born in Dallas where I was staying to help after the delivery, making travel to Denver for a candle vigil on July 23 nearly impossible to do.

Others After the Trial

Craig Silverman became a highly popular host of a radio talk show in Denver on station KHOW. He has commented on cases for Court TV, including the O.J. Simpson trial. He is a partner in Silverman-Olivas Law Firm, where he practices as a very successful defense attorney. Craig and his wife, Trish, live in Denver with their two sons, Benjamin and Samuel.

Pete Flye, when last we saw him in Denver, went to the cemetery with us. Pete had written poems and brought them for us to read. Quite serious about them, he wrote poems that were heartfelt and introspective, some about girls. Pete worked as a lighting specialist at a Denver theatre. Shortly after we saw him, he moved to Los Angeles. He told us he was moving to live with a cousin or a brother. Pete has not replied to my attempts to contact him on Facebook.

Kris Baehre stayed in Denver. For a time, he operated an Internet business from his home. More recently, he was manager of The Armory, a sports bar on Larimer.

In 2014, Kris Baehre had a major motorcycle accident sustaining severe injuries. He said that Craig Silverman had been helping above and beyond what an attorney might do, more in the category of a concerned and helpful friend.

Epilogue: What Happened in the Years After the End of the Trial?

Mitts Lee Married July 2, 1994

A difficult time for us was the day Mitts Lee married, about one year after Tom's murder. We were thinking a lot about how much fun Tom would have had during this event and how much trouble he would have given Mitts. Tom should have been there with us and probably was.

I wrote a poem about this.

A Toast from Tom
July 2, 1994

To Mitts:

Have fun! old chum
and have a good life.

It seems to me
you have a good wife.

I really wish
that I could be there—

your wedding day
I'd like to share.

But since I'm not,
here's this toast from YMOT:

A toast to Mitts
and to Kristie, too
I'll be up here looking out for you.

Live long, love well;
and be of good cheer;
just remember I'll always be near.

And when your time comes
to join me up here
we'll have good times like we used to do.

So, now have a glass
for times that are past,
and for your wonderful new life ahead.

First Candle Vigil, July 23, 1994

We returned to Denver on the anniversary of Tom's death to the spot where he bled to death on the sidewalk under the locust tree on Corona Street. For me this spot is sacred, much more important than the gravesite, since it is the place where Tom ascended with Kris Baehre holding his head.

Bloodstains in the sidewalk, now deep and black, were still visible. Rocks under the tree and a few straggly evergreens were littered with cigarette butts, aluminum-can pull tabs, broken glass, wrappers, chewed gum. We swept and cleaned the area.

Typical candle vigil showing dark spot on sidewalk, rocks cleaned of debris, flowers.

At dusk, we lit the candles, which were lovely among the rocks strewn with flowers. A fitting tribute: beauty where there had been ugliness and violence at the scene of Tom's murder. Rain showers earlier in the day had stopped, but at the time we assembled, a lovely rainbow appeared overhead. This was captured on Channel 4 TV News. Tom loved rainbows, and we talked of Tom's rainbow sign.

Candle Vigil July 23, 1995

On July 23, 1995—two years after Tom's murder, Howard and I cleaned the rocks near where Tom died, removing debris. We filled trash bags, which we hauled away and dumped in a trash bin. It was hot and sunny. We borrowed a broom and dustpan from Mary and Emily. Howard got a hose nozzle so we could wash the sidewalk and stones under the locust tree using water from the Shana Marie. We bought candles, flowers and chalk from King Soopers.

Someone had poured a dark substance over the area where Tom's blood had been, so now that spot on the sidewalk is permanently dark. Memory of that dark-red spot of Tom's blood on the sidewalk along Corona is one that still brings pain and tears to my eyes when I think of Tom's agonal death. Eric Baehre had helped early in the day by piling up rocks and sticking flowers and candles in and around them. He showed up with his blond, blue-eyed good looks in a sporty blue Audi, pulling into the parking lot beside where we were working on the rocks.

We missed connections with Christina to go to the cemetery together. When we left 9th and Corona and went to the grave, flowers and three candles were there, one obviously was Christina's. It was too windy to light them. Christina could not attend candle vigils since it was too upsetting for her to return to the scene of Tom's murder and her abduction and beating. We were hot and sweaty by the time we'd laid flowers on Tom's grave, so we returned to our hotel room to shower before dinner.

Nedra and Eric Baehre afternoon before candle vigil July 23, 1995

After dinner at McCormick's, as we returned to 9th and Corona, we saw a large, double rainbow sweeping over Denver. Could this be a Tom Rainbow Sign again?

Brian Maass and Chanel 4 cameramen were there, but they backed away when we arrived. They were being very respectful. Suzanne and Noel Waechter, Don and Nancy Dhonau were there.

We chatted with Noel and Suzanne Waechter about Karl and changes he'd experienced since Tom's murder. Others at the candle vigil were: Craig Silverman, Dan Dhonau, Danica Brown, Eric Baehre, and another man from Capitol Hill who introduced himself, but whose name I have forgotten. We started putting out flowers and lighting candles. Danica Darling was in Alaska, and Kris Baehre and Mike Evans were in Germany. A shy young man laid a rose on the rocks and kept walking. A man from Mayor Webb's office came and helped light candles.

A woman who works at Racine's with Danica Darling came with flowers, and we kept relighting candles with her cigarette lighter. A King Soopers security guard was on duty from 4 P.M. to 12:00 A.M. He came and chatted. He showed us how to use a child-proof, disposable lighter with one hand to relight candles that had blown out.

Christina visiting Tom's grave

Wind settled; the sky grew dark; candles took on a soft glow. We all stood around the candles and flowers remembering Tom and thinking about what had happened. We wrote chalk messages on the asphalt around the hearse, still parked in the same parking space as July 23, 1993.

✦

On July 23, 1995, I wrote in my journal, "Even though it's been two years, it still hurts. I am Tom's mother. I was there when he was born, and I want to be as close to his death as possible. I raised Tom to be honest, active and creative, and to experience the world and not be passive. I guess you could say that Tom did that. He walked to his own drummer and never did conform. We are still adjusting to our loss of Tom, a most positive influence in our lives. Nothing in your life prepares you for an event like the brutal, coldblooded murder of your son. Everyone has losses—grief of some kind, and in each there is also the gift of healing."

At iMi JiMi, Christina and Sissily, an employee, had decorated the window with a chartreuse overstuffed chair for the mannequins to sit in and on, with a chandelier overhead with all colors of bulbs. Eric had painted one of the counters, as well as arms, legs, and hands of mannequins with scrolls and flowers. Bunches of plastic grapes were hanging all over. The store was full of people, with a full staff on duty. Chris looked good. Her hair was pulled back, and she was barefooted. I had called Gloria and Al, who could not come to the candle vigil—still too difficult. Gloria said that Christina cries every time she talks about July 23, 1993.

Silverman asked me to do an interview about how prosecutors help victims, one that Christina refused to do. Discussing this with Christina later, she said she would never do it. She doesn't want to be dragged through events of the murder and trial again.

After this day, we went back to The Oxford Hotel to pack. I was very tired, but thought Tom's evening was a very nice, respectful tribute.

1996 Vigil

The tradition continued, and we held a candle vigil in Tom's memory July 23, 1996. In a letter I wrote to Christina the next day, "I'm sorry we missed you. It would have been nice to spend some time together on a very difficult day for both of us. Craig looked good at the vigil. Thinking I'd see you again, I brought some remedies for your cat, Annie, so I'll send them. I'm glad Speedboat and Spider (cats) are well. Our vigil was very nice. Quite a few people from the neighborhood came.

One was at Denver General when you were there. Earlier, we went to the grave, covered it with flowers, and I put my son to bed as I used to do so long ago. At the vigil, it was raining and too windy to light a candle. I like to see beauty where there was pain and violence and to know that Tom's soul is at rest and probably with us more than we know. It was good we were able to honor and remember Tom and grieve our loss.

Also, we grieved the loss of the happiness you two had and your hopes and dreams for the future. It was not just the loss of Tom, but all that you two had together that made us sad. He would want you to do what you are doing: making iMi jiMi a smashing success, a source of income and security for you, and to go on with your life, as the medium said that he said, "Find someone wonderful and have a good life."

Candles For Tom

Our small clusters of candles
light the grey of the night
a small energy spot
sent out to Tom.
He'll see our candles'
glow sent to him
from this place
so special
to me now:
9th and Corona
'neath a locust tree,
dark stain
on the sidewalk.
The place he parked
his black Honda;
tracing his last steps
before he died.
Honoring my son—
lighting candles in the night.
Tom, receiving our thoughts
and our love.

High Points

Every year, a handful of people, usually including Noel and Suzanne Waechter, Carole Malezija, Nancy and Don Dhonau, Danica Brown, and Craig Silverman loyally came to the candle vigil, as well as some from the Capitol Hill neighborhood on several occasions. Not sad affairs, the vigils were a way to keep Tom's memory alive, to help put events into perspective.

One year, Craig Silverman brought his two sons, Ben and Sam to the candle vigil. They played with a ball in the parking lot, something very appropriate that Tom would have liked—children playing.

Every year, signs appeared on the front door of iMi JiMi:

Christina could not return to the scene at 9th and Corona, but in 1999 on July 23, she and Gloria did go to Our Savior's Lutheran Church at 915 E. 9th Avenue, where once again, Reverend Don Dhonau led us in a lovely service for victims of violence. Laura Nissen, CSW, read *Growth and Healing*, which she had written; Chalise Jones and Adrian Baker sang *How Great Thou Art*.

Reverend Dhonau's words from this service were beautiful:

"God of many names and many peoples, your nature is to love, and you put us in this world to learn that love and share it with one another.

"From the midst of this world we call, O God, with voices made weak by sadness, voices made bold by anger, voices overwhelmed by the violence we have learned to visit upon each other, and the violence which has been visited upon those we love.

Reverand Don Dhonau talking to Gloria and Christina at Our Savior's Lutheran Church, July 23, 1999.

"Christ, our brother, guide and friend, you are the house in which we live, the house in which we look to share peace. You are the house in which we are called to act justly and honor all, both living and dead. We would live in you, and you in us, so that hope wouldn't be a stranger, and the end of violence we know would not be an empty dream.

"Spirit of Holiness, whose heart holds all who have gone before us, all whom we have loved and tonight are cared for, let love and memory and honor transform our every breath and action. Renew us by the power, which is born in love, and by the hope, which survives in truth, and by the vision, which is nurtured by caring. Strengthen us that we not falter in our steps toward righteousness, and lead us to perseverance in our work for justice.

"For the freedom to overcome our pain, our anger and our loneliness, and our witness for healing that begins in us, we are grateful.

"For courage to face our fear of evil and our confidence in choosing what is good, we are grateful. Keep us faithful to our living, so that we not forget those who have gone before us through indifference and discredit their integrity by our cynicism and despair."

At the candle vigil under the locust tree after the church service, I handed out the following benediction, which I read:

Go Now In Peace

Go now in peace
Light your candle
Find your way.

See the beauty
in simple things
Healing starts here
deep inside.

Dancing sunlight
Chirping birds
Laughing voices
Loving hearts

Move on from anger
Give up the blame
You've been wounded
You'll laugh again.

What this life was
and meant to you
becomes a crystal
in your heart.

Go now in peace
Light your candle
Find your way.

Candle Vigil For Capitol Hill, 1997

In 1997, a grisly murder occurred in Capitol Hill in June, one month before our usual candle vigil, and morale was down. A young woman, Jamie Benedict, had been raped and murdered in her Capitol Hill apartment by a serial rapist. I felt moved to broaden the scope of our little service to make it a healing service for Capitol Hill. Several people participated by reading parts of the service. We left invitations to attend the candle vigil early in the day on the rocks under the locust tree, and after it was over, we left copies of the healing prayers and poems on the rocks for residents to pick up.

Prayer for Capitol Hill 1997

Dear neighbors in Capitol Hill and people of the city of Denver,

May you come together now in this place to bring about healing of your hearts, your homes, your neighborhood.

May the beautiful blue Colorado skies soak deeply into your hearts to bring you beauty and healing.

May the warm light of the sun reach your souls to energize, cheer, and give you hope.

May the warm rains wash away old hurt, anger, and distrust to make a new space for caring, loving, creativity and happiness in this place.

May the breezes blow away the ugliness and fears to let you find peace in Capitol Hill.

May you know your neighbors, for this brings trust, security, and community, which we all need.

May the beauty of the place you are in: the majestic mountains, trees, flowers, and sounds of birds be part of you as it restores you.

Sweep old clutter and worries from your homes, and instead put new plants, rocks, art, beauty to become part of you.

Hear good music, wind chimes, soothing sounds to restore balance and serenity so you can be in touch with your souls.

We pray to God to reach this place
in all its corners of life
to clear dust and debris of the past
to make it a good and safe place to live
as it used to be.

Creative.Uplifting.
Full of happy spirit.
Amen.

Candle Vigil 1999 at 9th and Corona under the locust tree

Danica Brown (left) and Carole Malezija at Candle Vigil 1999

Each year for twelve years we went back to the place to have a candle vigil and to remember Tom on July 23. Each time we turned something ugly, where evil had been, into something solemn and beautiful, replacing the negative energy of violence with a calm and loving energy in tribute to Tom's memory.

More Aftermath of the Trial

Lanica Jones Accused of Perjury August 31, 1994

In an August 31, 1994, *Denver Post* article entitled, "Hollar Case Lying Count Filed," Howard Pankratz reported: "Lanica Jones, 20, girlfriend of convicted murderer Shane Davis, was accused of two counts of first-degree perjury.

The charges stemmed from her May 26 testimony before the jury considering murder charges against Davis and Steven Harrington. She denied then that she had ever identified a Casio watch and a small black-and-brown coin purse as belonging to Davis. The items had been found in Tom and Christina's hijacked car.

"That testimony contradicted a video-taped statement she'd made to Denver police Detectives Joe DeMott and Calvin Hemphill months before in which she positively identified the items as belonging to Davis," Pankratz reported.

Dee Baker Admits Perjury September 2, 1994

Howard Pankratz's article "Hollar Case Witness Admits Perjury," appeared on Friday, September 2, 1994. He said, "The Denver woman who provided one of Tom Hollar's killers with an alibi admitted yesterday that she lied to a Denver jury. ...Denver District Judge Jeff Bayless refused to lower the 35-year-old Baker's bond from $50,000, saying there is risk she might flee if released from jail."

Sentencing of Dee Baker, also known as Delores Mercado, was set for October 21.

Baker had entered into a plea bargain with Craig Silverman whereby she agreed to plead guilty in exchange for Silverman's dropping other charges.

The article quoted Silverman as saying he would ask for "an extremely serious prison sentence since had the jury believed Baker, Harrington would have walked out of court a free man....As Baker entered her pleas, her sobs often overtook her speech."

November 1994

We visited Margaret in Grand Rapids, Michigan, where she was still serving a year of internship at the hospital. Howard installed a green neon MSU sign, which Tom had made, in her apartment kitchen on an open shelf, where the sign could be seen from the living room. After Tom's murder she renamed her two black-and-white longhaired cats: Boulder and Springs, names of Colorado cities.

When we left for dinner at a favorite Italian restaurant, we noticed frozen rainbows on the edges of several clouds, something I hadn't seen before. It was a glowing iridescent array of pastel colors. We called it Tom's Rainbow Sign. Surely he'd watched as we'd placed his neon sign in Margaret's apartment. This made me smile.

Rodney Davis Sentenced

On December 29, 1994, *The Denver Post* article, "Hollar Case Sentencing Gets Vitriolic," by Mark Eddy, stated, "Rodney Davis, whose sister spat insults at Christina Hollar, the Prosecutor and Judge, was sentenced yesterday to six years in prison for lying in court during his brother's trial for murdering Hollar's husband....Hollar calmly endured the hateful shouts from Jacqueline Reece, Shane Davis's sister."

Reece shouted, "I hope you can sleep at night, Christina! I hope you can sleep at night!" as Christina left the courthouse after the sentencing. Christina handled the rude and unfair racially motivated outburst with dignity, an example to others.

Mark Eddy's article continued, "Rodney Davis, 28, has admitted he lied in order to protect his brother Shane and Harrington during their murder trial in June. The Hollar case made national news as the brutality of the crime became known."

My Letter To Judge Bayless March 17, 1995 Lanica Jones Case

We were told that our feelings about this case could be expressed in letters to the Judge. I wrote the following:

"Lanica Jones is a young girl, who has made stupid mistakes in her life. She deserves another chance, but she also deserves to pay for her illegal actions that harmed others. Nothing can make up for the pain and sadness caused by Lanica's actions in lying to try to protect Shane Davis.

As we sat there in court, we could not believe that she and others could dismiss the horribly brutal murder of my only son, Tom Hollar, and barbaric beating of Christina at the hands of Shane Davis and Steve Harrington. It was as if this cruelty were OK or even admired, as if the only important thing was to get away with it.

Lanica was flaunting her lies in the face of the court with no sense of right or wrong. I don't know if she can ever learn about such things.

If there is a program to try to rehabilitate someone like Lanica, who probably didn't know any better, then I would support that. Lanica needs to know what other choices she has in life, other than hanging out with murderers and gang members, who would only take advantage of her. Lanica needs to learn that she doesn't have to depend on a man for support or for a life, that she can take care of herself.

I would support some type of job training after a jail sentence. I do not know her well enough to know if she is a candidate for this."

Sentencing of Lanica Jones

When Lanica Jones was sentenced to five years in prison and three years probation on April 7, 1995, she was 21-years old and pregnant. Hers was the fifth conviction related to Tom's murder and Christina's beating. Steve Harrington and Shane Davis both received life sentences without possibility of parole for first-degree murder convictions. Delores Mercado, who willingly gave false alibi to try to protect Steve Harrington, and Rodney Davis, Shane Davis's older brother, were sentenced to spend six years in prison after being convicted of lying to the court, perjury.

Lanica Jones's sentence marked the end of Denver District Court proceedings related to Tom's murder and Christina's brutal beating.

In a letter dated April 10, 1995 Craig Silverman noted that, "Last Friday, April 7, 1995, Lanica Jones was sentenced to five years in prison for her perjury at the trial of People v. Davis and Harrington....Hopefully, this will be the final chapter in the trial court litigation of this tragic situation. ...The public will finance an appeal of People v. Davis and Harrington, which should be resolved (hopefully in our favor) in approximately a year."

This seemed to me like a terrific waste of taxpayers' money. Viewed from the side of the convicted murderers, it might seem fair to offer them this chance.

Good Friday, April 15, 1995

An article in *The Denver Post* on April 15, 1995, "Good Friday March Remembers Victims Of Violence," by Virginia Culver stated, "To Christians, Good Friday is a day of violent death. Yesterday, Denver Christians also remembered modern violent deaths—those who have died by gunfire.

"A group of Christians prayed and sang songs at nine metro area sites where people have been shot. ...The Reverend Alison Sawtell said, 'Jesus would, I think, rather we would do more than just walk, more than share the survivor's suffering. I think he would want us to help prevent future violence. There's no grace or glory in violence.' One sign the group carried showed a crucified Jesus with a handgun across his body.

"The unique event was sponsored by Washington Park United Church of Christ and included members of other congregations as well....The people prayed in the King Soopers parking lot in Capitol Hill."

I was pleased to hear of their efforts and that they prayed at the site of Tom's death. He was not forgotten.

Tom's Birthday, November 1995

I returned to Denver for Tom's birthday on November 6. He would have been 32-years-old.

I had had dinner with Tom and Chris on his 30th birthday, his last, while I was in Colorado Springs attending a medical conference and staying at the Broadmoor. Tom, Chris, and I ate in their formal dining room on his 30th birthday. I gave Tom a wool Colorado quilt with applique and embroidery of places of note in the state, such as Aspen, Vail, and Steamboat Springs ski resorts, Pike's Peak.

During this 1995 visit on November 6, Christina and I had dinner at Bella. She picked me up in the silver Mitsubishi pickup truck outside McCormick's bar on Wazee Street. I saw Craig Silverman and his brother dining at Mc-Cormick's that night, and they were planning to attend a memorial service for Yitzhak Rabin, Prime Minister of Israel, who had been murdered on November 5, after a peace rally. Rabin was an Israeli politician, statesman and general, who had been elected for two terms of office.

During dinner, Chris told me that her mother's family came from Tuscany. Knowing my interest in cooking, Chris told me that Gloria had a good recipe for ciappino made with chicken, shrimp, and ham which had come from New Orleans.

Christina said she can't go through any more hurt like she's been through. She said that she and Tom were very happy, never fought. Tom was loving and kind, and they had fun doing projects where they worked side-by-side till the wee hours of the morning sometimes, such as decorating windows at iMi JiMi. She said he liked money and was making plenty. They had been looking at houses and planning to buy one in the E. 6th Avenue area, near where she had been then living on Fairfax.

Early in 1996

A letter from Christina said, "I just remodeled at the store. It turned out OK. I wanted to send you the newest hats and iMi JiMi sunglasses. I'll talk to you soon." Christina had a way of understating her successes. She sent black-and-white iMi JiMi baseball caps and black Wayfarer sunglasses.

A note from Don Dhonau written on a receipt from 2609 Lawrence Street Home of Neighborly Service in January 1996, said, "Words will never be adequate to express what we all feel about Tom's life and untimely death. The events of July changed us all forever, in very different ways, but forever. I thank you for allowing me to be with you and your family. While we'll never understand Tom's senseless death, I will always thank God for Tom's life and friendship and his spirit—a rare gift to many of us."

I loved Don Dhonau's words here!

In a letter from Craig Silverman dated May 24, to the Family of Tom Hollar, he wrote, "I just got back from a pleasant visit with Christina, where we had a healthy repast of onion rings, French fries and a Bud Light. (Sorry, Nedra)"

iMi JiMi Anniversary Party
Saturday, August 17, 1996

CHRISTINA WROTE that the 10th Anniversary of iMi JiMi party held at City Spirit Café on Blake Street "turned out OK. It was a lot of fun. There were about 300-400 people, and they all looked smashing." This was her usual understatement of her own successful party. Her printed invitation read, "Champagne toast at 10:00 P.M.; Smashing attire requested." The party was held from 9:00 until midnight at the café, but after that, a few friends and family gathered at Christina's home on Cook St., where more than five people were staying. Photos I have from this party showed both Margaret and Greg Schneider wearing a pink Afro wig. Christina also wrote that things at the store were going well.

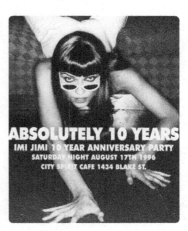

Invitation to iMi JiMi's 10 year anniversary party.

In another letter from Christina before the iMi JiMi party, she wrote, "I've been getting ready for the party. I'm glad Margaret is able to come out. While everyone is in town we will also be celebrating my mom's 60th birthday."

iMi JiMi Sold,
2002

IN 2002, AFTER having successfully managed the store for nine years
after Tom's death, Christina sold iMi JiMi. She'd not only carried on the
spirit and attitude of iMi JiMi, she'd created ads and bought merchandise
that allowed iMi JiMi to be even more successful.

New owner, Stephanie Fast said, "You wouldn't believe how many people
still come in and want to talk about Tom and what had happened. People are
constantly coming in with memories of this place."

In 2009 *Westword Newspaper* referred to iMi JiMi as: "That 13th Avenue
Institution," in an article that stated: "Clothes encounters: That 13th Avenue
institution, iMi JiMi, is getting a makeover, with new owners and a new
look."

But in fact, the driving force behind iMi JiMi, which was Tom and Christina's vibes, then Christina's alone, was intangible; could not be sold.

The new manager, Jodi Ulrich, was quoted in *Westword*, "We're changing
to be a little more price-friendly for the neighborhood. We're doing more
street-friendly, as well as some of the higher-end stuff. We're still going to
carry Free People and some of the other lines, but we're also bringing in some
lower-priced points like Juicy."

Jodi managed iMi JiMi for Stephanie Fast, who sold the store to Kendra DeHaven, owner of Thrifty Stick and Thrifty Stick II, a fitting transfer considering the original iMi JiMi sold skate boards.

The *Westword* article reported, "Fast had taken the reins from Christina Hollar, who ran the store for nine years after her husband, Tom, was murdered in 1993 near the King Soopers at 9th Avenue and Corona Street." Remarried, with a child, she moved to another city where she works in retail.

Jodi Ulrich was quoted by *Westword* as saying, "The store will not be significantly different. We're keeping the same name and the history."

Free On Own Recognizance,
February 28, 1997

ROD MITCHELL, media-relations representative for a group named Strike Back! contacted me. He told me that the Colorado legislature was considering a bill which would allow accused criminals who are a risk   to society to go free on their own recognizance. He wanted me to speak to the Legislature.

Steve Harrington and Shane Davis had been charged with three cases of felony car theft and were free on their own recognizance at the time they murdered Tom and beat Christina. They had repeatedly failed to appear for court dates set for them. Had the current system worked, they would have been in jail the night of July 23, 1993, and Tom would be alive; Christina would not have had to endure the pain, stress, sorrow of his death and her injuries.

I was told that the two gang-members had a long record in Los Angeles and were out to show Denver what real Los Angeles brutality and viciousness can be. Tom was killed according to gang standards, having been shot in the chest, then again after he fell to the ground. Gang members admire murder and rape.

I said, "Who are you kidding when you believe people like Steve Harrington and Shane Davis after they have repeatedly lied and broken all rules of human decency?

"Purely economic motivations cannot measure against the cost of precious human life. Since jails are full, you might consider swifter use and implementation of the death penalty. These people do not deserve to live, let alone be allowed to go free to go out and do it again. These people do not understand words or a slap on the wrist; they laugh at the system. You cannot, in good conscience, allow vicious criminals, persons with no social responsibility, no basis for living decent lives, no training in right and wrong, no nurturing, no hope for redemption, to go free! It is unthinkable."

As it happened, Laura and I were on our way home from attending a medical conference in Las Vegas, so we stopped in Denver to appear before the Legislature. We wouldn't have made this trip separately had we not already been planning to be in Denver at that time.

I told the Legislature that my family and I were still grieving; our lives would never be the same; I was, in fact, in Denver to put flowers on my son's grave. Denver was his home. He was happy here with his wife of one year, where he had had a successful business and a good life, many friends. He is buried in Denver, rather than in Michigan because this is where he was with his life. He and Christina had been looking at houses, planned to buy one and to start a family. Tom said he wanted ten kids. We were feeling very good about Tom's life and the direction it was taking, the kind of person he was—a good person, helping others, spreading cheer, good will, and joy.

We come back often to visit the grave, to leave flowers or something from home like pine cones from the many conifers in our yard, and as often as possible, we hold a candle vigil at the scene of his death on July 23. The stress, pain, and sadness Christina had gone through were unimaginable. She had to start her life all over again, despite serious injuries and emotional trauma from the brutal beating at the hands of the violent offenders allowed back out on the streets by the current system.

The system allowed for secured pre-trial release of accused defendants, whom courts allow to be released on bail. Secured release is handled by bail agents, who require cash or property as payment on the bail. A defendant may be released once a bail is set and posted or paid. This is a temporary pass from jail.

The bail agent is accountable for the released defendant, and both the defendant and his family have a financial interest in seeing that he appears for his court date. Bail agents may check a defendant's background and gather information before issuing a bail bond.

General guidelines for release from jail without paying for bail include that the Defendant must:

- Not be able to afford to post bail
- Be a U.S. citizen with a local, established residence
- Be a first-time offender, charged in a non-violent, victimless crime, such as white-collar crime or simple misdemeanor
- Have NO prior history of failure to appear for scheduled court dates

Clearly Shane Davis and Steve Harrington didn't meet requirements for being allowed back on the streets of Denver without posting bail. Had the system worked, my son wouldn't have been killed at their hands, and Christina wouldn't have been beaten.

It seems that the over-burdened courts might set a bail, then another court might reduce it, and then another abandon it altogether, and then a judge might allow defendants to go free on their own recognizance. All this may be done to clear the court dockets of heavy caseloads, but it is not the best answer for citizens.

Shane Davis was charged with two car thefts in a three-month period, not enough to keep him off the streets. After a charge of aggravated motor-vehicle theft, bond was set at $10,000, which was reduced to $2,500 by another court, and then reduced to personal recognizance with a promise to appear for the court date. But Shane Davis didn't show up, so courts sent out a bench warrant for his arrest. If only the police had been able to pick him up on that warrant before he had the opportunity to attack Tom and Christina—

Appellate Court Denied Appeals, May 1997

Steven Harrington had filed an appeal to overturn the judgment of conviction for first-degree murder citing errors and racial discrimination in jury selection. The Appellate Court affirmed the conviction and found no errors in jury selection. Likewise, Shane Davis appealed the judgment of his conviction and the Appellate Court affirmed it.

Canyon Ranch Clairvoyant, 1998 — WHY?

I was fortunate to be able to stay at Canyon Ranch in Tucson, where I had a session with a clairvoyant, who helped me with answers to my question, "Why?"

She said, "His life was about his childhood and about having fun. He was never intended to become an old man." This seemed to be the way it was, providing me with comfort of sorts.

In fact, his childhood never ended: Tom never did stop playing. This did not keep him from handling serious issues responsibly, and working hard to run a successful business. He made Denver his new back yard, gathering people around him the same way he did while growing up. He had a happy marriage and plans for having a family.

One time Tom took us over the railroad tracks to an area behind Union Station where he had hung a big, black bungee cord over structures for a billboard, a place where he could jump up and down on the cord as he used to do under the box elder tree at his home in Michigan.

Another time, he took us to a bar in this same area on a Saturday afternoon.

Others knew him, coming to our table to chat with him. He told us that soon that bar would become popular, a place to be seen. He enjoyed showing off for us that he was known around town and was a leader among peers.

Another time, we drove around LoDo in the black Honda. Tom would pull up to the curb, not properly parking, jump out of the car, run over to put iMi JiMi stickers on light posts, bike racks or sign posts. I recall him doing this at the corner of Wynkoop and 18th Street where the Wynkoop Brew Pub is located. He stuck iMi JiMi stickers on bike racks there. We liked to have lunch or dinner at Wynkoop Brew Pub since it is walking distance from The Oxford Hotel, and during the trial, groups of extended family sometimes had dinner there.

Dangerous Experiences

The clairvoyant at Canyon Ranch also said, "Tom could have died a few years earlier, but he stayed on for some reason without having a vision of himself later on, no plans for a career, since he wasn't going to be here." I believe that Tom lived beyond the time he could have died to have this final, special upward spiral of his karma, this Camelot time with Christina.

An earlier death could have come when he was 22 working at the ranch and cut a deep gash in his left leg just above the knee, bleeding into his boot, although this is unlikely.

Another death could have happened while playing "Chicken" with his used black Honda at Western Michigan University with Mitts in the passenger seat. He was very fortunate that he'd totaled his car while it was traveling at slow speeds inside the city of Kalamazoo, rather than outside on country roads where he'd raced at fast and dangerous speeds.

Another death could have happened when he, Mitts, and Jeff traveled from Wyoming to go skiing in Colorado, and then traveled south through New Mexico to Texas where the three, crowded into the single seat in his black Dodge truck, survived an incident where Tom may have fallen asleep at the wheel, and hit a curb causing the truck to be momentarily airborne before landing without incident on the same side of the busy road. His truck could easily have veered into oncoming traffic.

September 12, 2002 Colorado Victim Services

A letter from Colorado's Office of Attorney General informed us that Steve Harrington had made an appeal requesting review by another court. He was appealing the denial of his motion for post-conviction relief. The letter was signed by Judy Page, Victim Services Coordinator. A booklet was included, which explained the rights of victims of violent crime in Colorado to be informed, present, and heard, to be treated with fairness, respect, and dignity. Colorado was striving to provide "the finest crime-victim services possible." In our case, we were treated well and kept informed before, during and for years after the trial.

FORGIVENESS

ABOUT THIS TIME, I had a dream, which I remember quite well. In the dream, Steve Harrington with his bushy Jeri-curled hair was sitting on a golden throne a few steps up from where I was.

I walked over to the throne and up the steps, and raised my arms over his head in a gesture to forgive him. I had been deeply saddened by his terrible life.

Ten Years

ON JULY 23, 2003, the tenth anniversary of Tom's murder and Christina's beating, we gathered together with those closest to the event at the home of Nancy and Don Dhonau. They hosted a luncheon, while I distributed most of the remaining iMi JiMi *End the Violence* T-shirts and sweatshirts I still had. The sizes were all large or extra-large, an idea that came from Tom. He figured that most people could wear a large, even if it was a little baggy, and ordering fewer sizes made it easier.

On July 23, 2003, many of Tom and Christina's contemporaries came to sit and chat, and Christina came with her baby daughter and husband. Craig Silverman was able to attend as well.

We held a candle vigil that evening, as we had done every year so far, at the spot where Tom's blood stained the sidewalk. *Rocky Mountain News* carried an article by John C. Ensslin on July 24, 2003, entitled, "Decade of Grief, Lifetime of Love." Ensslin wrote: "They arrived early in the day, an older couple from Michigan, who had come to sweep a section of the sidewalk of the 900 block of Corona Street and splash water over it in the middle of a summer afternoon.

"Later, around dusk, few people coming and going from the nearby King Soopers paid much attention as the couple, now joined by family and friends, started lighting candles. They were holding a vigil on the spot where 10 years ago Wednesday night, on July 23, 1993, two men shot and killed Tom Hollar and attacked his wife, Christina." Ensslin went on to describe the attack and the summer of violence.

Twenty Years

DESPITE COLORADO GOVERNOR Romer's attempts to control gang violence in Denver in 1993, gang members continued to murder people in Denver.

Reported in Fred Brown's *Denver Post* article "Gang Fear Lurks in Shadows" posted July 15, 2007: On January 1, 2007, a drive-by shooting killed Bronco's cornerback Darrent Williams after he'd left a New Year's party. Members of the Tre Tre Crips, an east Denver street gang, were implicated in the crime.

In 2003, Denver Police had estimated there were 14,000 gang members in 220 gangs in Denver.

On July 23, 2013, a gathering assembled at The Oxford Hotel to remember the events of July 23, 1993. Participants included Prosecutors Craig Silverman and Tom Clinton, Denver Police Officers Vince Lombardi and Scott Hartvigson, Police Detectives Dan Wycoff, Dave Neil, and John Priest, Detective Robert Gomez from the Prosecutor's Office, Carole Malezija, our Victim's Assistant, Noel and Suzanne Waechter, Don and Nancy Dhonau, Christina, her husband, and her two friends, Minica and Nicole (last names unavailable) Kris Baehre, Steve Simmons, Howard and me.

When speaking with Detectives Wycoff and Neil, I commented that one of my patients is a prison counselor, who told me that many convicted criminals change in prison, express remorse, and adopt redeeming social values which could allow re-entry into society.

One of the two detectives replied, "Not these two."

Danica Brown was unable to attend. She had steadily improved her situation in life by going back to school. She worked for a long time with Native Americans in the Denver area as a social worker and counselor. As of July 2015, she had completed one year toward her Ph.D. in social work in Oregon. We have stayed in touch with Danica, who took time to come to our candle vigils most years until she moved to Portland in 2012.

Danica Brown wrote from Oregon, "It is really hard to believe that it has been 20 years. In some ways it seems like a lifetime ago; in other ways it seems like just yesterday. I can still close my eyes and see Tom's face …that night." She had said earlier that when she first went down to where Tom lay on the sidewalk dying, his eyes were open and he was looking at her. She held him, and his eyes closed. Then Kris Baehre replaced her.

"I know that this is still a hard memorial for so many. They say that time heals all wounds, but this is a deep, deep wound. I have been in contact with Double D (Dan Dhonau), and I might see if he wants to light a candle that night with me. I will be thinking of all of you. I wish I could be there to celebrate the life of such a wonderful, creative and caring friend. Send my love to all, and I hope everyone finds some peace and love in this memorial."

Christina and her husband discussed whether it would be healthier for them to attend or not attend the 20-year reunion at The Oxford Hotel's Plum Room. They opted to go back to Denver for this day, which couldn't have been fun for her husband, who handled it with poise, and was certainly stressful for Christina to revisit events of July 23, 1993.

At the twenty-year reunion, Vince Lombardi and Scott Hartvigson greeted Christina, whose life they most likely saved since they were in the police car that found her in the alley in northeastern Denver the night of July 23,

398

1993. She had a chance to thank them.

I could not imagine two more professional police officers—men you'd be glad to have your daughter bring home—clean cut, good looking, professional demeanor. Scott was a strong, silent type. He had a thick, brown mustache, was tall and handsome in the dark-blue uniform he wore with probably 30 or more small silver medals pinned on the left shoulder. He'd come straight from work at Denver International Airport without taking time to change, so he could attend the luncheon at The Oxford Hotel.

After lunch, the crowd lingered in the Plum Room at The Oxford Hotel, people brought together by sharing a momentous, tragic event twenty years prior, still bonded by the event and their roles in it.

People Remember Tom

Denver's mayor, Wellington Webb, described Tom as an example of young leadership sorely needed by people in America's cities.

Tom liked to help people. A man who had been homeless came to me outside the Monarch Society in July 1993. He told me that Tom had given him a job repairing skateboards in 1989 or so, and this started him on a path toward employment and a better life.

Though Tom was not an academic star, he was basically good and—with freedom—he shone. When he was permitted to follow his whims and to realize his dreams, his joy and spirit abounded like gifts to everyone around him.

He had solid family ties, and the routine of traditions including holidays and birthdays, and coming home for dinner. He knew we had expectations of him. He had role models in his father, Howard, Clair Smoker, Juan Reyes, and John Milnor. He had security, care, and nurturing. He had limits, which he pushed and bent, but never broke. He carried the energy of the moment with its unknown finish and drew from the energy of his companions. He loved people. And all this paid off in building him into the man he was.

Shana Holman lived in the apartment building named after her, The Shana

Marie, when Tom and Chris were there. She wrote: "Tom so deserves re-membering. He was a unique and very special individual. I know many who admired him. He had a tendency of taking people under his wing and caring for them."

"We were all very happy when he fell in love with Christina; we thought he had met his match. She is adorable, but so strong and a force to be reck-oned with. They were just kind and happy and very, very cool. People loved his store, his…black Cadillac hearse. I remember both their faces, kind eyes, always smiling. There was something very centered about their existence."

"Tom had the greatest sense of timing and humor. I remember just hang-ing out with him, Kris, Dan, at 9th and Corona. I was younger and sort of in awe of them all."

In a letter, Greg Schneider wrote: "We all miss Tom. Michael and I talk about it. It's amazing how many times we saw Tom in his last year, consider-ing he lived in Denver—six times."

"And he had become our brother, Chris's husband—someone we liked, loved, and trusted. He was clever and had a wit that fit in with us. He was creative and had a wild side, yet he was gentle and considerate. We looked forward to a lifetime with him. Most importantly he truly loved Chris, and they made each other so happy. They glowed together."

Windup

No one is immune from violence. It can happen to anyone at any time. This story is not intended to be about violence and horror, but to tell Tom's story, the ordinariness of a good life. It is about my personal journey and the quiet victory of recovery. In telling this story, I was not a part of Tom's Denver life, but I have the perspective of knowing who he was before and after his new self emerged in Denver. This story is about large issues—living through unexpected great loss, recovery, the comfort of an ordinary life.

TWENTY THREE YEARS

When we returned to Denver for probably our last candle vigil on July 23, 2016, we found that the city had changed!

Crowded with people, traffic jamming the streets, hundreds of people populating Union Station- now one large cocktail lounge, with others dining under colored umbrellas outside along with sleeping dogs and children running barefoot through the fountains- Denver kept no traces of Tom. This is still a young, energetic, and attractive city.

His old store at 609 E. 13th Avenue had been remodeled into a much nicer, upscale location, sporting good windows with professional lettering. No more hand-painted signs made by Tom. The store, a tattoo parlor, was not open when we were there, so we could not check inside. FashioNation which used to be next door had moved to South Broadway, and Pegasus Restaurant, formerly across the street, is no longer there.

Likewise, the dark stain on the sidewalk at 9th and Corona is gone.

We returned this July 23 on the 23rd anniversary of Tom's murder and Christina's beating partly because it coincided with the first printings of this book about Tom's life and death.

Craig Silverman is enjoying himself with his Saturday morning radio show on KNUS from 9:00 to 12:00. Graciously, he invited me to be on the show on the 23rd, so I was able to connect with his vast listening audience. As a result, new faces appeared at the candle vigil. At the same time, some old faithful friends were unable to attend due to health problems. Howard and I picked up Don and Nancy Dhonau since Don is now legally blind and no longer drives. So it goes as we age. I posted the following on Facebook when we returned home:

We had a great time in Denver. We remembered Tom who was murdered there 23 years ago. Craig Silverman chose to help KNUS listeners remember the event and to help me promote my book about Tom's life and death on his Saturday, July 23 radio show. This interview was reposted on When Tom Went West Facebook page and website. He interviewed me for one hour during this show which Christina was able to listen to. He has been a great friend and supporter all these years. My book: When Tom Went West, is only available at Tattered Cover Book Store in Denver. We connected with old friends as well as new people at the candle vigil we held at the place where Tom bled to death on the sidewalk, including Craig, Dan Wycoff, a detective who worked on the case, Eric and Kris Baehre, the Dhonaus, Noel Waechter, Julian Martinez, Shandra Hartvigson, whose father Scott was one of the two Denver policemen who found badly beaten Christina in the Black Honda that had been hidden in a Denver alley. As we left Denver International Airport this morning, Scott came to our gate to chat for a few minutes as we were about to board the plane. He works at DIA. I didn't say we had a happy time, but a great and memorable time where we were warmed by support from the Denver community. There were quite a few others at the candle vigil whose names I don't recall, plus I signed a few books. I didn't take any pictures.

Obituary—Local in Michigan

Thomas Edward Hollar, born November 6, 1962, died July 23, 1993. He graduated from Flushing High School and attended Western Michigan University. Tom was the owner of iMi JiMi, a clothing store in Denver, Colorado.

A memorial service was held in Washington Park, Denver, on July 27, 1993 and burial was in Fairmount Cemetery on July 29, 1993. Thomas is survived by his wife, Christina, his sisters Laura Kovalcik of Flint, and Margaret Hollar, D.O., and his parents, Nedra Downing, D.O. of Clarkston and Edward Hollar, D.D.S. of Montrose.

Obituary—Denver

The Monarch Society, 1534 Pearl, 303-837-8712, listed the following obituary in their column in the Denver Post:

> Thomas Edward Hollar, Denver. Survived by his wife, Christina; his sisters, Laura Kovalcik and Margaret Hollar, and his parents Dr. Edward Hollar and Dr. Nedra Downing. Visitation, Monday 4:30-7:30, Tuesday 10:00 A.M. - 2:00 P.M. Memorial service, Tuesday 6:30 P.M., Washington Park.
>
> Contributions can be made to the Thomas Hollar Memorial Fund, c/o iMi JiMi, 609 E. 13th Ave., Denver, Colorado, 80203.

Made in the USA
Coppell, TX
25 July 2020